English Algorithmic Grammar

English Algorithmic Grammar

Hristo Georgiev

continuum

Continuum
The Tower Building
11 York Road
London SE1 7NX

15 East 26th Street
New York
NY 10010

First published 2006

British Library Cataloguing-in-Publication Data
A catalogue record for this book is available from the British Library.

ISBN: 0-8264-8777-7 (hardback)

Typeset by BookEns Ltd, Royston, Herts.
Printed and bound in Great Britain by MPG Books Ltd, Bodmin, Cornwall

Contents

Preface

The main purpose of this book is to bridge the gap between traditional and computational grammar, showing how traditional grammar can be turned into computational without losing readers. There have been no previous attempts made in this direction, since all computational linguists have used Artificial Languages for their algorithmic notation. By doing so they have excluded those readers who are unfamiliar with formal languages and computers and how they operate, but are eager to learn. Some of those readers are English language students and teachers.

A computational grammar can be read and understood by humans and by computers only if it is written in a language they can both comprehend. For the humans, this is the Natural Language (in our case, English); for the computers, this is the rigid and unequivocal algorithmic language. When the algorithmic language is expressed in Natural Language, say English, it can be made legible for humans and at the same time it can be easily turned into a computer software program using one of the artificial languages to program it.

So, in this book we will provide a formal description of English grammar (syntax) for the computer, in two parts. In Part 1 we will introduce procedures for automatic recognition (disambiguation) of the Parts of Speech in a text. Part 2 will deal with the sentence and the interrelationships of its constituent elements, including Parsing and Pronominal Reference.

The algorithmic approach to grammar is a step by step approach, in line with the digital thinking of the computer. Such an approach leaves nothing unresolved, since the computer cannot take a step further without having first solved the task presented at the previous step. The algorithmic approach leaves no room for errors. Errors accumulate if not corrected in time and frustrate the operation of the whole system. The functioning of the algorithm, and hence the performance of the computer software program, is entirely dependent on the formal method of description of the language. If this method is inadequate, if it cannot describe every word and every sentence, then this method is useless to the computer. The algorithmic approach, unlike other methods, can be verified. We can check each step of the algorithm manually and be personally convinced whether the decision taken by the computer at this step is true or false.

English grammar, as seen through the digital eyes of the computer, looks like an endless chain of operations (instructions) and decisions aimed at resolving a particular grammatical or semantic task.

The present grammar is designed for text analysis, not for text synthesis, though, after some additions and exclusions, it can be used for the latter purpose if one is willing to generate syntactically correct but meaningless sentences on a computer. In the classroom, for teaching purposes, the students may use it to generate meaningful sentences by adding words to the list of syntactical structures. *English Algorithmic Grammar* has a very wide scope of application. It can be used to study, teach and exercise English grammar (syntax) at all levels. It could serve to introduce the linguist at under-graduate, postgraduate or faculty level to computers and to the computer way of thinking and decision-making, and the computer scientist or hobbyist to linguistics. Many Natural Language Processing teams in the world may find its algorithms preferable for implementation. *English Algorithmic Grammar* is both a textbook and a reference book. It is accompanied by a Dictionary of Segments, available for free download on the Internet (see Internet Downloads at the end of the book), containing some 27,000 syntactically correct structures permitted by English grammar. The structures are pre-parsed and can be used for reference by English speakers and non-English speakers alike. The reader needs no special knowledge of the related fields (mathematics and computational linguistics) in order to be able to understand this book.

PART ONE

1 Algorithmic recognition of the Verb

In the present study an attempt is made to describe the Verb in the English sentence formally for the computer, by means of flow charts. The flow charts are procedures for text analysis. These procedures are based on the formal grammatical and syntactical features called 'markers' present in the text. The procedures, in the form of instructions (in English), show how to disambiguate those wordforms which potentially belong to more than one Part of Speech, one of which is a Verb. The implementation of the present algorithmic description will help improve the quality of Machine Translation where English is the input language.

1 Introduction

The advent and the subsequent wide use of formal grammars for text synthesis and for formal representation of the structure of the Sentence could not produce adequate results when applied to text analysis. Therefore a better and more suitable solution was sought. Such a solution was found in the algorithmic approach for the purposes of text analysis. The algorithmic approach uses series of instructions, written in Natural Language and organized in flow charts, with the aim of analysing certain aspects of the grammatical structure of the Sentence. The procedures – in the form of a finite sequence of instructions organized in an algorithm – are based on the grammatical and syntactical information contained in the Sentence.

The method used in this chapter closely follows the approach adopted by the all-Russia group Statistika Rechi in the 1970s and described in a number of publications (Koverin, 1972; Mihailova, 1973; Georgiev, 1976). It is to be noted, however, that the results achieved by the algorithmic procedures described in this study by far exceed the results for the English language obtained by Primov and Sorokina (1970) using the same method. (To prevent unauthorized commercial use the authors published only the block-scheme of the algorithm.)

2 Basic assumptions and some facts

It is a well known fact that many difficulties are encountered in Text Processing. A major difficulty, which if not removed first would hamper any further progress, is the ambiguity present in the wordforms that potentially belong to more than one Part of Speech when taken out of context. Therefore it is essential to find the features that disambiguate the wordforms when used in a context and to define the disambiguation process algorithmically.

As a first step in this direction we have chosen to disambiguate those wordforms which potentially (when out of context, in a dictionary) can be attributed to more than one Part of Speech and where one of the possibilities is a Verb. These possibilities include Verb or Noun (as in *stay*), Verb or Noun or Adjective (as in *pain*, *crash*), Verb or Adjective (as in *calm*), Verb or Participle (as in *settled*, *asked*, *put*), Verb or Noun or Participle (as in *run*, *abode*, *bid*), Verb or Adjective or Participle (as in *closed*), and Verb or Noun or Participle or Adjective (as in *cut*).

We'll start with the assumption that for every wordform in the Sentence there are only two possibilities: to be or not to be a Verb. Therefore, only provisionally, exclusively for the purposes of the present type of description and subsequent algorithmic analysis of the Sentence, we shall assume that all wordforms in the Sentence which are not Verbs belong to the non-verbal or Nominal Word Group (NG). As a result of this definition, the NG will incorporate the Noun, the Adjective, the Adverb, the Numeral, the Pronoun, the Preposition and the Participle 1st used as an attribute (as in *the best selected audience*) or as a Complement (as in *we'll regard this matter settled*). All the wordforms in the Sentence which are Verbs form the Verbal Group (VG). The VG includes all main and Auxiliary Verbs, the Particle **to** (used with the Infinitive of the Verb), all verbal phrases consisting of a Verb and a Noun (such as *take place*, *take part*, etc.) or a Verb and an Adverb (such as *go out*, *get up*, *set aside*, etc.), and the Participle 2nd used in the compound Verbal Tenses (such as *had arrived*).

The formal features which help us recognize the nominal or verbal character of a wordform are called 'markers' (Sestier and Dupuis, 1962). Some markers, such as *the*, *a*, *an*, *at*, *by*, *on*, *in*, etc. (most of them are Prepositions), predict with 100 per cent accuracy the nominal nature of the wordform immediately following them (so long as the Prepositions are not part of a phrasal Verb). Other markers, including wordform endings such as *-ing* and *-es*, or a Preposition which is also a Particle such as *to*, etc., when used singly on their own (without the help of other markers) cannot predict accurately the verbal or nominal character of a wordform. Considering the fact that not all markers give 100 per cent predictability (even when all markers in the immediate vicinity of a wordform are taken into consideration), it becomes evident that the entire process of formal text analysis using this method is based, to a certain degree, on probability. The question is how to reduce the possible errors. To this purpose, the following procedures were used:

a) the context of a wordform was explored for markers, moving back and forth – up to three words to the left and to the right of the wordform;
b) some algorithmic instructions preceded others in sequence as a matter of rule in order to act as an additional screening;
c) no decision was taken prematurely, without sufficient grammatical and syntactical evidence being contained in the markers;
d) no instruction was considered to be final without sufficient checking and tests proving the success rate of its performance.

The algorithm presented in Section 3 below, numbered as Algorithm No 1 (Georgiev, 1991), when tested on texts chosen at random, correctly recognized on average 98 words out of every 100. The algorithm uses Lists of markers.

3 Algorithm for automatic recognition of verbal and nominal word groups. Algorithm No 1

The block-scheme of the algorithm is shown in Figure 1.1.

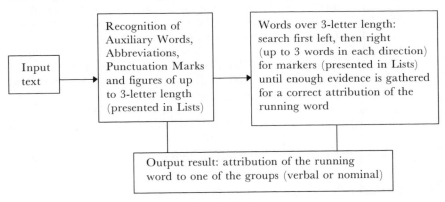

Figure 1.1   Block-scheme of Algorithm No 1
Note: The algorithm, 302 digital instructions in all, is available on the Internet (see Internet Downloads at the end of the book).

3.1 Lists of markers used by Algorithm No 1

(i)   List No 1: for, net, two, one, may, fig, any, day, she, his, him, her, you, men, its, six, sex, ten, low, fat, old, few, new, now, sea, yet, ago, nor, all, per, era, rat, lot, our, way, leg, hay, key, tea, lee, oak, big, who, tub, pet, law, hut, gut, wit, hat, pot, how, far, cat, dog, ray, hot, top, via, why, Mrs, ..., etc.

(ii)   List No 2: was, are, not, get, got, bid, had, did, due, see, saw, lit, let, say, met, rot, off, fix, lie, die, dye, lay, sit, try, led, nit, ..., etc.

(iii)   List No 3: pay, dip, bet, age, can, man, oil, end, fun, dry, log, use, set, air, tag, map, bar, mug, mud, tar, top, pad, raw, row, gas, red, rig, fit, own, let, aid, act, cut, tax, put, ..., etc.

(iv)   List No 4: to, all, thus, both, many, may, might, when, Personal Pronouns, so, must, would, often, did, make, made, if, can, will, shall, ..., etc.

(v)   List No 5: when, the, a, an, is, to, be, are, that, which, was, some, no, will, can, were, have, may, than, has, being, made, where, must, other, such, would, each, then, should, there, those, could, well, even, proportional, particular(ly), having, cannot, can't, shall, later, might, now, often, had, almost, can not, of, in, for, with, by, this, from, at, on, if, between, into, through, per, over, above, because, under, below, while, before, concerning, as, one, ..., etc.

(vi)   List No 6: with, this, that, from, which, these, those, than, then, where, when, also, more, into, other, only, same, some, there, such, about, least, them, early, either, while, most, thus, each, under, their, they, after, less, near, above, three, both, several, below, first, much, many, zero, even, hence, before, quite, rather, till, until, best, down, over, above, through, Reflexive Pronouns, self, whether, onto, once, since, toward(s), already, every, elsewhere, thing, nothing, always, perhaps, sometimes, anything, something, everything, otherwise, often, last, around, still, instead, foreword, later, just, behind, ..., etc.

(vii)   List No 7: Includes all Irregular Verbs, with the following wordforms: Present, Present 3rd person singular, Past and Past Participle.

(viii) List No 8: -ted, -ded, -ied, -ned, -red, -sed, -ked, -wed, -bed, -hed, -ped, -led, -ved, -reed, -ced, -med, -zed, -yed, -ued, ..., etc.

(ix)   List No 9: -ous, -ity, -less, -ph, -'s (except in *it's, what's, that's, there's*, etc.), -ness, -ence, -ic, -ee, -ly, -is, -al, -ty, -que, -(t)er, -(t)or, -th (except in *worth*), -ul, -ment, -sion(s), ..., etc.

(x)   List No 10: Comprises a full list of all Numerals (Cardinal and Ordinal).

3.2 Text sample processed by the algorithm

Text	Word Group
She	NG
nodded	VG
again and	NG
patted	VG
my arm, a small familiar gesture which always	NG
managed to convey	VG
both understanding and dismissal.	NG

3.3 Examples of hand checking of the performance of the algorithm

Let us see how the following sentence will be processed by Algorithm No 1, word by word:

Her apartment was on a floor by itself at the top of what had once been a single dwelling, but which long ago was divided into separately rented living quarters.

First the algorithm picks up the first word of the sentence (of the text), in our case this is the word *her*, with instruction No 1. The same instruction always ascertains that the text has not ended yet. Then the algorithm proceeds to analyse the word *her* by asking questions about it and verifying the answers to those questions by comparing the word *her* with lists of other words and Punctuation Marks, thus establishing, gradually, that the word *her* is not a Punctuation Mark (operations 3–5), that it is not a figure (number) either (operation 5–7), and that its length exceeds two letters (operation 8). The fact that its length exceeds two letters makes the algorithm jump the next procedures as they follow in sequence, and continue the analysis in operation No 31. Using operation No 31 the algorithm recognizes the word as a three-letter word and takes it straight away to operation No 34. Here it is decreed to take the word *her* together with the word that follows it and to remember both words as a NG. Thus:

Her apartment   =   NG

Then the algorithm returns again to operation No 1, this time with the word *was* and goes through the same procedures with it till it reaches instruction No 38, where it is seen that this word is in fact *was*. Now the algorithm checks if *was* is preceded (or followed) by words such as *there* or *it* (operation No 39, which instructs the computer to compare the adjacent words with *there* and *it*), or if it is followed up to two words ahead by a word ending in *-ly* or by such words as *never*, *soon*, etc., none of which is actually the case. Then, finally, operation No 39d instructs the computer to remember the word *was* as a VG

was   =   VG

and to return to the start again, this time with the next word *on*. Going through the initial procedures again, our hand checking of this algorithm reaches instruction No 9 where it is made clear that the word is indeed *on*. Then the algorithm checks the left surroundings of *on*, to see if the word immediately preceding it was recognized as a Verb (No 10), excluding the Auxiliary Verbs. Since it was not (*was* is an Auxiliary Verb), the procedure reaches operation Nos 12 and 12a, where it becomes known to the algorithm that *on* is followed by *a*. The knowledge that *on* is followed by an Article enables the program to make a firm decision concerning the attribution of the next two words (12a): *on* and the next two words are automatically attributed to the NG:

on a floor   =   NG

After that the program again returns to operation No 1, this time to analyse the word *by*. The analysis proceeds without any result till it reaches operation No 11, where the word *by* is matched with its recorded counterpart (see the List enumerating the other possibilities). In a similar fashion (see *on*), operation No 12b instructs the computer to take *by* and the next word blindfoldedly (i.e. without analysis) and to remember them as a NG. Thus we have:

by itself = NG

We return again to operation No 1 to analyse the next word *at* and we pass, unsuccessfully, through the first ten steps. Instruction No 11 enables the computer to match *at* with its counterpart recorded in the List (*at*). Since *at* is followed by *the* (an Article), this enables the computer to make a firm decision: to take *at* plus *the* plus the next word and to remember them as a NG:

at the top = NG

We deal similarly with the next word – *of* – and since it is not followed by a word mentioned in operation No 12, we take only the word immediately following it (12b) and remember them as a NG:

of what = NG

Since the next word – *had* – exceeds the two-letter length (operation No 7), we proceed with it to operation No 31, but we cannot identify it till we reach operation No 38. Operation No 39 checks the immediate surroundings of *had*, and if we had listed *once* with the other Adverbs in 39b, we would have ended our quest now. But since *once* is not in this list, the algorithm proceeds to the next step (39d) and qualifies *had* as a VG:

had = VG

Now we proceed further, starting with operation No 1, to analyse the next word, *once*. Being a long word, *once* jumps the analysis destined for the shorter (two- and three-letter) words and we arrive with it at operation No 55. Operations No 55 and 57 ascertain that *once* does not coincide with either of the alternatives offered there. Through operation No 59 the computer program finds *once* listed in List No 6 and makes a correct decision – to attribute it to the NG:

once = NG

Now we (and the program) have reached the word *been* in the text. The procedures dealing with the shorter words are similarly ignored, up to operation No 61, where *been* is identified as an Irregular Verb from List No 7 and attributed (No 62b) to the VG:

been = VG

Next we have the word *a* (an Indefinite Article) which leads us to operations No 11 and 12 (where it is identified as such), and with operation No 12b the program reaches a decision to attribute *a* and the word following it to the NG:

a single = NG

Next in turn is *dwelling*. It is somewhat difficult to tag, because it can be either a Verb or a Noun. We go with it through all the initial operations, without significant success, until we get to operation No 69 and receive the instruction to follow routines No 246–303. Since *dwelling* does not coincide with the words listed in operation No 246, is not preceded by the syntactical construction defined in No 248 and does not have the word surroundings specified by operations No 250, 254, 256, 258, 260, 262, 264, 266, 268, 270, 272, 274, 276, 278 and 280, its tagging, so far, is unsuccessful. Finally, operation No 282 finds the right surrounding – to its left there is, up to two words to the left, an Article (*a*) – and attributes dwelling to the NG:

dwelling = NG

However, in this case *dwelling* is recognized as a Gerund, not as a Noun. If we were to use this result in another program this might lead to problems. Therefore, perhaps, here we can add an extra sieve in order to be able to always make the right choice. At the same time, we must be very careful when we do so, because the algorithms are made so compact that any further interference (e.g. adding new instructions, changing the order of the instructions) might well lead to much bigger errors than this one.

Now, in operation No 3, we come to the first Punctuation Mark since we started our analysis. The Punctuation Mark acts as a dividing line and instructs the program to print what was stored in the buffer up to this moment.

Next in line is the word *but*. Being a three-letter word it is sent to operation No 31 and then consecutively to Nos 34, 36, 38 and 40. It is identified in No 42 and sent by No 43 to the NG as a Conjunction:

but = NG

Next, we continue with the analysis of the word *which*, starting as usual from the very beginning (No 1) and gradually reaching No 55, where the real identification for long words starts. The word *which* is not listed in No 55 or No 57. We find it in List No 6 of operation 59 and as a result attribute it to the NG:

which = NG

The word *long* follows, and in exactly the same way we reach operation No 55 and continue further comparing it with other words and exploring its surroundings, until we exhaust all possibilities and reach a final verdict in No 89:

long = NG

Next in turn is the word *ago*. As a three-letter word it is analysed in operation No 31 and the next operations to follow, until it is found by operation No 46 in List No 1, and identified as a NG (No 47):

ago   =   NG

Following is the word *was*, which is recognized as such for the first time in operation No 38. After some brief exploration of its surroundings the program decides that *was* belongs to the VG:

was   =   VG

Next in sequence is the word *divided*. Step by step, the algorithmic procedures pass it on to operation No 55, because it is a long word. Again, as in all previous cases, operations No 55, 56, 57, 59, 61 and 63 try to identify it with a word from a List, but unsuccessfully until, finally, instruction No 65 identifies part of its ending with *-ded* from List No 8 and sends the word to instructions No 128–164 for further analysis. Here it does not take long to see that *divided* is preceded by the Auxiliary Verb *was* (No 130) and that it should be attributed to the VG as Participle 2nd (No 131):

divided   =   VG

The Preposition *into* comes next and since it is not located in one of the Lists examined by the instructions and none of its surroundings correspond to those listed, it is assumed that it belongs to the NG (No 89):

into   =   NG

Next, the ending *-ly* of the Adverb *separately* is found in List No 9 and this gives enough reason to send it to the NG (No 64):

separately   =   NG

Now we come to a difficult word again, because *rented* can be either a Verb or an Adjective, or even Participle 1st. Since its ending *-ted* is found in List No 8, *rented* is sent to instructions No 128–164 for further analysis as a special case. With instructions No 144 and 145 the algorithm chooses to recognize *rented* as a Participle (1st) and to attribute it to the NG:

rented   =   NG

Next comes *living*. At first it also seems to be a special case (since it can be Noun, Gerund, Verb – as part of a Compound Tense – Adjective or Participle). Instruction No 69 establishes that this word ends in *-ing* and No 70 sends it for further analysis to instructions No 246–303. Almost towards the end (instructions No 300 and 301), the algorithm decides to attribute *living* to the NG:

living   =   NG

acknowledging that it is a Present Participle. If the program were more precise, it would be able also to say that *living* is an Adjective used as an attribute.

The last word in this sequence is *quarters*. The way it ends very much resembles a verbal ending (3rd person singular). Will the algorithm make a mistake this time? Instruction No 67 recognizes that the ending -*s* is ambiguous and sends *quarters* to instructions No 165–245 for more detailed analysis. Then the word passes unsuccessfully (unrecognized) through many instructions till it finally reaches instruction No 233, where it is evidenced that *quarters* is followed by a Punctuation Mark and this serves as sufficient reason to attribute it to the NG:

quarters   =   NG

Finally, our algorithmic analysis of the above sentence ends with commendable results: no error.

However, in the long run we would expect errors to appear, mainly when we deal with Verbs, but these are not likely to exceed 2 per cent. For example, an error can be detected in the following sample sentence:

Not only has his poetic fame – as was inevitable – been overshadowed by that of Shakespeare but he was long believed to have entertained and to have taken frequent opportunities of expressing a malign jealousy of one both greater and more successful than himself.

This sentence is divided into VG and NG in the following manner:

Text	*Word Group*
Not	VG
only	NG
has	VG
his poetic fame	NG
– as	NG
was	VG
inevitable –	NG
been overshadowed	VG
by that of Shakespeare	NG
but he	NG
was long believed to have entertained	VG
and	NG
to have taken	VG
frequent opportunities of expressing	NG
a malign jealousy of one both greater	NG
and	NG
more successful than himself.	NG

As is seen in the above example, the word *long* was wrongly attributed to the VG (according to our specifications laid down as a starting point for the algorithm it should belong to the NG).

The reader, if he or she has enough patience, can put to the test many sentences in the way described above (following the algorithmic instructions), to prove for himself (herself) the accuracy of our description.

Though this is a description designed for computer use (to be turned into a computer software program), nevertheless it will surely be quite interesting for a moment or two to put ourselves on a par with the computer in order to understand better how it works. Of course, that is not the way we would do the job. Our knowledge of grammar is far superior, and we understand the meaning of the sentence while the computer does not. The information used by the computer is extremely limited, only that presented in the instructions (operations) and in the Lists.

Further on we will try to give the computer more information (Algorithm No 3 and the algorithms in Part 2) and correspondingly increase our requirements.

4 Conclusion

- Most of the procedures to determine the nominal or verbal nature of the wordform, depending on its context, are based on the phrasal and syntactic structures present in the Sentence (for example, instructions 11 and 12, 67 and 68, 85, etc.), i.e. structures such as Preposition + Article + Noun; *will* (*shall*) + *be* + (Adverb) + Participle; *to* + *be* + (*not*) + Participle 2nd + *to* + Verb; *-ing* + Possessive Pronoun + Noun, etc. (the words in brackets represent alternatives).
- When constructing the algorithm it was thought to be more expedient to deal first with the auxiliary and short words of two-letter length, then with words of three-letter length, then with the rest of the words – for frequency considerations and also because they represent the main body of the markers.
- The approach presented in this study is not based on formal grammars and is to be used exclusively for text analysis (not for text synthesis). One should not associate the VP (Verbal Phrase) with the VG and the NP (Noun Phrase) with the NG – for these are completely different notions as has been shown by the presentation.
- The algorithm can be checked by feeding in texts through the procedures (the instructions) manually and if the reader is dissatisfied he or she may change the instructions to improve the results. (See Section 3.3 for details of how the performance of the algorithms can be hand checked.)

    The algorithm can be easily programmed in one of the existing artificial languages best suited for this type of operation.
- The algorithm presented in this study was mentioned, only as a block-scheme, in a previous publication as Algorithm No 1 (Georgiev, 1991).

2 Division of the sentence into phrases

1 Introduction

For multiple purposes, in Text Processing and Machine Translation, often there is a need to divide the sentence into smaller units that can be processed more easily than the whole sentence, especially when the sentence happens to be a long one. To that purpose we have devised an efficient algorithm based on the assumptions presented in the next section.

2 Presentation

When we say that we are going to divide the sentence into phrases, we must state first how we will define the phrase and what our understanding of the phrase will be – where it starts and where it ends. For the purposes of the present algorithm (and not for any other, especially theoretical, purposes) the phrase is delimited on its left and on its right by Punctuation Marks and Auxiliary words. The phrase usually starts with an Auxiliary word and ends with the appearance of a Punctuation Mark or an Auxiliary word.

The Auxiliary words, marking the boundaries of the phrases, are presented in tables (Lists). Each table lists Auxiliary words of a particular type. It was observed that some Auxiliary words (as well as some sequences of consecutively used Auxiliary words) start usually longer and more independent phrases than others. For example, in a sentence like

It is often difficult to seek solutions through the curtailment of consumption.

the Auxiliary word *through* followed by the Article *the* (another Auxiliary word) starts a phrase that ends with the appearance of a Punctuation Mark, while the Auxiliary word *of* starts a sub-phrase which is part of a longer phrase. In our algorithm (see Algorithm No 2 in Section 3) this subdivision of the sentence into longer phrases and the subdivision of the longer phrases into smaller constituent phrases is expressed by leaving different lengths of space between one phrase and another. The longer the space left before the phrase, the more self-sufficient and independent the phrase is thought to be. In this study we have established five types of phrases, depending on their relative independence within the sentence. This independence is expressed by a particular Auxiliary word (or words) or by a Punctuation Mark. The longest and the most self-sufficient and relatively independent phrase starts and ends with a Punctuation Mark. The second most independent phrase starts with a word from List No 1 and ends with a Punctuation Mark or with the appearance of another Auxiliary word from List No 1. For example:

(6 spaces left) *One US government study estimated*
(5 spaces left) *that there are 68 large manufacturing complexes*
(4 spaces) *in the region*
(5 spaces left) *that have significant idle capacity.* (end)

The full stop at the start of the sentence is equivalent to six spaces. In other words, a smaller space following after a larger space to the left means that the phrase starting after the smaller space is dependent on, and a constituent of, the larger phrase. The smaller space in the example above (4 spaces) shows that the phrase following after it is dependent on the previous phrase *that there are 68 large manufacturing complexes* and explains it (or brings additional information about it, here location), while the five spaces left after *region* signify that the next phrase is dependent on the previous large phrase (the one that has a longer space left in front), in this case *One US government study estimated that there are 68 large manufacturing complexes*.

The space left between the phrases depends on the actual Preposition (or Punctuation Mark) used or on the sequence of Punctuation Mark and/or Auxiliary words, as specified (for more details see the instructions for Algorithm No 2 below).

3 Algorithm for division of the sentence into phrases. Algorithm No 2

The block-scheme of the algorithm is shown in Figure 2.1.

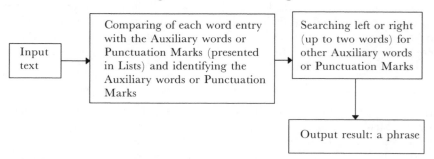

Figure 2.1 Block-scheme of Algorithm No 2
Note: The algorithm (27 digital instructions in all) is available for free download on the Internet (see Internet Downloads at the end of the book).

3.1 Lists used by Algorithm No 2

NB The words not registered in the Lists are recorded as they follow, in the same sequence, after those registered in the Lists.

(i) List No 1: besides, therefore, however, whereas, thus, hence, though, despite, with, nevertheless, throughout, through, during, that, only, but, if, otherwise, again, which, although, thereby, already, against, unless, thereafter, ..., etc.

(ii) List No 2: over, as, what, toward(s), for, into, about, by, so, from, at, above, under, beside, below, onto, since, behind, in front of, beyond, around, before, after, then, altogether, among(st), between, beneath, ..., etc.

(iii) List No 3: both, neither, none, ..., etc.

(iv) List No 4: of, to (as Preposition)

(v) List No 5: the, a, an

(vi) List No 6: so much as, so far as, so far, as long as, as soon as, so long as, in order that, in order to, lest, as well as, and, or, nor, ..., etc.

(vii) List No 7: such, than, onto, until, all, near, even, when, while, within, last, next, also, less, more, most, whether, much, once, one, any, many, some, where, another, other, each, then, whose, who, whoever, till, until, what, across, whence, according, due to, owing, whereby, prior, wherever, whenever, already, moreover, likewise, however, ..., etc.

(viii) List No 8: out, in, on, down, ..., etc.

3.2 Some examples of the performance of Algorithm No 2

Below we will present a text divided into phrases according to the instructions for the algorithm:

(i) *Many countries also have established or have   under construction   a free zone, where exporters have access   to shipping facilities, a pool   of labour and freedom from exchange controls.*

(ii) *The Caribbean Basin Initiative, a US package   of aid and trade incentives to encourage manufacturing, has given   an added boost   to industrial development   in this region.*

The analysis of the sentence starts with checking the contents of the memory and taking to print any information stored up to this moment (this is done at the start of each new sentence), also with ascertaining whether the sentence has ended or not and recording the analysed word in the memory if it is not recorded yet (a procedure carried out after each word). Then the algorithm reads the next word (in No 4a), which in the case of (i) above is *many*, and proceeds to analyse it in 5. Since it is not a full stop or any other Punctuation Mark (5, 7), nor a word specified in 9, 11, 13, 15, 17 or 19, the analysis yields no result until the program gets to operation No 21, where the word *many* is located in List No 7. Here the program, through operation No 22, checks whether *many* is followed by yet another word from the Lists. Operation 22ab certifies that it is not, and instructs the program to cut the sentence at this point and to leave three spaces (before *many*) when recording it, then to return to operation No 2 to start the analysis of the next word. The next word, *countries*, could not be identified (it is not registered in the Lists), therefore operation 27 instructs the program to record it in the memory as the next consecutive word of the phrase and to return to 2 to continue the analysis of the sentence.

The word *also* follows next. The program cannot locate the word and proceeds further, after registering it. The next words *have* and *established* are dealt with in a similar way. Next comes the Conjunction *or*. The program locates the word in operation No 17, then it checks if other words from the Lists follow (18). A single space is left before recording it (No 18b). The word *have* is registered next and the program reaches *under* (15) to draw a dividing line by leaving four spaces (16ab), and this carries on till the end of the text.

These procedures can be applied to any English language texts. The actual users of the algorithm can improve it by adding new words to the Lists or by changing the dividing lines to suit other strategies and other interpretations of the boundaries of the English phrase.

4 Discussion

Algorithm No 2 was developed with the special purpose of aiding the overall automatic analysis of the sentence. The division of the sentence into smaller units helps us understand better its meaning, though the division, as presented in this section, is not based on meaning but on formal features. The reader will find somewhat different and much more accurate interpretation of the existing boundaries within a sentence in Part 2.

In the course of this study it was observed that each foregoing phrase finds further interpretation of its meaning in the next phrase. In other words, the first phrase of a sentence carries a certain meaning, which with each successive phrase becomes more and more clear and complete – the next phrase simply adds more information to the meaning of the previous phrase. The phrases have varied mutual interdependence, which we tried to express with a margin left between them. We will express this graphically in Figure 2.2, which considers two sentences.

The brackets show the dependence of each succeeding phrase both on the previous one and on all preceding ones. In the second sentence, the phrases are separated with equal space left between them. In those cases where the space left is smaller, this means that the tie with the previous phrase is stronger (i.e. the next phrase is an integral part of the preceding one). A sudden surge of the interval signals the division between two phrases, as in the example in Figure 2.3. In this example, the second large phrase (Clause) explains the meaning of the first. This is indicated with the interval left and with the brackets.

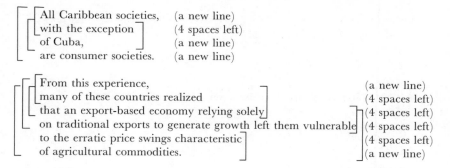

All Caribbean societies,   (a new line)
with the exception   (4 spaces left)
of Cuba,   (a new line)
are consumer societies.   (a new line)

From this experience,   (a new line)
many of these countries realized   (4 spaces left)
that an export-based economy relying solely   (4 spaces left)
on traditional exports to generate growth left them vulnerable   (4 spaces left)
to the erratic price swings characteristic   (4 spaces left)
of agricultural commodities.   (a new line)

Figure 2.2 Graphic representation of interdependence of phrases

(6 spaces)   The US quota system actually affords little protection
(4 spaces)   against the volatile world market
(5 spaces)   that sets
(2 spaces)   the price
(4 spaces)   of most exported sugar.

Figure 2.3 Representation showing division between two large phrases

3   Algorithmic recognition of Parts of Speech

One of the first grammatical difficulties found in using English as an input language in a computerized Text Processing system is the recognition of Parts of Speech in a text. In this chapter, an algorithmic procedure is offered for recognition of Parts of Speech in the text, capable of yielding 99.93 per cent correct results. The algorithmic procedure is based on the contextual analysis of every running word in the sentence. The contextual analysis is carried out on the level of Parts of Speech. All available grammatical, syntactical and some lexical and semantic information is used in the process.

1   Introduction

In a language like English, almost every individual word belongs to more than one Part of Speech when taken out of context and placed in a dictionary.

Since every Text Processing system inevitably uses a dictionary, the task of disambiguating the grammatical meaning of the words when used in a text is of primary importance for any further success in grammatical and semantic text analysis. It is well known that the wordforms (the running words, or the word from space to space) are unambiguous with respect to their Part of Speech. The way, however, that humans and computers disambiguate the wordforms when they see them in the text is essentially different.

The computers don't know the language: they don't know the grammatical structure and the meaning of the sentence unless humans teach them this. As a result, the computer knows as much as we are able to tell it using a language it can understand, a language capable of explaining step by step (because the computer is digital) what to do in order to recognize the Part of Speech of a word when in a text. In this case we will provide the explanation in English, in the form of flow charts (algorithmically) so that everybody can read it and understand it. The flow charts can be easily programmed later in one of the existing computer languages most suitable for the task, or programmed directly into machine language.

In the first chapter, an algorithm was presented for 98 per cent correct recognition of the Verb in a text, using the so-called 'markers' present in the context of a wordform. In this chapter, in order to determine the Part of

Speech of every running word in the text a different procedure is used, based on the actual or possible attribution of the adjacent wordforms (left or right from the wordform under consideration) to one (or more) Part(s) of Speech. As a result, the rate of successful recognition has been improved considerably – it is 99.93 per cent correct.

So, our aim in this chapter is to teach the computer to recognize, algorithmically, the following Parts of Speech: Verb, Noun, Adjective (Attribute, Predicative), Participle, Adverb, Pronoun, Numeral, Auxiliary word (Particle, Preposition, Conjunction) and Interjection. Particular emphasis is laid on the Verbs, the Nouns, the Participles and the Adjectives, since almost all of them have more than one homograph.

2 Presentation

The present algorithmic procedure is constructed on the assumption that the computer uses, as a reference table, a full and comprehensive dictionary of the English language in which every wordform is marked according to its membership of one or more Part(s) of Speech.

2.1 *Presentation of the electronic Dictionary of Wordforms*

a) Those words in the Dictionary that belong to only one Part of Speech are marked as follows: Noun only, Adjective only, Verb only, Preposition only, Numeral only, Personal Pronoun Nominal Case (PPNC), Reflexive Pronoun (Refl. Pr), Personal Pronoun Objective Case (PPOC), Reciprocal Pronoun (Rec. Pr), Possessive Pronoun (Poss. Pr), Demonstrative Pronoun (Dem. Pr), Interrogative Pronoun (Inter. Pr), Relative Pronoun (Rel. Pr), Indefinite Pronoun (Indef. Pr), Indicative Pronoun (Indic. Pr.), Particle, Participle 1st, Participle 2nd, Gerund, Conjunction, Interjection, Adverb, Person – human being (d), Geographical name (r), Abbreviation (Abbr.), Punctuation Mark.

b) Those wordforms in the Dictionary that belong to more than one Part of Speech are marked as follows: Noun or Adjective (NA), Adjective or Verb (AV), Noun or Verb (NV), Adjective or Noun or Verb (ANV), Verb or Adjective or Participle (VAP) – all wordforms ending in *-ed* and all past Participles of the Irregular Verbs – Participle or Adjective or Noun or Verb (PANV) – all words ending in *-ing* – Participle or Adjective or Verb (PAV) – all words ending in *-ing* – Participle or Adjective (PA) – words ending in *-ed* and Past Participles of the Irregular Verbs – Participle or Verb (PV), Adverb or Adjective (AA), Verb or Noun or Participle (VNP) – for example *run, abode*. The reader can find more examples in any English language dictionary that lists the Part(s) of Speech of a word.

NB Explanation of the terms covered by PANV and PAV:
1. Participle -1, as a Verb in a Compound Tense:

He was building a house.
2. Gerund -1 (functioning as Noun):
   The building of a new society ...
3. Gerund -2 (operating as a Verb) (= *to* + Verb):
   ... an important way of keeping them together ..., ... start speaking ...
4. Present participle -2: – operating as a Verb in a non-finite clause:
   Walking in the street, he saw ...
5. Present participle -3 (a variant of 4):
   ... adult men staying at a hotel ..., ... people gathering in front of ...
6. Present participle -4 (another variant of 4):
   He spoke without winking.
7. Noun:
   A new building

N.B. This distinction was made to facilitate translation into other languages.

c) With a view to the above-mentioned codes, the electronic Dictionary used
by the computer program would be presented as follows:

Wordform	Part of Speech
answer	NV
answers	NV
answering	PAV
answered	VAP
....	....
arrive	V (Verb)
arrives	V
arrived	PV
arriving	PANV
arrival	N (Noun)
....	
building	PANV
buildings	N
....	
calm	ANV
calming	PANV
calmness	N
calmly	Adv (Adverb)
....	.... etc.

Geographical and personal names are also recorded in the Dictionary and
coded respectively. All abbreviations like *I'm, can't, won't,* etc. are also listed
and their full forms registered.

2.2 Presentation of Algorithm No 3

The algorithm uses routines (instructions) directing the computer to take a
running word from the text and to compare it with the wordforms recorded in

the Dictionary. When the corresponding word in the Dictionary is found, the computer takes its grammatical record for further examination (the computer also keeps a record of the grammatical information of the words preceding the word under scrutiny, up to several words to the left). If the word under scrutiny belongs to only one Part of Speech, there is no need to analyse this word any further and the computer proceeds to the next word. If the word belongs to more than one Part of Speech, then this word is sent for further analysis in the respective subroutine of the algorithm.

Apart from the Dictionary, the algorithm uses also tables (Lists) of words. These Lists include lists of the Possessive Pronouns, PPNC, PPOC, Prepositions, Conjunctions, Adverbs, etc. These Lists are not presented here since they can be found elsewhere in the literature. For the purposes of the present algorithm, the Punctuation Marks are regarded as separate words.

When a search is carried out (in order to collect additional information) to the left or to the right of the word under scrutiny, this search should stop as soon as a Punctuation Mark is reached, unless specified otherwise. When the search is carried out to the left of the wordform under examination, it is assumed that the words to the left are already 'recognized' with respect to their contextual Parts of Speech (unless for specific purposes their original Parts of Speech – as registered in the Dictionary – are preferred). Therefore, in the algorithm these words (the words to the left of the word under examination) are mentioned with the Parts of Speech which they have in that particular context after recognition, for example N, Adj, V, etc. This means that their Parts of Speech are already established and known to the computer. Sometimes, however, when analysing the words to the left of the wordform under examination, it is necessary to use the Part(s) of Speech of particular words as registered in the Dictionary (before the analysis carried out by the algorithm): NV, ANV, AV, PANV, etc.

When the search is carried out to the right of the wordform under examination, the words are named as they are before the analysis (since their attribution to a particular Part of Speech is not known yet): Adj only, N, V, NV, PAV, AV, NA, PANV, VAP, etc.

When, in the algorithm, we use the phrase *Is this word followed (or preceded) by*: ..., it should be understood 'immediately' (unless specified otherwise); the enumerated words following the colon are alternatives.

Some of the Lists (of words) used by the present algorithm are presented at the end of the algorithm, in Section 6 below.

3 Algorithm for recognition of Parts of Speech. Algorithm No 3

This algorithm was presented (Georgiev, 1991) only as a block-scheme and was referred to as Algorithm No 3. The block-scheme of the algorithm is shown in Figure 3.1.

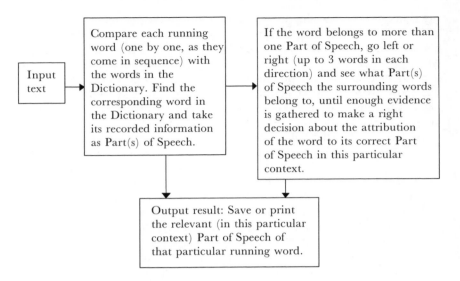

Figure 3.1 Block-scheme of Algorithm No 3
Note: The algorithm, 1701 digital instructions in all, including the Lists it uses for reference, can be downloaded from the Internet (see Internet Downloads at the end of the book).

4 Discussion

The present algorithm does not satisfactorily recognize: *in, out, over, up, down, away*, ..., etc., because these words can be an integral part of the Phrasal Verbs or they can be used as Prepositions or Adverbs. The ambiguity arising on this purely grammatical level can be overcome at a later stage.

In this study, we have also given a more specific interpretation of the '-ing' forms to facilitate their translation into other languages.

This algorithm recognizes correctly (hand checked) 993 words out of every thousand. The other methods known to the author could not achieve better results. This makes the algorithm suitable for implementation in Text Processing systems, especially for Machine Translation, where English is used as a source language. The algorithm will resolve the existing ambiguity on the level of Parts of Speech, and thus will narrow the choice of the relevant word in a particular context. For example, if the word *conflict* is used as a Noun in a specified context, the computer will ignore its meanings as a Verb (recorded in the Dictionary alongside its meanings as a Noun), and will have to choose only between its meanings as a Noun: *struggle, quarrel, collision*.

5 Examples of the performance of the algorithm

Below we have provided an example obtained at the output after an input text was processed by the above algorithm. The input text is in the left column, the results are shown in the right column:

Wordform	Part of Speech
from	Preposition
the	Article
window	Noun
all	Indefinite Pronoun
that	Demonstrative Pronoun
could	Auxiliary Verb
be	Auxiliary Verb
seen	Participle 2nd
was	Auxiliary Verb
a	Article
receding	Adjective
area	Noun
of	Preposition
grey	Noun

We will give yet another example to show how the performance of Algorithm No 3 can be hand checked in order to prove its accuracy on randomly chosen texts. Let's analyse the following text:

With the first peep of day I opened my eyes, to find myself in a great chamber, hung with stamped leather, furnished with fine embroidered furniture, and lit by three fair windows.

The algorithm (or the program developed on its basis) reads the first word of the text and takes it to the Dictionary to find its match there and to see its grammatical record (the reader can use any full English language dictionary that records the grammatical information of the words, but must comply with our abbreviations for it). In this case, the first word is *with*. In our Dictionary there will be only one possibility registered – a Preposition:

with   =   Preposition

Then the algorithm picks up the next word, *the*, and finds it in the Dictionary. There it is registered as an Article:

the   =   Article

Next comes the word *first*. This word can be either an Adjective or a Noun or a Numeral. Since the Numeral Ordinal can be a Noun too, we will find the following grammatical record in the dictionary: NA (Noun or Adjective). From this point on we deal only with the grammatical information of the word, not with the word itself. Then we compare the grammatical information of the word with the grammatical information required by the algorithmic instructions, step by step: it is not a full stop (No 3), it is not a Preposition or an Article (No 5), it is not a figure or a Numeral (No 7), etc., till we finally arrive at operation No 87, where the algorithm asks for just this particular grammatical information – NA. The next instruction (88) sends NA for further analysis in subroutine 370–466.

Starting with 370, all the next steps establish the environment of the word under examination (*first*). Finally, operation 388 matches the exact environment required for a correct decision: an Article to the left of the word (*the*) and a word that can be either an Adjective or a Noun or a Verb (ANV) on its right side (*peep*). Instruction No 389 declares that this is an Adjective:

first   =   Adjective

and reverts the analysis back to operation No 1.

Next the algorithm reads the word *peep*, and sees (in the Dictionary) that its grammatical information equals ANV (Adjective or Noun or Verb). Again the procedures carry the word through all the initial steps, until operation No 93 identifies the grammatical information as correct and sends it (94) for further analysis to subroutines 880–1124. Here it does not take long to match the environment of *peep*. Operation No 884 requires a Preposition to follow (List No 1) and an Adjective to precede. As a result, a decision is triggered (885):

peep   =   Noun

The next word *of* can only be a Preposition, so the analysis goes on to the word following it. This is another Noun or Adjective (NA), *day*. We will omit how we arrive at the right place – subroutines 370–466. Here again a search starts for matching surroundings and it does not take long to find out that the Preposition *of* enforces a pre-determined decision (372–373):

day   =   Noun

Next comes the Personal Pronoun Nominal Case (PPNC), *I*, and since it can be PPNC only, it requires no further attention:

I   =   PPNC

Coming next is the word *opened*. It can be a Verb or an Adjective or a Participle (VAP). Of course, we know what it is, because we are humans, but the computer knows nothing yet. Therefore the computer must process VAP till at long last it reaches operation No 1212, which requires a PPNC to precede, so that a correct decision (1213) is finally taken:

opened   =   Verb

The next word *my* can only be a Possessive Pronoun:

my   =   Possessive Pronoun

The word coming next is *eyes*. It can be either a Noun or a Verb (NV), therefore it is dispatched to operations No 550–874, where in 552 an easy solution is found for it – a Noun, because it is preceded by a Possessive Pronoun and followed by a Punctuation Mark (from List No 1). So we record:

eyes   =   Noun

Now we have arrived at a difficult (for the algorithm) point, because our next word *to* can be either a Preposition or a Particle used as Infinitive of the Verb (85). Subroutine 330–365 will decide what exactly. One of the questions asked (356) is if the next word can be NV, AV or ANV. Since *find* can be either Noun or Verb (NV), the condition is met and the decision is taken (357):

to   =   Particle (Infinitive)

Then the ambiguity of *find* is resolved by operations 656–657b. After eliminating numerous other possibilities it is being thought that since *find* is preceded by *to* and does not end in -*s* (*finds*), it must be a Verb:

find   =   Verb

Of course this decision could have been taken automatically, as soon as it was known that *to* is an Infinitive, but then, if the algorithm was wrong, it would have made two errors at the same time. Procedures like this one are designed to reduce the possibility of errors.

Since the following words *myself*, *in*, *a* etc. are unambiguous we will omit them and concentrate on the word *hung*, which can be either a Participle or a Verb (PV). This is one of the difficult grammatical ambiguities in the English language that has to be described for the computer. However, in this case, the algorithm finds a quick solution – it takes only a few steps to see (1663) that since *hung* is preceded by a comma it must be Participle 1st.

hung   =   Participle 1st

If this rule is not 100 per cent secure, then we must raise serious doubts about the freedom of use of Punctuation Marks and Participles.

At this point we will leave the rest of the above text to the readers in the hope that they will not be satisfied with this example and will check the performance of the algorithm on other texts.

An algorithm for recognition of the Verbal Tenses can easily be constructed on the basis of the results obtained by the present algorithm (see further for details).

6 Lists of words used by Algorithm No 3

(i)   List No 1: Conjunctions, Prepositions, Particles, Auxiliary words, Punctuation Marks, the Article, Pronouns, Interjections, Adverbs, all words registered in the Dictionary as VAP or PV, and all Verbs (Auxiliary included)

(NB List No 1 is used by Algorithms No 3, No 4 and No 5, in Part 1 only.)

(ii)   List No 2: All Prepositional Verbs (used with *in, up, out, down, over, away, aside, at, on, . . .*, etc.)

(iii) List No 3: All Phrasal (or Compound and Separable Compound) Verbs (Verbs that are sometimes used in combination with another word, e.g. *take place, take part, become evident* (*or clear*), *there is* (*or are, was, were*), *make clear* . . ., etc.)

(iv)   List No 4: besides, therefore, however, whereas, thus, hence, though, despite, with, nevertheless, throughout, through, during, that, only, but, if, otherwise, again, which, although, thereby, already, against, unless, thereafter, over, as, what, toward(s), for, into, about, by, so, from, at, above, under, beside, below, onto, since, in, behind, in front of, beyond, around, before, after, about, against, then, altogether, among, between, beneath, both, neither, none, of, Article, so much as, so far as, so far, as long as, as soon as, so long as, in order that, in order to, lest, as well as, and, or, nor, such, than, onto, until, all, near, even, when, while, within, last, next, also, less, more, most, whether, much, once, one, any, many, some, where, another, other, each, then, whose, who, till, what, across, whence, hence, according, due to, owing, whereby, prior, wherever, despite, already, moreover, likewise, however, out, down, over . . ., etc.

(v)   List No 5: no, what, how, much, some, any, into, in, where, when, how, while, after, more, most, less, least, each, against, Possessive Pronouns, but, as, from, Article, on, at, with, without, by, to, for, of, if, neither, nor . . ., etc.

(vi)   List No 6: any, with, such, without, for, no, from, much, many, less, least, how, more, most, where, when, after, before, lest, of, at, on, other, another, toward(s), Possessive Pronouns, same, every, Article, in, into, per, a word ending in *-'s* or *-s'* . . ., etc.

(vii) List No 7: would(n't), will, won't, shall, shan't, should(n't), can(not), can't, could(n't), not, may, may not, might(n't), must(n't), ought(n't), . . . ought to . . ., etc.

(viii) List No 8: Article, a word ending in *-'s* or *-s'* – genitive of the Noun, Possessive Pronouns, every, where, when, how, all, no, some, against, by, for, after, before, beyond, at, under, other, as, in, into, of, any, for, on, onto, from, such, same, only, with, another, toward(s) . . .

(ix)   List No 9: no, no use, beyond, in, into, with, without, any, before, after, what, how, how much, where, some, each, from, as, about, and, while, on, onto, since, by, to, for, of, much . . .

(x)   List No 10: am, am not, is(n't), are(n't) was(n't), were(n't), . . ., etc.

7 Algorithmic procedure to determine the use of Adjectives, Nouns, Participles, Numerals and Adverbs as attributes to the Noun

After the analysis of the text with Algorithm No 3, each wordform receives its correct Part of Speech, depending on the context. But, as we know, the Parts of Speech represent the most general level of description of the language. The Parts of Speech are word groups formed on the basis of our study of both text and vocabulary. As such, the Parts of Speech provide very general information about the word relationships within the sentence. This information is not sufficient when we come to sentence level and want to establish the role of each individual word in the sentence. On sentence level many Nouns, Adverbs, Participles and Numerals can be used as Adjectives (attributes to the Noun), while the Adjective can be used either as an attribute to the Noun or as a Predicative. Let's consider the following examples:

(i)   *She has ten suitcases.*

(where *ten* is used as an Adjective and as an attribute to the Noun) or

(ii)   *She looks nice.*

(where *nice* is used as a Predicative). Compare the other use of *nice* as an attribute to the Noun in:

(iii)   *She is a nice girl.*

The following algorithm (No 5) is designed specifically for this purpose – to analyse the sentence and to decide whether the Nouns, the Participles, the Numerals and the Adverbs play an adjectival and attributive or predicative role. Algorithm No 5 cannot be used without Algorithm No 3 and Algorithm No 4. Algorithm No 4 splits the sentence into smaller parts to facilitate the operation of Algorithm No 5.

7.1 Algorithm No 4. A preparatory procedure for Algorithm No 5

1.   Read the words from left to right as they follow in the text, one by one. After reading each consecutive word the following question is asked about it:
2.   Has the text ended?
3.   Yes. Stop. End operation.
4.   No. Record this word in the memory. The words are stored in the memory, one after another, as they follow in the text.
4a.   Read the next word and proceed to 5.
5.   Is this a Punctuation Mark?
6.   Yes. Cut the sentence just before the Punctuation Mark, leaving five spaces before recording the next word in the memory. Go to 2.
7.   No. Is this a word from List No 1 (see List No 1 in Algorithm No 3)? NB Exclude from List No 1 all Punctuation Marks and add to it all words

registered as PANV and PAV (in the Dictionary), in order to make it suitable for the procedures that follow below.

8.   Yes. Is this word followed by another word from List No 1?

8a.   Yes. Is this second word followed by yet another word from List No 1?

8aa.   Yes. Cut the sentence just before the word in question and leave five spaces before recording this word and the other two words that follow it in the memory. Go to 2.

8ab.   No. Cut the sentence just before the word in question and leave five spaces before recording this word and the word following it in the memory. Go to 2.

8b.   No. Cut the sentence just before the word in question leaving five spaces before recording it in the memory. Go to 2.

9.   No. Record the word in the memory. Go to 2 (all words that are not registered in List No 1 are recorded in the memory as they follow, without leaving extra space between them).

A sample of the output of the algorithm is presented below:

He was pleased   , too   , about the scheduled return   by air   next Saturday   .

7.2 Algorithm No 5 – a procedure to determine the attributes and the predicatives in a sentence

NB In this algorithm by *a word from List No 1* should be understood the margin of five spaces left at the output of Algorithm No 4.

1.   Read the next word (till the end of the text is reached).

2.   Is this an Adjective?

3.   Yes. Go to subroutine 1–37.

4.   No. Is this a Noun?

5.   Yes. Go to subroutine 39–51.

6.   No. Is this a Participle?

7.   Yes. Go to subroutine 52–62.

8.   No. Is this a Numeral?

9.   Yes. Go to subroutine 78–82.

10.   No. Is this an Adverb?

11.   Yes. Go to subroutine 63–77.

12.   No. Is this a name, or an abbreviation, or a capital letter word (excluding the first word of the sentence)?

13.   Yes. Go to subroutine 83–91.

14.   No. Is this a Gerund, or Participle '-ing'?

15.   Yes. Is it preceded by a word from List No 1 (the original List for Algorithm No 3, not the one modified for Algorithm 4 and 5) and at the same time followed by an Adjective, which in turn is followed by an Adjective or by a Noun?

15a.   Yes. Record in the memory against it: an Adjective. Go to 1.

15b.   No. Go to 1.

16.   No. Is this **all**, **that**, ... etc.?

17. Yes. Is it preceded by **is(n't)**, **was(n't)**, **be**, and at the same time followed by a word from List No 1?

17a. Yes. Record in the memory against **all** or **that** . . ., etc.: a Predicative. Go to 1.

17b. No. Record in the memory against **all** or **that** . . ., etc.: a Pronoun. Go to 1.

18. No. Go to 1.

subroutine 1–37 (for the Adjective)

1. Is the Adjective (Adj) preceded by a word from List No 1 and at the same time followed by a Noun, which in turn is followed by a word from List No 1?

2. Yes. Record in the memory against the Adj: an Adjective. Go to 1.

3. No. Is the Adj preceded by **and**, which in turn is preceded by a Predicative?

4. Yes. Record in the memory against the Adj: a Predicative. Go to 1.

5. No. Is the Adj preceded by an Adverb, which in turn is preceded by a Punctuation Mark and at the same time followed by **to**, which in turn is followed by a Verb?

6. Yes. Record in the memory against the Adj: a Predicative. Go to 1.

7. No. Is the Adj preceded by a word from List No 1 and at the same time followed by an Adjective, which in turn is followed by a word from List No 1?

8. Yes. Record in the memory against the Adj: a Predicative. Go to 1.

9. No. Is the Adj preceded by an Adjective, which in turn is preceded by a word from List No 1 and at the same time followed by a word from List No 1?

10. Yes. Record in the memory against the Adj: a Predicative. Go to 1.

11. No. Is the Adj preceded by a Verb (Auxiliary included) or by a Participle 1st and at the same time followed by a word from List No 1?

12. Yes. Record in the memory against the Adj: a Predicative. Go to 1.

13. No. Is the Adj preceded by a comma and at the same time followed by a word from List No 1?

14. Yes. Record in the memory against the Adj: a Predicative. Go to 1.

15. No. Is the Adj preceded by an Adverb, which in turn is preceded by the word **only** and at the same time followed by a word from List No 1?

16. Yes. Record in the memory against the Adj: a Predicative. Go to 1.

17. No. Is the Adj preceded by an Adverb, which in turn is preceded by: **not**, **is(n't)**, **am**, **am not**, **are(n't)**, **was(n't)**, **were(n't)** and at the same time followed by a word from List No 1?

18. Yes. Record in the memory against the Adj: a Predicative. Go to 1.

19. No. Is the Adj preceded by a word from List No 1 and at the same time followed by a word from List No 1?

20. Yes. Record in the memory against the Adj: an Adjective. Go to 1.

21. No. Is the Adj preceded by: **most**, **more**, **less**, **least** . . ., etc., which in turn is preceded by a Verb and at the same time followed by a word from List No 1?

22.   Yes. Record in the memory against the Adj: a Predicative. Go to 1.
23.   No. Is the Adj preceded by an Adverb, which in turn is preceded by a Verb and at the same time followed by a word from List No 1?
24.   Yes. Record in the memory against the Adj: a Predicative. Go to 1.
25.   No. Is the Adj preceded by an Adverb and at the same time followed by a word from List No 1 (excluding the word **and** from the List)?
26.   Yes. Record in the memory against the Adj: a Predicative. Go to 1.
27.   No. Is the Adj preceded by **of** and at the same time followed by a word from List No 1?
28.   Yes. Record in the memory against the Adj: a Predicative. Go to 1.
29.   No. Is the Adj preceded by a comma and at the same time followed by a Verb?
30.   Yes. Record in the memory against the Adj: a Predicative. Go to 1.
31.   No. Is the Adj preceded by an Article, which in turn is preceded by: **is(n't)**, **be**, **am**, **am not**, **are(n't)**, **was(n't)**, **were(n't)** and at the same time followed by a Noun?
32.   Yes. Record in the memory against the Adj: a Predicative. Go to 1.
33.   No. Is the Adj preceded by **still**, which in turn is preceded by: **not**, **is(n't)**, **are(n't)**, **am**, **be**, **was(n't)**, **were(n't)** . . ., etc., and at the same time followed by a word from List No 1?
34.   Yes. Record in the memory against the Adj: a Predicative. Go to 1.
35.   No. Is the Adj preceded by: **not**, **be**, **is(n't)**, **are(n't)**, **am**, **am not**, **was(n't)**, **were(n't)** . . ., etc. and at the same time followed by a word from List No 1?
36.   Yes. Record in the memory against the Adj: a Predicative. Go to 1.
37.   No. Go to 1.

subroutine 39–51 (for the Noun)
39.   Is the Noun (N) preceded by: an Adjective, Numeral, Participle 1st (used as attribute), Participle '-ing', Gerund . . ., etc., which in turn is preceded by a word from List No 1 and at the same time followed by a Noun, which in its turn is followed by a word from List No 1?
40.   Yes. Record in the memory against N: an Adjective. Go to 1.
41.   No. Is N preceded by **no**, which in turn is preceded by a Verb and at the same time followed by a word from List No 1?
42.   Yes. Record in the memory against N: a Predicative. Go to 1.
43.   No. Is N preceded by an Article or Possessive Pronoun and at the same time followed by an Adjective, which in its turn is followed by a Noun?
44.   Yes. Record in the memory against N: an Adjective. Go to 1.
45.   No. Is N preceded by an Adjective, which in turn is preceded by an Article, which in its turn is preceded by: **is(n't)**, **are(n't)**, **be**, **am**, **am not**, **was(n't)**, **were(n't)** . . ., etc. and at the same time followed by a word from List No 1?
46.   Yes. Record in the memory against N: a Predicative. Go to 1.
47.   No. Is N followed by a Noun and at the same time preceded by a word from List No 1?
48.   Yes. Record in the memory against N: an Adjective. Go to 1.

49.   No. Is N preceded by: an Article, **am**, **am not**, **is(n't)**, **are(n't)**, **was(n't)**, **were(n't)** ..., etc., and at the same time followed by a word from List No 1?

50.   Yes. Record in the memory against N: a Predicative. Go to 1.

51.   No. Go to 1.

subroutine 52–62 (for Participle 1st)

52.   Is Participle 1st (P1) – the past participle of all regular and irregular Verbs – preceded by a word from List No 1 and at the same time followed by a Noun?

53.   Yes. Record in the memory against P1: an Adjective. Go to 1.

54.   No. Is P1 followed by **and**, which in turn is followed by P1, which in its turn is followed by a Noun?

55.   Yes. Record in the memory against P1: an Adjective. Go to 1.

56.   No. Is P1 preceded by an Adjective or an Adverb and at the same time followed by a Noun?

57.   Yes. Record in the memory against P1: an Adjective. Go to 1.

58.   No. Is P1 preceded by a Participle '-ing' or Gerund, and at the same time followed by a word from List No 1?

59.   Yes. Record in the memory against P1: a Predicative. Go to 1.

60.   No. Is P1 preceded by a word from List No 1 and at the same time followed by a word from List No 1?

61.   Yes. Record in the memory against P1: a Predicative. Go to 1.

62.   No. Go to 1.

subroutine 63–77 (for the Adverb – **b**)

63.   Is the Adverb (b) preceded by an Article or an Adjective and at the same time followed by a Noun?

64.   Yes. Record in the memory against b: an Adjective. Go to 1.

65.   No. Is b preceded by a Punctuation Mark and at the same time followed by **to**, which in turn is followed by a Verb?

66.   Yes. Record in the memory against b: a Predicative. Go to 1.

67.   No. Is b preceded by a comma and at the same time followed by a Noun, which in its turn is followed by a comma?

68.   Yes. Record in the memory against b: an Adjective. Go to 1.

69.   No. Is b preceded by a word from List No 1 and at the same time followed by an Adjective, which in its turn is followed by a Noun?

70.   Yes. Record in the memory against b: an Adjective. Go to 1.

71.   No. Is b preceded by **of** and at the same time followed by a Noun?

72.   Yes. Record in the memory against b: an Adjective. Go to 1.

73.   No. Is b preceded by a word from List No 1 or an Adjective and at the same time followed by a Noun or by a Participle 1st?

74.   Yes. Record in the memory against b: an Adjective. Go to 1.

75.   No. Is b followed by **and**, which in turn is followed by an Adverb, which in its turn is followed by a Participle 1st or a Noun?

76.   Yes. Record in the memory against b: an Adjective. Go to 1.

77.   No. Go to 1.

subroutine 78–82 (for the Numeral – **M**)

78.   Is the Numeral (M) preceded by an Article and at the same time followed by a Noun (or by an Adjective, which in its turn is followed by a Noun, as second alternative)?

79.   Yes. Record in the memory against M: an Adjective. Go to 1.

80.   No. Is M preceded by a word from List No 1 and at the same time followed by a Noun or by an Adjective?

81.   Yes. Record in the memory against M: an Adjective. Go to 1.

82.   No. Go to 1.

subroutine 83–91 (for names, abbreviations, capital letter words)

83.   Is the Abbreviation (F) or name (Name) preceded by a word from List No 1 and at the same time followed by an Adjective, which in its turn is followed by an Adjective or a Noun?

84.   Yes. Record in the memory against F or N: an Adjective. Go to 1.

85.   No. Is F or N preceded by an Adjective or a Numeral and at the same time followed by a Noun or an Adjective?

86.   Yes. Record in the memory against F or N: an Adjective. Go to 1.

87.   No. Is F or N preceded by a dash (–), which in its turn is preceded by a name or by an abbreviation and at the same time followed by a Noun?

88.   Yes. Record in the memory against F or N: an Adjective. Go to 1.

89.   No. Is F or N preceded by a word from List No 1 and at the same time followed by a dash, which in its turn is followed by an abbreviation or a name, which in its own turn is followed by a Noun?

90.   Yes. Record in the memory against F or N: an Adjective. Go to 1.

91.   No. Go to 1.

7.3 A text sample showing the performance of Algorithms 4 and 5

We will return to the text from Section 5 which we have already analysed with Algorithm No 3. At the output of Algorithm No 4 this text will look like this:

> *With the first peep   of day I opened my eyes,   to find myself in a great chamber, hung   with stamped leather,   furnished   with fine embroidered furniture,   and lit   by three fair windows.*

Let's now see how Algorithm No 5 will manage to determine the role of the following words in the sentence: *first* (Numeral), *stamped* (Participle 1st), *embroidered* (Adjective) and *three* (Numeral).

Operation 78 asks if the word *first* has an Article on its left and a Noun on its right, if so, then *first* is an Adjective (79). The same question is asked (52) for the word *stamped* and we have the same answer: an Adjective (53). The surroundings of the word *embroidered* are slightly different, but it is found by operation 56 and the word is declared to be an Adjective (57). The surroundings of the word *three* are spotted by operation No 80 and the word is recognized as an Adjective. Note that the Adjectives in the sentence are attributes to the Noun.

7.4 *How some of the algorithmic instructions look when programmed in C (C + +)*

```
case 34: // in a *.c or *.cpp file
   if (!stricmp(wrd- > inword, "the")){
      wrdm- > syn  =  'N';
      wcount  =  copysyn(que, wp);
      i  =  mpos; continue;
   }
   if (wrd- > numb  = =  wrdm- > numb){
      i = mpos; continue;
   }
   break;
      {"S < A > Z",   "S$V", 34},   // in the *.h file
```

N denotes a **Noun**, **Z** denotes the ambiguity **Noun or Verb**, **V** denotes a **Verb**, **S** denotes an **Article** or **Indicative Pronoun**, and **< A >** and **$** denote the possibility of an intervening Adjective, which may be positioned between **S** and **Z**. The code **wrd** denotes the preceding word; **wrdm** denotes the word immediately following. In other words, this rule says that if the analysed word is ambiguous (Noun or Verb), in this particular context it is a **Noun** if preceded by the Article **the**. In another example:

```
case 41: /*** in a *.c or *.cpp file ***/
   if (wrd- > e.V.controli  = =  0){
      if (!strrchr(wrdm- > cw, 'N'))   /* Noun or Adjective */
         wrdm- > syn  =  'A';
      else
         wrdm- > syn  =  'N';
      copysyn(que, wp);
      i  =  mpos; continue;
   }
   break;
      {"[EV] < TAO > [#N]Z",     $.V", 41},   /*** in the *.h file ***/
```

case 41 says that if the word is ambiguous (Noun or Adjective), it is an Adjective if preceded by a Verb or Participle **[EV]** and followed by another ambiguous word (Noun or Verb) **Z**. The sign **< TAO >** denotes possible intervening words (Article **T**, Adjective **A**, Possessive Pronoun **O**).

Some rules are expressed only in the respective *.h file. For example

```
      {" 'a'NZ[PXxU]", "@AN", },
```

means that if the Noun **N** is preceded by Indefinite Article **'a'** and followed by another ambiguous word **Z** (Noun or Verb), which in turn is followed by a Preposition or by an Auxiliary Verb **[PXxU]** then, in this context, this Noun **N** plays the role of an Adjective **A** and at the same time, this rule resolves the ambiguity of **Z** (Noun and Verb), declaring it to be a Noun **N**.

We have used this programming code only to illustrate how closely it matches our algorithmic rules.

4 Algorithmic recognition of the Tenses

In this chapter we'll present an algorithmic procedure for automatic recognition of the Verbal Tenses in English texts, on the understanding that the computer has already determined the Part of Speech of every running word of the text to be processed (by means of Algorithm No 3).

1 Presentation

Having processed the text using Algorithm No 3, and having attributed the running words of the text to a particular Part of Speech, we proceed as follows: all words marked as Verbs, together with the Personal Pronoun Nominal Case (PPNC) attached to them (or personal name, if there is such a name), are taken out of the sentence, preserving their order of occurrence in the sentence and the distance between them (measured in words).

Those Verbs that are separated from the rest of the sentence by dashes are analysed separately – the computer is instructed to ignore (to jump) the dashes and to find the remaining part of the Verbal Tense (if there is one). For example:

> *Not only has his poetic fame – as was inevitable – been overshadowed by that of Shakespeare, but he ...*

In the example shown above, the algorithm will ignore *was* and connect *has been overshadowed*.

In the present analysis we use the following types of Verbs: (i) the Auxiliary; (ii) the Verb Proper (Present form); (iii) the Verb in its Past form; (iv) the Verb ending in '-ing' (Participle '-ing'), as part of a Compound Tense; and (v) the Verb in its Participle form, as part of a Compound Tense.

The Auxiliary Verbs are presented in Tables (Lists). The Verbs Proper and their Past and Participle forms are presented in the Dictionary used by Algorithm No 3 to disambiguate the Verbs and their Past and Participle forms (if according to the Dictionary they face more than one attribution).

The present algorithm uses a Table for the Verbal Tenses such as:

am (are, is) + *-ing* form of the Verb = Present Continuous Tense
was (were) + *ing* form of the Verb = Past Continuous Tense
has (have) + Participle 2nd = Present Perfect Tense
had + Participle 2nd = Past Perfect Tense
... etc.

2 Presentation of the algorithm. Algorithm No 6

1.   Read the next word (till the end of the sentence is reached). (Then read the next sentence word by word, etc.)

2.   Is this a Present form of the Verb (Verb or Participle – PV)?

3.   Yes. Is it preceded by a PPNC or by a name?

3a.   Yes. Record in the memory against it: Present Simple Tense. Go to 1.

3b.   No. Is it preceded by: **should(n't)**, **would(n't)**?

3c.   Yes. Record in the memory against it (RM): Future in the Past, Present Conditional Mood. Go to 1.

3d.   No. Is it preceded by **to**?

3e.   Yes. RM: an Infinitive. Go to 1.

3f.   No. Is it preceded by: **shall**, **will**, **shall not (shan't)**, **will not (won't)**?

3g.   Yes. RM: Future Simple Tense. Go to 1.

3h.   No. RM: Present Simple Tense. Go to 1.

4.   No. Is this a past form of the Verb (Participle or Verb – PV)?

5.   Yes. Is it preceded by a PPNC or by a name (the appearance of an Auxiliary verb stops the search)?

5a.   Yes. RM: Past Simple Tense. Go to 1.

5b.   No. RM: Past Simple Tense. Go to 1.

6.   No. Is this a Participle 2nd (or Past Participle of an Irregular Verb, or Past form of the Verb)?

7.   Yes. Is it preceded by **have**?

7a.   Yes. Is **have** preceded by: **shall**, **will**, **shall not (shan't)**, **will not (won't)**?

7aa.   Yes. RM: **shall**, **will** (etc.) + **have** + Participle 2nd = Future Perfect Tense. Go to 1.

7ab.   No. Is **have** preceded by: **should(n't)**, **would(n't)**?

7ac.   Yes. RM: **should(n't)**, **(would(n't)** + **have** + Participle 2nd = (i) Perfect Tense in Conditional Mood, (ii) Future Perfect in the Past. Go to 1.

7ad.   No. RM: **have** + Participle 2nd = Present Perfect Tense. Go to 1.

7b.   No. Is it preceded by **been**?

7c.   Yes. Is **been** in turn preceded by **have(n't)**?

7ca.   Yes. Is **have(n't)** in its turn preceded by: **shall**, **shan't**, **will**, **won't**?

7caa.   Yes. RM: **shall**, **will** (etc.) + **have** + **been** + Participle 2nd = Future Perfect Tense. Go to 1.

7cab.   No. Is **have(n't)** in its turn preceded by: **should(n't)**, **would(n't)**?

7cac. Yes. RM: **should**, **would** (etc.) + **have** + **been** + Participle 2nd = Future Perfect in the Past. Go to 1.

7cad. No. RM: **have(n't)** + **been** + Participle 2nd = Present Perfect Tense. Go to 1.

7d. No. Is it preceded by **being**?

7e. Yes. Is **being** preceded by: **was(n't)**, **were(n't)**?

7ea. Yes. RM: **was(n't)**, **(were(n't)** + **being** + Participle 2nd = Past Continuous Tense, Passive Voice. Go to 1.

7eb. No. Is **being** preceded by: **am**, **am not**, **is(n't)**, **are(n't)**?

7ec. Yes. RM: **am** (etc.) + **being** + Participle 2nd = Present Continuous Tense, Passive Voice. Go to 1.

7f. No. Is it preceded by **be**?

7g. Yes. Is **be** in turn preceded by: **should(n't)**, **would(n't)**?

7ga. Yes. RM: **should(n't)**, **would(n't)** + **be** + Participle 2nd = Future in the Past, Passive Voice. Go to 1.

7gb. No. Is **be** in turn preceded by: **shall**, **shan't**, **will**, **won't**?

7gc. Yes. RM: **shall** (etc.) + **be** + Participle 2nd = Future Tense. Passive Voice. Go to 1.

7gd. No. Is **be** preceded by to?

7ge. Yes. RM: **to** + **be** + Participle 2nd = Infinitive, Passive Voice. Go to 1.

7h. No. Is it preceded by: **am**, **am not**, **is(n't)**, **are(n't)**?

7i. Yes. RM: **am** (etc.) + Participle 2nd = Present Tense, Passive Voice. Go to 1.

7j. No. Is it preceded by: **has(n't)**, **have(n't)**?

7k. Yes. RM: **have(n't)** or **has(n't)** + Participle 2nd = Present Perfect Tense. Go to 1.

7l. No. Is it preceded by **had**?

7m. Yes. RM: **had** + Participle 2nd = Past Perfect Tense. Go to 1.

7n. No. RM: Past Simple Tense. Go to 1.

8. No. Is this **-ing** form of the Verb?

9. Yes. Is it preceded by **been**?

9a. Yes. Is **been** in turn preceded by **have(n't)**?

9aa. Yes. Is **have(n't)** in its turn preceded by: **should(n't)**, **would(n't)**?

9aaa. Yes. RM: **should(n't)**, **would(n't)** + **have** + **been** + Participle -ing = Future Perfect Continuous in the Past. Go to 1.

9aab. No. Is **have(n't)** in its turn preceded by: **shall**, **shan't**, **will**, **won't**?

9aac. Yes. RM: **shall** (etc.) + **have(n't)** + been + Participle '-ing' = Future Perfect Continuous Tense. Go to 1.

9aad. No RM: **have(n't)** + **been** + Participle '-ing' = Present Perfect Continuous Tense. Go to 1.

9ab. No. Is **been** preceded by: **has(n't)** or **have(n't)**?

9aba. Yes. RM: **has(n't)**, **have/n't)** + **been** + Participle '-ing' = Present Perfect continuous Tense. Go to 1.

9abb. No. Go to 1.

9b. No. Is it preceded by **be**?

9c. Yes. Is **be** in its turn preceded by: **should(n't)**, **would(n't)**?
9ca. Yes. RM: **should(n't)**, **would(n't)** + **be** + Participle '-ing' = Future Continuous in the Past. Go to 1.
9cb. No. Is **be** in turn preceded by: **shall**, **shan't**, **will**, **won't**?
9cc. Yes. RM: **shall** (etc.) + **be** + Participle '-ing' = Future Continuous Tense. Go to 1.
9cd. No. Go to 1.
9d. No. Is it preceded by: **am**, **am not**, **are(n't)**, **is(n't)**?
9e. Yes. RM: **am** (etc.) + Participle '-ing' = Present Continuous Tense. Go to 1.
9f. No. Go to 1.
10. No. RM: unrecognized Tense. Ask the operator for help. Go to 1.

3 Discussion

At this stage of description and recognition it is not always possible to differentiate some of the Verbal Tenses, especially for example when homographs such as *put*, *cut*, etc. are involved, therefore the algorithm states both Tenses: (i) Past or Present Simple Tense; (ii) Perfect Tense in Conditional Mood, or Future Perfect in the Past.

All the above-mentioned homographs are arranged in a separate Table, for reference. The ambiguity arising on this level of description can be resolved with other algorithms, using semantic information. For example, compare the sentences:

(i) *I put my hat on my head every day.* (Present Simple Tense)
(ii) *I put my hat on my head a few minutes ago.* (Past Simple Tense)

This algorithm, when tested manually on randomly chosen texts yields perfect results (100 per cent correct recognition). Note that Algorithm No 6 was programmed and incorporated in the English parsing program SYNTPARSE (see Internet Downloads at the end of the book).

PART TWO

5 Syntactical structure of the sentence

1 Introduction

In Part 2 we will continue with the algorithmic description of English grammar. Our focus will be English syntax for the computer – syntax, without lexical semantics. The presentation of knowledge will be similar to that in Part 1 – flow charts and a database accessible to both human and artificial intellects. The expected results at the output will be:

- to recognize each word's grammatical role in the sentence:
  a) as Part of Speech – Noun, Verb, Adjective, Adverb, Particle, Pronoun, Numeral, Preposition, Conjunction, Interjection. The algorithmic procedures offered here do not duplicate those presented in Part 1, Algorithm No 3. The method used in Part 2 is completely different and has much wider application. In Part 2 the same goal is achieved with fewer instructions and greater accuracy.
  b) as Part of the Sentence – Subject, Object (Direct and Indirect), Complement Subject and Object, Infinitival Complement, Predicative, Verb, Verbal Tense, Infinitive, Adverb, etc. Differentiation is made between attributive and predicative adjectives, adjuncts and disjuncts.
- to offer a satisfactory algorithmic solution of Pronominal Reference (procedures based entirely on syntax with the aim of finding the Nouns to which the Pronouns refer, with minimal error);
- to present the syntactic structure of the sentence in a programmable way, so that the computer can:
  a) recognize all simple sentences;
  b) recognize the Independent and the Dependent Clauses, including the Adverbial Clauses in a Complex or Compound Sentence;
  c) connect all disconnected syntactic structures (phrases) within the sentence;
  d) transform the sentence into simple statements each of which expresses one single aspect of the meaning of the sentence.

All this done, the computer will become intelligent enough to be able to understand, without difficulty, some aspects of English grammar and syntax.

However, at this level of knowledge, the computer cannot understand the meaning of the sentence, cannot reason yet – cannot make logical inferences, cannot make independent decisions, cannot assess the meaning of the text as a whole and cannot judge its significance and meaning in relation to other texts.

What the computer can do in fact, at this stage, is simply to identify a portion of the text (a sequence of words) with what is being registered in its memory as a portion of English syntax (a sequence of syntactical elements). Still, this is an excellent achievement, because since the advent of Computational Linguistics, the computational identification of the syntactical structure of the sentence has not transcended its experimental stage – only 50 per cent correct results are reported by McEnery (1992: 82) in his reviewal of the Constituent Likelihood Grammar (Garside, 1986).

It should be noted, however, that some ambiguities on the syntactic level still remain, but the computer will recognize an ambiguity and ask the operator for help.

The algorithmic description of English grammar, presented in Part 1 and Part 2, is not simply something which ought to be applied in a Text Processing System: it is a Text Processing System itself.

2 Syntactic Structures

The idea of Syntactic Structures is closely associated with an earlier work in the field (Chomsky, 1957) and ever since then it has found wide interpretation and application, mainly in the construction of artificial languages. But although this idea was derived from the structure of the natural language it was never applied fully to it (to cover every possible sentence and utterance), for two reasons:

a) because the representation of the sentence as a sequence of Noun Phrases (NP) and Verbal Phrases (VP), though universal in truth and simple to understand, has only a theoretical, not a practical value (Shanks, 1993: 27–31);
b) because of the enormous diversity of the syntactic structures involved – their number was thought to be practically infinite, taking into account the combinatorics of their constituent elements, the Parts of Speech.

Artificial Intelligence in general, and Machine Translation and Information Retrieval in particular, require a suitable procedure to analyse and understand natural language texts on a computer if mankind wants to make further progress in these fields.

In an attempt to satisfactorily resolve this outstanding problem algorithmically, we propose the formal definition given below of a Syntactic Structure that would apply to every individual sentence.

A syntactic structure begins with one of the following Punctuation Marks ; . : ! ? ( ) – or with one of the words listed in List No 1 (in this section List

No 1 includes all Auxiliary words – excluding the Auxiliary Verbs – see further for details) and ends just before one of the above-mentioned Punctuation Marks or just before a word listed in List No 1. Often, the new structure begins at the point where a Prepositional Adverbial Clause has ended. Then there is no need of a Punctuation Mark or of a word from List No 1 to signal the start of the new structure (see further for examples). In this case, the ensuing structure can start with any Part of Speech.

The structures encompassed within these left and right boundaries do not always coincide with the Syntactic Structures in the traditional sense. They are of the following types:

a) Syntactic Structures, as known traditionally in the literature – all grammatically correct and simple sentences (i), or Independent (Main) Clauses (ii) of the sort:
   (i)   *Peter eats an apple.*
   (ii)   *she is reading a book*

b) structures that coincide with the Dependent (Subordinate) Clauses of the sentence:
            (*He told me*)
   (iii)   *that she was asked to attend the conference.*
            (Predicative Clause)

   (iv)   *by a man; at an adjacent table*, etc.
            (Prepositional Adverbial Clauses)

            (*The man,*)
   (v)   *who was invited to attend the party*, ...
            (Relative Clause)

c) structures that play an appositional role in the sentence, such as:
            Peter Smith,
   (vi)   *a writer of romantic fiction*, ...

d) incomplete structures, like those used for enumeration (vii), or a structure interrupted by a comma or by another structure (viii), etc.:
   (vii)   ..., *sings, laughs, cries*, ...
   (viii)   *The book on the table is mine.*
   (viii a) *is mine.*

e) grammatically incorrect structures, permitted sometimes in texts.

Therefore, to avoid any misunderstanding, we propose to call all structures mentioned above 'portions of the text' (the sentence) or 'strings of words'.

Each natural language word in such a portion can be substituted by its equivalent Part of Speech. Then the abbreviated representation of a portion of a text (of a sentence) as a sequence of Parts of Speech will be called a segment (see further for details).

3 The segment

The term segment used in this study has a vague resemblance to, but is distinct from, that used by Hausser (1989).

As a result of our formal definition of the segment, we were able to reduce the text (the sentence) to a finite number of segments and to list those segments in a Dictionary (see: Dictionary of Segments, available for download on the Internet, in the chapter Internet Downloads at the end of the book). This type of Dictionary has a full right to existence on a par with all other dictionaries. Not only can it be used by the computer, it can also be used by anyone who studies or teaches English as a native or foreign language and by anyone who wants to have a better and more varied style of writing.

The segments listed in the Dictionary of Segments were extracted manually from the text, on a statistical basis. The text consisted of two million running words, divided into 40 samples. The text samples were taken from various sources, the object being to cover all possible styles.

However, some less common and rare segments are not listed. Some incomplete or grammatically incorrect segments are listed and marked with the sign *.

We hope that with the use of the Dictionary of Segments in the Text Processing System or at home on a personal computer the missing segments will take their due place.

At present, the segments listed in this study represent 98 per cent of all possible segments in English texts (or sentences). We deem this database to be quite sufficient to write an English Algorithmic Grammar based on it and also to prove our belief that segments, like morphemes and words, can be enumerated and can be used as individual units of expression of syntax and grammar, in the same way, for example, as words or morphemes are used to express lexical meaning and grammar.

The segments are sequences of grammatical and syntactical elements represented simultaneously on three different language levels:

1. On the level of natural language wordforms only. These segments have fixed terminological, phrasal or idiomatic meaning, therefore they are left as they are used in natural language. Their constituent words cannot (or rather, should not) be substituted with Parts of Speech. For example:

   (i)   *in any case*; *in a way*; *by no means*, etc.

2. On the level of Parts of Speech only: Noun, Verb, Adjective, etc. Here, for example, all Nouns are marked with **n**, all Verbs are marked with **v**, all Adjectives are marked with **G**, etc. All Nouns form a set of Nouns; all Verbs form a set of Verbs, etc. When we register a segment using only the abbreviations of Parts of Speech to replace the constituent words of a portion of a text, we mean that any Noun can be placed in the position marked by **n**, any Verb can be placed in the position marked by **v**, etc. For example:

(ii)   n v n
(iii)   n v G n

The segments are a substitute for a great number of English language sentences (statements, phrases, Clauses, even single words), for example:

(iv)   *People like presents.*   =   d v n
(v)   *Peter eats apples.*   =   d v n
(vi)   *Ann speaks good English.*   =   d v G n
(vii)   *Come!*   =   v

(**d** is a subclass of the Noun, marking all words denoting a human being.)

Since the gender and number of the Nouns and Pronouns and the person of the Verbal Tense were not specified, the segments can generate grammatically incorrect utterances. Here are some examples of grammatically incorrect sentences that can be formed on this basis:

(v a)   *Peter eat apple.*   =   d v n
(vi a) *Ann speak good English.*   =   d v G n

because the third person singular of the Present Tense of the Verb was not marked specifically (**v** stands for all forms, Present and Past Simple) and because **n** stands for both singular and plural of the Noun, while **d** stands for singular and plural, masculine and feminine. However, syntactically, the segments show the correct sequence of Parts of Speech as permitted by English grammar.

The fact that some grammatical features (concord, agreement) within the segment were not specified should not be regarded as a failure, because this was done to reduce the number of the segments and because the segments were designed for text analysis, not for text synthesis. This means that the segments would be used to match grammatically correct and meaningful sentences, and not to generate such.

If we were to use the segments for text generation, we would have to add the missing grammatical information. For example, we can use **v'** to mark third person singular Present Tense, **n'** to mark the plural of the Noun, and **k** to mark human being, female, etc. This will undoubtedly treble the present list of 27,000 segments.

3. Mixed level. On this level, the segments are expressed using natural language wordforms, the abbreviations for Parts of Speech and the abbreviations for semantic groups. The semantic group is a set of words sharing the same meaning and fitting a particular position specified in the segment. As such, the semantic group is a subset of the respective Part of Speech. For example, the semantic group marked with **d** (all words denoting people, including proper names and PPNC) is a subclass of all words marked with **n**. The semantic group marked with FB (year, month, second, moment, season, etc.) is also a subclass of **n**. In order to make the segments more specific in meaning, in many cases we have preferred to use the abbreviation of a semantic group instead of the abbreviation for a Part of Speech. For example:

(viii) v R UF = *tell me something, give us everything, ask him nothing,* etc.,

instead of

(ix) v R n = *teach us English, give him money,* etc.

where UF (something, nothing, etc.) is a subset of **n** and this means that no other **n** can assume this position in the segment, except those Nouns which belong to the semantic group UF. Let's take another example:

(x) on the S of FB-BE = *on the first of January*

where **S** is a Numeral Ordinal and FB-BE is a subset of **FB**, and as such no other word from FB can assume this position in the segment, except those belonging to FB-BE. Therefore the semantic subgroup restricts the choice of the words that can be used in a specified position in a segment. The use of a natural language wordform instead brings this choice down to a single word. In the above example (x) *on* is a natural language word, a Preposition, and no other word can take its place in this segment.

The mixed level of representation of the segment resembles a pulsation with gradual surges and declines, and brings the segment nearer to the natural language text by balancing the entropy and the redundancy inherent in Natural Language. The pulsation reflects the choice of natural language words permitted by the grammar at a specified position in the segment.

The Auxiliary words, especially the Prepositions and the Conjunctions, play a special role in the formation of the Sentence (and in our case, of the segment) by bringing the choice down to zero; therefore they deserve particular attention.

As part of this mixed-level representation, each Verbal Tense was presented separately, with its own abbreviations, with some exceptions (for more details see Section 3.1.1 in the next chapter). For example, Present Simple and Past Simple Tense were both marked with **v** (see also the Index of Abbreviations) because being Simple, they function syntactically in an identical way.

The simultaneous representation of the segments on three different language levels is simply a reminder that these levels coexist in the text; it is only the grammarians that delineate them to study them better.

Below we list more examples of the mixed level of presentation of the segment:

(xi)   by means of G n

(used instead of *by n of G n*), where **by** and **means** are English language words and no other word can take their place in this position and in this segment; or, another example:

(xii)   d has also P2 A n of EBB

(used instead of *d has also P2 A n of n*), where **d** is a human being, **has** stands for the **have** paradigm (excluding *having*), **also** stands for *also, not,* Adverb, etc. (see the Index of abbreviations), **P2** stands for Participle 2nd, **A** marks the Article, **of** is the irreplaceable Preposition *of* used in genitive constructions, **n** is a Noun and **EBB** is a semantic group (*somebody, someone, nobody*, etc.). No other natural language words, semantic groups or grammatical categories can assume the specified positions in this segment (xii), except those indicated.

On this mixed level of presentation of the segment, some positions allow greater choice (like that of **n**), other positions considerably restrict the choice (like that of **d**, or even more so that of **EBB**, because **EBB** is a subclass of **d**) and still other positions allow no choice – there is only one possibility, a specific English word (such as *of, on, by, means*, etc.).

In the present study, we have preferred the mixed level of presentation of segments for two reasons:

a) because it is impossible to enumerate all sequences of natural language words (all portions of texts);
b) because using only Parts of Speech, as substitutes for the natural language words, makes the segment very generalized in its syntactical meaning. For example, if we were to mark all Prepositions with **C** and substitute them with **C**, we would not be able to differentiate the Prepositional Adverbial Clauses for time, place, means, etc.

4 Presentation of the segment

The interrelation between the constituent elements of a segment is predetermined by the very construction of the segment. This relation is pretty obvious to the grammarian, but it is not understood by the computer. To make the computer understand the interrelation of the constituent elements of a segment, we have marked the interrelation using different signs (see the Index of Abbreviations). For example **Sj** stands for Subject, **Od** for Object Direct, " means that the second word marked with " relates (or refers) to the first one marked with ", etc.

Each segment is followed by its Parsing (on the line below). For example:

(i)   d v A G n
         Sj v Od

When several segments in a row have the same Parsing, we have shown it under the last segment. For example:

(ii)   d v O G G n
(iii)   d v O G n
(iv)   d v O n
(v)   d v O n of n
(vi)   d v O n of G n
       Sj v Od

(**O** is a Possessive Pronoun)

In those cases where the Parsing of a segment is not presented, we have placed a sequence of dots:

(vii)   and b to v
(viii)   and b v
....
(**b** is an Adverb)

In those cases where a segment has more than one possible Parsing, the next alternative Parsing is shown on the line below. The Parsing of the segment is predetermined. The Verbal Tenses are presented individually. The reader can find more about the presentation of the Verbal Tenses in Chapter 6, Section 3.1.1.

The Parsing of the segments is discussed in greater detail in Chapter 7, Section 2.

NB Those words that have the same abbreviation can assume only the syntactical position marked with the abbreviation (unless specified otherwise). In addition, some words can belong to a group (as in (ix) below) and at the same time be stand-alone words (as in (x)):

(ix)   *Merry will go on with this.*
        d   shall v up with I

Here *on* is part of a larger group abbreviated with **up** (see the Index of Abbreviations: up = *on, with, at, up, off,* etc.).

(x)   *Merry arrived on time.*
        d   v   on FB

Here **on** marks the Preposition *on* – the only alternative permitted, or in other words **on** = *on*. In example (ix) *with* is also a stand-alone word and marks the only alternative permitted.

6 Composition of the segments

1 Introduction

The segment is the grammatical and syntactical framework within which the semantic (lexical, grammatical, syntactical, etc.) meaning finds expression in communication. It is a grammatical norm, like many other norms in the language, that keep it from falling apart. The acquisition of this syntactical framework starts from the very early stages of childhood and runs parallel with the acquisition of the vocabulary. It is, in a sense, a syntactical word and those people who learn English as a first or second language should, eventually, know all the syntactical words in the language. Some English writers are more versatile – they use a wider range of syntactical words (segments) – than others. Some writers have a preference for certain syntactical expressions. Therefore, it can be said that the segments are an integral part of the style of writing. It takes some effort, but it can be easily proven that about 80 per cent of the segments reappear within the first 100 pages of a novel.

The syntactical framework expressed by the segments is not something permanent in the language: it changes slowly over the centuries. For example, in primitive expression (Curme, 1955: 106) the predicate Noun, the Adjective and the Adverb were used as a Complement Subject without a linking Verb. The introduction of linking Verbs was a marked improvement of speech.

A comprehensive List of the segments existing in the English language, under the heading Dictionary of Segments, can be downloaded from our homepage on the Internet (see Internet Downloads at the end of the book). The list comprises some 27,000 segments, which represent 98 per cent of all possible segments in English. This fact was proven statistically, by comparing the segments from an unknown text with those listed in the Dictionary of Segments. In order to make this calculation, we took one hundred texts (from various sources), each containing one hundred segments and went through the Dictionary of Segments to locate each one of the segments. On average, two segments out of every hundred were not registered in the Dictionary of Segments. These usually were rare, odd or grammatically incorrect syntactical constructions used, sometimes, in writing. The latter can be found more often in speech (speech was beyond our scope of study).

2 Examples of manual extraction of segments from a text

Below we will list several sentences and show how they divide into segments (see Sections 2 and 3 of the previous chapter for the dividing rules).

Ann ran past her, through the kitchen and into the hall. Her footsteps slowed as she reached the door of Mr Paton's room, and she stood outside it for a moment, her heart thumping. Mr Paton was a bad man and he had left them in the cellar to die.

The portion of the text is shown first. Then each portion of text is presented as a sequence of Parts of Speech (words, semantic groups) – the segment. Then the segment is followed by its Parsing.

(i)   *Ann ran past her,*
        d   v   up R
        Sj v   Od

(ii)   *through   the kitchen*
        through A n
        bdl: (Adverbial phrase for direction and location)

(iii)   *and*
        and
        (Conjunction)

(iv)   *into the hall.*
        into A n
        bdl

(v)   *Her footsteps slowed*
        O   n   v
        Sj   v

(vi)   *as*
        as
        (Conjunction)

(vii)   *she reached the door of Mr Paton's room,*
        d   v   A n   of N''s   n
        Sj v   Od

(viii) *and*
        and
        (Conjunction)

(ix)   *she stood*
        d   v
        Sj v

(x)   *outside it*
        outside R
        bdl

(xi)   *for a moment,*
        for A FB
        bm (Adverbial clause for time)

(xii)   *her heart thumping.*
O n   Pi
Sj   Cs

(xiii) *Mr Paton was a bad man*
d   am A G n
Sj   v   Cs

(xiv) *and*
and
(Conjunction)

(xv)   *he had left them*
d had P2 R
Sj v   Od

(xvi) *in the cellar*
in A n
bdl

(xvii) *to die.*
to v

Later on in this study it will be shown how the computer program can connect *to die* to *he had left them*.

In the next example, the segments will be separated by /:

(xviii) *Suddenly | there came a flashing light |*
b   there v A G   n
into his clouded mind. | It shot clear | across
into O G   n   it v j   across
the perplexed field of the consciousness. | Like a
A G   n of A n   like A
bursting thunderbolt clarifying the murky
G   n   Pi   A G
atmosphere | it burned away the little thoughts
n   it v   up A G n
and fears.
and n

We leave the task of Parsing the above segments to the reader.

3 Types of segments

In this section the reader will find a detailed description of the segments listed in the Dictionary of Segments and more information on how to interpret and use them in practice.

According to the initial element of the segment, the segments can be subdivided into three major categories:

1) *Nominal segments.* These are the segments that begin with one of the following Parts of Speech or Natural Language words:

(i)	An Article (**A**-segments);
(ii)	Numeral (**M**-segments);
(iii)	Noun (**n**-segments);
(iv)	Indicative Pronoun (i-segments);
(v)	**all** – plural quantifier and plural indefinite determiner (**all**-segments);
(vi)	Noun denoting a human being (**d**-segments);
(vii)	**it** – PPNC, neutral (**it**-segments);
(viii)	Adjective (**G**-segments);
(ix)	**who** – relative or interrogative pronoun (**who**-segments);
(x)	**both** – pronoun (**both**-segments);
(xi)	**which** – determiner, also interrogative determiner (**which**-segments);
(xii)	**whose** – determiner for possessiveness, also interrogative determiner (**whose**-segments);
(xiii)	**whom** – one of the relative pronominal forms and interrogative pronoun (**whom**-segments);
(xiv)	**whoever** – relative pronominal form (**whoever**-segments);
(xv)	Possessive Pronoun or genitive of the Noun (**O**-segments, **N"s**-segments);
(xvi)	**other** – pronoun (**other**-segments);
(xvii)	**such** – pronoun (**such**-segments);

2) *Verbal segments.* These segments begin with a proper (Main) or an Auxiliary Verb, an Infinitive starting with the Particle **to** (to + Infinitive), or with a Participle.

Most of these segments constitute the Predicative. The Predicative includes the second argument, the Object, the Complement (Subject, Object) and the Infinitive, following after the Main or the Auxiliary Verb. In this case, the Predicative is cut off from the Nominal part representing the Subject by an intervening segment. Some of those Verbal Segments that start with a Main Verb are Imperative. A certain number of those segments that start with an Auxiliary Verb are Interrogative. Other segments start with the Infinitive used as a Subject.

According to their first element, the Verbal segments are classified as:

(i)	Participle -**ing** (**Pi**-segments);
(ii)	Verb proper, including **have** and **do** (excluding *doing*) paradigms (**v**-segments);
(iii)	**am** – the **be** paradigm, but excluding *be* and *being* (**am**-segments);
(iv)	**to** – as an Infinitive to the Verb (**to v**-segments);
(v)	Second argument (such as *busy, ready*, etc., usually used after a word from the **be** paradigm) (**j**-segments);
(vi)	Participle 1st (**P1**-segments);
(vii)	**did** – comprising *do, does* and *did* (**did**-segments);
(viii)	**has** – the **have** paradigm, but excluding *having* (**have**-segments);

(ix)   **can** – modal auxiliary Verb comprising *can, could, may, might, shall, should, will, would, would better, ought to, must, have to* (**can**-segments);

(x)   **should** – modal auxiliary Verb comprising *should, will, would, may, might, shall, must* (**should**-segments);

(xi)   **not** – particle for negation (**not**-segments);

(xii)   **there are** – comprising *there are, there v, there was, there were, there is* (**there are**-segments);

(xiii) **there has** – comprising *there has, there had, there have* (**there has**-segments);

(xiv)   **there can** – comprising *there can* (and the other modal verbs), *there seem(s), there seemed* (**there can**-segments).

Note: *be, being, called, calling* and *noted* are listed with the Auxiliary segments.

3) *Auxiliary segments.* These segments begin with an Auxiliary word (Preposition, Conjunction, Interjection), Verb (*be, being, called, calling*), Adverb, or some of the quantifiers and modifiers, etc. When the Preposition is not an integral part of a Phrasal Verb it is used to start a Prepositional Adverbial Clause.

NB The Prepositions and the Conjunctions listed here are part of List No 1 used by Algorithms No 2 and No 3 in Part 1 and all other algorithms in Part 2. The Auxiliary words presented below represent List No 1 used by Algorithms No 2 and No 3 (Part 1) and Algorithms No 7 and No 20 (Part 2).

(i)   **from** – Preposition (**from**-segments);
(ii)   **over** – Preposition (**over**-segments);
(iii)   **of** – Preposition (**of**-segments);
(iv)   **at** – Preposition (**at**-segments);
(v)   **on** – Preposition (**on**-segments);
(vi)   **with** – Preposition (**with**-segments);
(vii)   **without** – Preposition (**without**-segments);
(viii)   **within** – Preposition (**within**-segments);
(ix)   **by** – Preposition (**by**-segments);
(x)   **into** – Preposition (**into**-segments);
(xi)   **in** – Preposition (**in**-segments);
(xii)   **onto** – Preposition (**onto**-segments);
(xiii)   **for** – Preposition (**for**-segments);
(xiv)   **to** – Preposition (**to**-segments);
(xv)   **past** – Preposition (**past**-segments);
(xvi)   **next** – Preposition (**next**-segments);
(xvii)   **against** – Preposition (**against**-segments);
(xviii) **through** – Preposition (**through**-segments);
(xix)   **under** – Preposition (**under**-segments);
(xx)   **only** – Conjunction, Adverb (**only**-segments);
(xxi)   **between** – Preposition (**between**-segments);

(xxii)   **above** – Preposition (**above**-segments);

(xxiii)   **than** – Conjunction (**than**-segments);

(xxiv)   **that** – Conjunction (**that**-segments);

(xxv)   **although** – Conjunction (**although**-segments);

(xxvi)   **or** – Conjunction (**or**-segments);

(xxvii)   **and** – Conjunction (**and**-segments);

(xxviii)   **if** – Conjunction (**if**-segments);

(xxix)   **even** – Conjunction (**even**-segments);

(xxx)   **though** – Conjunction (**though**-segments);

(xxxi)   **but** – Conjunction (**but-**segments);

(xxxii)   **so** – Conjunction (**so**-segments);

(xxxiii)   **because** – Conjunction (**because**-segments);

(xxxiv)   **as** – Conjunction (**as**-segments);

(xxxv)   **since** – Conjunction, Preposition (**since**-segments);

(xxxvi)   **before** – Preposition (**before**-segments);

(xxxvii)   **after** – Preposition (**after**-segments);

(xxxviii) **when** – Conjunction, Pronoun (**when**-segments);

(xxxix)   **where** – Conjunction, Pronoun (**where**-segments);

(xxxx)   **why** – Conjunction, Interrogative Pronoun (**why**-segments);

(xxxxi)   **what** – Relative Pronoun used as Conjunction (**what**-segments);

(xxxxii) **then** – Conjunction (**then**-segments);

(xxxxiii) **just** – Adverb used as Conjunction (**just**-segments);

(xxxxiv) **until, till** – Conjunction, Preposition (**until**-segments);

(xxxxv) **while** – Conjunction (**while**-segments);

(xxxxvi) **yet** – Adverb used as Conjunction (**yet**-segments);

(xxxxvii) **once** – Adverb used as Conjunction (**once**-segments);

(xxxxviii) **about** – Conjunction, Preposition (**about**-segments);

(xxxxix) **how** – Conjunction, Interrogative Pronoun (**how**-segments);

(l)   **aboard** – Preposition, Adverb (**aboard**-segments);

(li)   **anything** – comparative modifier (**anything**-segments);

(lii)   **according to** – Conjunction (**according to**-segments);

(liii)   **across** – Preposition (**across**-segments);

(liv)   **ahead of** – Preposition (**ahead of**-segments);

(lv)   **albeit** – Conjunction (**albeit**-segments);

(lvi)   **almost** – Conjunction (**almost-**segments);

(lvii)   **alone** – Adverb (**alone**-segments);

(lviii)   **along** – Preposition (**along**-segments);

(lix)   **already** – Conjunction (**already**-segments);

(lx)   **also** – Conjunction (**also**-segments);

(lxi)   **altogether** – Conjunction (**altogether**-segments);

(lxii)   **always** – Adverb (**always**-segments);

(lxiii)   **among** – Preposition (**among**-segments);

(lxiv)   **any** – comparative modifier (**any**-segments);

(lxv)   **anyway** – Conjunction (**anyway**-segments);

(lxvi)   **apart from** – Conjunction (**apart from**-segments);

(lxvii)	**around** – Preposition (**around**-segments);
(lxviii)	**away from** – Preposition (**away from**-segments);
(lxix)	**be** – Auxiliary Verb *be* (**be**-segments);
(lxx)	**behind** – Preposition (**behind**-segments);
(lxxi)	**being** – Participle (**being**-segments);
(lxxii)	**beside** – Preposition (**beside**-segments);
(lxxiii)	**besides** – Conjunction (**besides**-segments);
(lxxiv)	**better** – Adjective, Comparative (**better**-segments);
(lxxv)	**beyond** – Preposition (**beyond**-segments);
(lxxvi)	**called** – Participle (**called**-segments);
(lxxvii)	**calling** – Participle (**calling**-segments);
(lxxviii)	**depending on** – Conjunction (**depending on**-segments);
(lxxix)	**despite** – Conjunction (**despite**-segments);
(lxxx)	**down** – Preposition (**down**-segments);
(lxxxi)	**during** – Preposition (**during**-segments);
(lxxxii)	**e.g., i.e.** – Conjunction (**e.g.**-segments);
(lxxxiii)	**each** – modifier (**each**-segments);
(lxxxiv)	**earlier** – Adjective (**earlier**-segments);
(lxxxv)	**either** – Conjunction (**either**-segments);
(lxxxvi)	**enough** – Conjunction (**enough**-segments);
(lxxxvii)	**every** (incl. *everybody, everyone*) – modifier (**every**-segments);
(lxxxviii)	**except** – Conjunction (**except**-segments);
(lxxxix)	**far enough** (incl. *far from* and *far less*) (**far**-segments);
(lxxxx)	**given** – Conjunction (**given**-segments);
(lxxxxi)	**halfway** – Conjunction (**halfway**-segments);
(lxxxxii)	**having** – Participle (**having**-segments);
(lxxxxiii)	**hence** – Conjunction (**hence**-segments);
(lxxxxiv)	**however** – Conjunction (**however**-segments);
(lxxxxv)	**indeed** – Conjunction (**indeed**-segments);
(lxxxxvi)	**inside** – Preposition (**inside**-segments);
(lxxxxvii)	**instead** – Conjunction (**instead**-segments);
(lxxxxviii)	**irrespective (of)** – Conjunction (**irrespective**-segments);
(lxxxxix)	**last** – Adverb (**last**-segments);
(c)	**late(-r)** – Adjective (**later**-segments);
(ci)	**less** – modifier (**less**-segments);
(cii)	**let, let's** – Verb (**let**-segments);
(ciii)	**more** – comparative modifier (**more**-segments);
(civ)	**moreover** – Conjunction (**moreover**-segments);
(cv)	**most** – comparative modifier (**most**-segments);
(cvi)	**near** – Preposition (**near**-segments);
(cvii)	**needless** – Conjunction (**needless**-segments);
(cviii)	**neither** – Conjunction (**neither**-segments);
(cix)	**nevertheless** – Conjunction (**nevertheless**-segments);
(cx)	**nice** – Adjective (**nice**-segments);
(cxi)	**nonetheless** – Conjunction (**nonetheless**-segments);
(cxii)	**nor** – Conjunction (**nor**-segments);

(cxiii)   **noted** – Participle (**noted**-segments);
(cxiv)   **nothing** – determiner (**nothing**-segments);
(cxv)   **now** – Adverb (**now**-segments);
(cxvi)   **often** – Adverb (**often**-segments);
(cxvii)   **oh** – Interjection (**oh**-segments);
(cxviii)   **please** (**please**-segments);
(cxix)   **one** – Numeral, Pronoun, Noun (**one**-segments);
(cxx)   **others** – Noun (**others**-segments);
(cxxi)   **otherwise** – Conjunction (**otherwise**-segments);
(cxxii)   **out** – Adverb (**out**-segments);
(cxxiii)   **overall** – Adjective, Adverb (**overall**-segments);
(cxxiv)   **per** – Preposition (**per**-segments);
(cxxv)   **perhaps** (**perhaps**-segments);
(cxxvi)   **quite** – Adverb (**quite**-segments);
(cxxvii)   **prior** – Preposition (**prior**-segments);
(cxxviii) **rather** – Adverb, Conjunction (**rather**-segments);
(cxxix)   **regarding** (also *concerning*) – Preposition (**regarding**-seg-
           ments);
(cxxx)   **round** – Preposition (**round**-segments);
(cxxxi)   **some** – quantifier, determiner (**some**-segments);
(cxxxii)   **somehow** – Adverb (**somehow**-segments);
(cxxxiii) **somewhat** – Adverb (**somewhat**-segments);
(cxxxiv)   **somewhere** – Adverb (**somewhere**-segments);
(cxxxv)   **thereby** – Conjunction (**thereby**-segments);
(cxxxvi)   **therefore** – Conjunction (**therefore**-segments);
(cxxxvii) **throughout** – Preposition (**throughout**-segments);
(cxxxviii) **thus** – Conjunction (**thus**-segments);
(cxxxix)   **together** – Adverb (**together**-segments);
(cxxxx)   **toward(s)** – Preposition (**towards**-segments);
(cxxxxi)   **too** – Adverb (**too**-segments);
(cxxxxii) **unless** – Conjunction (**unless**-segments);
(cxxxxiii) **upon** – Preposition (**upon**-segments);
(cxxxxiv) **via** – Preposition (**via**-segments);
(cxxxxv)   **whatever** – Conjunction (**whatever**-segments);
(cxxxxvi) **whenever** – Conjunction (**whenever**-segments);
(cxxxxvii) **whereas** – Conjunction (**whereas**-segments);
(cxxxxviii) **whether** – Conjunction (**whether**-segments);
(cxxxxix) **up** – Adverb, including *up, off, out, down, over, in* at the start of
           the segment (**up**-segments);
(cl)   **like** – Conjunction, Preposition (**like**-segments);
(cli)   **b** – Adverb (**b**-segments)

There are also some other Auxiliary Clauses listed only in the Dictionary of
Segments, namely those starting with **been**, **FB**, **following**, **P** (Gerund), **P2**,
S (Numeral Ordinal), **T**, **very**, **well**, **X** (Reflexive Pronoun) and **yes**. The
list also includes a number of semantic groups used as a first element of the

segment to restrict the choice of words at this initial position (EAL, EAW, EBB, EBI, EBK, EBL, EBO, EBR, UF, UG, UI, UK).

The above List is used by Algorithm No 7 to identify the first element of the segment before starting to identify the next element, etc.

The above listed words and Parts of Speech either interrupt the previous segment (if that is not already done by a Punctuation Mark) or appear because the previous segment has ended, so that they can start a new segment. Then, as soon as the segment started by one of them ends, the end signals the beginning of a new segment (regardless of whether there is a Punctuation Mark or not to make the interruption) and the search for a new beginning starts, going through the above List again, and so on, from full stop to full stop.

These beginnings of segments (about 150 in all) are formal features (again we shall call them 'markers') which turn out to be quite useful in text processing.

In addition, these 150 beginnings have approximately 27,000 possible continuations (the total number of entries in the Dictionary of Segments).

3.1 Nominal segments

The first element(s) of a Nominal segment is (are) always a Subject (Sj), provided that the nominal start is followed by a Verb (Verbal Tense) (see vii–x below). If not (if there is no Verb to follow and the Nominal segment ends), then the Nominal segment can be either a Subject or an Object (Od) (i–vi below). An algorithmic procedure must determine which by analysing the context.

(i)   A b G n of i G n (e.g. *the undoubtedly excellent performance of this German gymnast*)

(ii)   all A n of n (e.g. *all the presents of Jim*)

(iii)   n of O G n of n (etc.)

(iv)   i n

(v)   d of n of n

(vi)   Sj or Od

(vii)   A b G n shall also v

(viii) d has P2

(ix)   O n are to v

(x)   Sj v

In those cases when the nominal start is followed by a Verbal Tense, the conjugation of the Auxiliary Verb is presented in an abbreviated form:

(xi)   d are P2

(xii)   O G n are P2

        (where **are** stands for *is, are, were, was*)

(xiii) i n has been P2

(xiv)   O n of n has been P2

        (where **has** stands for *has, have, had*)

The abbreviated conjugation comes as a result of the abbreviated Noun – it is not known whether the Noun is used in the singular (or what person in the singular) or in the plural – and also as a result of the abbreviated Tense (it is not specified whether it is Present or Past, or what person), and room has been allowed for all possibilities. The Verbal Tense will be discussed in detail below.

The third part of the Nominal segment, the one following after the Verbal Tense, represents the Predicative and can be either an Object or a Complement:

(xv)   n has also to be P2 to v A n

(xvi)   all I n v R

(xvi a) d am Pi A n
         Sj v   Od

(xvii) d shall also v R A n

(xviii) d should have also P2 R A n
         Sj v   Oi Od
         Sj v   Od Co

(xix)   d v A n of n Pl
         d v to v R Pl
         Sj v   Od Co

(xx)   d has also been A n of A G n

(xxi)   M of A G n has also been j

(xxii) O n are j

(xxii a) d am j

(xxii b) d am n

(xxii c) d am A G n
         Sj v Cs

(xxiii) d shall v R to v O n

(xxiv) d has P2 O n v to v A G n
         Sj v   Od   Ic

(xxv) d shall v G

(xxvi) A n shall v S
         Sj   v   Pr

As was seen from the above examples, the complement can be a Complement Sj (xxi, xxii), Complement Object (xvii, xviii, xix), or an Infinitival Complement (xxiii, xxiv). The Object can be Object Direct (xvii, xviii, xix) or Object Indirect (xvii, xviii). In those cases (xvii, xviii) where it is not known if we have Object Indirect or Complement Object, further algorithmic analysis is needed before a decision is taken.

The Nominal segments xvi a, xx, xxi, xxii and xxii a bear examples of the use of the second argument (the second argument follows after the Auxiliary Verb). The Nominative agreement, using the paradigm of the Auxiliary Verb **be**, is exemplified by xxii b and xxii c.

In many cases the nominal part preceding the Verbal Tense is identical to the nominal part following after the Tense:

(xxvii) O n v O n
(xxviii) d v A S G n of n
A S G n of n v O n

This means that we have to select the identical patterns (O n, A S G n, A S G n of n, etc.) that compose the segments (their number will be only a few thousand) and use them in studying and teaching the language, in the same way as the morphemes are used in studying and teaching the composition of the word. A suitable name for this branch of syntax would perhaps be Morphology of Syntax. (The identical patterns in this study will be called Syntactical Words. The Syntactical Words are the building blocks of the segment and of the sentence.)

The second part of the Nominal segment is taken up by the Verbal Tense. In the next section we will briefly review the Tenses and explain the abbreviations used to code them.

3.1.1   Verbal Tenses and constructions. The Infinitive

The Verbal Tenses in the Nominal segment, as well as in all other types of segments, are presented as follows:

a) The Present Simple and the Past Simple Tense are marked with **v** (no differentiation is made between them). For example:

(i)   A n v A n

can mean either

(i a)   *The boy takes the money.* or
(i b)   *The boy took the money.*

Present Tense third person singular is not specified.

b) All forms of the Future Tense, the Future in the Past and the Present Conditional are marked with **shall v** (no distinction is made between them). For example:

(ii)   d shall v

can be interpreted as

(ii a)   *You will work.*
(ii b)   *You would work.*
(ii c)   *We do work.*
(ii d)   *He did work.*

The first person (singular and plural) is not differentiated from the second and the third person – **shall** stands for all, also for all modals that can assume this position, and for the **do** paradigm, with the exception of *doing*.

c) The Present and the Past Continuous Tenses are marked with **am Pi**. For example:

> (iii) d am Pi
> (iii a) *Jim is practising.*
> (iii b) *Ann was sleeping.*

The Auxiliary Verb **am** stands for the whole **be** paradigm with the exception of *be* and *being*.

d) No differentiation is made between the Future Continuous and the Future Continuous in the Past. Both tenses are marked with **shall be Pi**. For example:

> (iv) A n shall be Pi

can be equivalent to

> (iv a) *The engine will be working.*
> (iv b) *The engine should be working.*

No differentiation is made between first, second and third person, and **shall** stands for all modals that can assume this position.

e) The Present Perfect and the Past Perfect are also marked identically, for example:

> (v) O n has P2

which can be interpreted as

> (v a) *Her husband has arrived.*
> (v b) *Their car had stopped.*

f) The Future Perfect, the Future Perfect in the Past and the Perfect Conditional are marked identically with **shall have P2**. For example:

> (vi) d shall have P2

can mean

> (vi a) *You will have worked.*
> (vi b) *You should have worked.*

(**shall** represents all modals that can assume this position; **have** stands for **have**)

g) The Present Perfect Continuous Tense and the Past Perfect Continuous Tense are also marked identically with **has been Pi**. For example:

> (vii) i n has been Pi

can mean

(vii a) *This man has been sleeping.*
(vii b) *Such people had been playing.*

(**has** represents the paradigm, *having* is excluded)

h) The Future Perfect Continuous Tense and the Future Perfect Continuous in the Past are also marked with an identical sign. For example:

(viii)   d shall have been Pi

can mean

(viii a) *I shall have been reading.*
(viii b) *You would have been staying.*

(**shall** represents all modals specified in the Index)

i) The Present Tense and the Past Tense in the Passive Voice are marked identically, with **am P2**:

(ix)   d am P2

can mean

(ix a) *I am asked ...*
(ix b) *He was asked ...*

j) The Future Tense and the Future in the Past, Passive Voice, are also marked identically:

(x)   M n shall be P2

which can mean

(x a)   *Ten items will be chosen.*
(x b)   *Several boxes should be opened.*

(**shall** stands for all modals that can assume this position)

k) The Present Continuous Tense and the Past Continuous Tense, Passive Voice, are not differentiated. They are denoted with **am being P2**. For example:

(xi)   d am being P2

can be interpreted as

(xi a) *We are being asked ...*
(xi b) *He was being asked ...*

(**am** represents the paradigm, *be* and *being* are excluded; **being** = *being*)

l) The Present Perfect Tense and the Past Perfect Tense, Passive voice, are also marked identically:

(xii)   n has been P2

which can mean

> (xii a) *Food has been eaten.*
> (xii b) *Wine had been drunk.*

(**has** represents the **have** paradigm, with the exception of *having*)

All those Tenses that are marked in an identical way have an identical syntactical role in the sentence and occupy identical positions in the segments. Another reason for merging those Tenses was to compress the description of the segment (and hence, the description of English grammar for the computer), using the entire paradigm of an Auxiliary Verb or several such paradigms in a single, specified position in the segment. This fully accorded with the grammatical and syntactical rules governing the construction of the sentence.

The difference in meaning as a result of bringing all modals together (under **shall**, **can** or **should**) and placing them in one single position is ignored. Compare:

> (xiii a) *I shall come.* (plan, belief, etc.)
> (xiii b) *I could come.* (possibility)
> (xiii c) *I must come.* (necessity, etc.)

Our purpose was to capture the underlying grammatical (syntactical) construction

> (xiii)   d shall v

identical for all those meanings.

Similarly, we have incorporated in **also** all Adverbs including the negation expressed by *not*

> (xiv)   d shall also v

to represent segments (portions of text) such as

> (xiv a) *I could not come.*
> (xiv b) *I must surely come.*

regardless of the ensuing difference of meaning. The important thing was that all these portions of text or simple sentences, have the same underlying syntactical construction.

The segments can be in the Active or Passive Voice:

> (xv) d v G n (e.g. *Chris achieved remarkable results*)
>   d v to v j (etc.)
>   d v to v b G n
>   d v to v G n
>   A G n v A n A n

are Active Voice segments.

(xvi) A n should have been P2 (e.g. *The food should have been eaten.*)
       A n has been P2 (e.g. *A decision has been taken.*)
       d am P2 (e.g. *I was asked.*)

are Passive Voice segments.

Those segments that contain a Possessive Pronoun or a Genitive of the Noun are Gentive segments:

(xvii) O n are b j (e.g. *Her horses are always ready.*)
        N''s n are j (etc.)
        A G N''s n are j

Following the above description, the reader can easily identify all constructions and the Tenses found both in the text (any English language text) and in the Dictionary of Segments.

The Verbal Tense is often followed by a Participle '-ing', a Gerund, or an Infinitival Complement used as an Object of the Verb (xviii):

(xviii a) d has P2 Pv (*started practising*)
(xviii b) d has P2 Pi
(xviii c) d has P2 P
(xviii d) d v to v (*to sing*)
           Sj v Ic

The **to** Infinitive (expressed with the Particle **to**) can be Present (xix) or Passive (xx):

(xix)   *They will have to do the painting of the house.*
        d   shall v   to v A n   of A n
(xx)   *The chairman agreed to be re-elected.*
        A   n   v   to be P2

The **to** Infinitive can be positioned before the Object (xxi) or after it (xxii), used with a Verbal Tense (xxiii), or used in a Prepositional Adverbial Clause (xxiv):

(xxi)   A n v to v A G G n
          A n should have to be Pi to v A G n
          d am also to v A G n
(xxii)   A n v G n to v A G n
(xxiii)   d am P2 to v M G n
(xxiv)   for A n to v
(xxiv a) with R to v A n

The Verbs that may be followed by an Infinitive or Gerund can be found listed in Graver (1971: 157–65) or Hornby (1958: 48–9).

3.1.2 **A**-segments

The **A**-segments start with an Article (definite or indefinite). The Article is followed most often by the following sequences of Parts of Speech (up to the start of the Verbal Tense):

(i)	A b G	(xviii)	A n of A n Pl b
(ii)	A b G G G n	(xix)	A n of A n Pl
(iii)	A G G G n	(xx)	A n of A n Pi
(iv)	A G G G n of n	(xxi)	A n of A N''s G G n
(v)	A G G m n	(xxii)	A G n of all A n
(vi)	A G G G n of A G n	(xxiii)	A G n of all i
(vii)	A G G n of	(xxiv)	A n of b G G n
(viii)	A G G n of G n	(xxv)	A n of G G G n
(ix)	A G G n of i n	(xxvi)	A n of i G n (where i = I)
(x)	A G G n of m n	(xxvii)	A n of M n
(xi)	A G G n of O G n	(xxviii)	A n of P A G n
(xii)	A G G n Pi A G n	(xxix)	A n Pi A m G n
(xiii)	A G n Pi G G n	(xxx)	A n Pi G G n
(xiv)	A G n b	(xxxi)	A n Pi i G n
(xv)	A G n of A n of A G n	(xxxii)	A n Pi A n of O N''s n
(xvi)	A n of A n of G G n	(xxxiii)	A N''s G G n
(xvii)	A G n of A G n	(xxxiv)	A S G n

S, M, m and **N''s** can always be equated with **G** and **G** can be optional – it can be omitted from the position specified for it.

For example:

(xxxi a)   *The man selling this beautiful house.*
(xxxi b)   *The man selling this house.*

It is worth noting that all sequences starting with an Article (A) must end with a Noun (n) before another Part of Speech or another sequence is allowed to proceed. The only Parts of Speech allowed to intervene between the Article and the Noun are the Adjective (G), the Adverb (b), the Participle 1st and the Numeral, only as attributes to the Noun:

A (G) (G) (G) n
A (G) (G) (m) n
A b G (G) n
A b Pl n

The choice in brackets is optional; the attribute after the Adverb is obligatory. There can rarely be more than three attributes in a row between **A** and **n**.

The above nominal patterns (syntactical words) can be used by all English language students, whether in the classroom or at home, to exercise their knowledge of English by filling them with words. This will be a preparatory exercise before trying to fill a whole segment with words.

The Nominal sequence before the Verbal Tense is always a Subject (viii). Often, the Subject can be followed by a Complement Subject (xix, xxxii). If the Nominal sequence is not followed by a Verbal Tense, it can be interpreted either as Subject or as Object (viii).

(viii)   *the pillars of wisdom*
    A   n   of n   (G omitted)

(xix)   *The leaves of the trees fallen*
    A   n   of A   n   Pl
    Sj   Cs

(xxxii)   *The dust covering the yard of his brother's house ...*
    A   n   Pi   A   n   of O N''s   n
    Sj   Cs

(xxxii a)   *The man reading the book is hungry.*
    A   n   Pi   A   n   are j
    Sj   Cs   v Cs

The segments xxxii and xxxii a are examples of a Reduced Relative Clause in the role of Complement Subject. Compare:

(xxxii b)   *The man who reads the book is hungry.*

Since the Verbal Tenses were discussed in the previous section (they are identical for all Nominal, Verbal and Auxiliary segments), we will omit them and will start to describe the second part of the A-segment, that coming after the Verbal Tense. Below is a list of the most characteristic sequences met after the Verbal Tense:

(xxxv)	A G G n b	(lvii)	A n up
(xxxvi)	A G G n m	(lviii)	A S G n to v
(xxxvii)	A G G n of m n	(lix)	A S Pl
(xxxviii)	A G G lx to v A n	(lx)	A S to v
(xxxix)	A G n b	(lxi)	b G
(xxxx)	A G n of A G n	(lxii)	b j
(xxxxi)	A G n of all i n	(lxiii)	b Os
(xxxxii)	A G n of b G G G n	(lxiv)	G
(xxxxiii)	A G n of n Pl to v G n	(lxv)	G G G n
(xxxxiv)	A G n of R	(lxvi)	G n
(xxxxv)	A G n Pl	(lxvii)	G n of G n
(xxxxvi)	A G n to v	(lxviii)	j
(xxxxvii)	A G n to v up	(lxix)	j of n
(xxxxviii)	A G n up	(lxx)	j to v
(xxxxix)	A G N''s n	(lxxi)	j to v A G n
(l)	A G P2	(lxxii)	j to v G n
(li)	A m G n Pl b	(lxxiii)	less j
(lii)	A n of G G n	(lxxiv)	less P2
(liii)	A n of i G G n	(lxxv)	M G n of A G n
(liv)	A n of M n	(lxxvi)	M n
(lv)	A n of R	(lxxvii)	M n to v A n
(lvi)	A n Pl to v	(lxxviii)	n of A G n

(lxxix)	O G G n		(lxxxvii)	R A n
(lxxx)	O less G n		(lxxxviii)	R all
(lxxxi)	O N''s n		(lxxxix)	R all up
(lxxxii)	of A G G n		(lxxxx)	R M n
(lxxxiii)	of G n		(lxxxxi)	R n
(lxxxiv)	Os		(lxxxxii)	R up
(lxxxv)	R		(lxxxxiii)	X
(lxxxvi)	R A G n of G G n			

The **G, b, up** and **M** are optional; **M** is equal to **G**. Some of the sequences used before and after the Verbal Tense coincide.

What is characteristic of the third part of the A-segment? Most of all the use of the Personal Pronoun Objective Case (PPOC), marked as R, and the positioning of the Adverb (**b, up**) at the very end of the sequence. At the very end we also find positioned the **up** part of the Prepositional and Phrasal Verb (compare *bring up, take off, put aside*, etc.). This last feature hampers considerably the automatic processing of English texts, because the Preposition, as part of a Prepositional Verb, can be easily mistaken for a Preposition at the start of an Adverbial segment.

The nominal sequence following after the Verbal Tense can be either an Object (liii a, lxvi, lxxxi a) or a Complement Subject (liii b, lx, lxxxi b). Some sequences can be both, depending on the Verb that precedes them. Those sequences that start with PPOC (R) are always the Object of the segment. When R is followed by a Noun, then R is the Indirect Object (lxxxxi).

(liii a)
(He saw)
the president of this small mountainous country.
A n   of i G   G   n
Od

(liii b)
(He is)
the president of this small mountainous country.
A n   of i G   G   n
Cs

(lxvi)
(He likes)
sweet wine.
G   n
Od

(lxxxi a)
(He bought)
his sister's house.
O N''s   n
Od

(lxxxii b)
(This is)
his sister's house.
O N''s   n
Cs

(lx)   *(I am)*
        the first to arrive.
        A S   to v
        Cs
        (I gave)
(lxxxxi) *him money.*
        R n
        Oi Od

Below is a sample extract from the **A**-segments of the Dictionary of Segments:

A b G n shall also v A G n
A b G n shall also v A G n b
A b G n shall also v A n
A b G n shall also v A n b
A b G n shall v A G n
A b G n shall v A G n b
A b G n shall v A n
A b G n shall v A n b
  Sj v Od
A b G n v
A b G n v off
  Sj v
A b G n v O n
  Sj v Od
A b G n'' Pi'' n v
  Sj Cs v
A b G n'' Pi'' ' n'
A b G
  Sj
  Od
A d NAME = d
A d of A d of Os = d
A d of A G d = d
A d of A G n = d
A d of A G N''s G G n = d
A d of A G N''s G n = d
A d of A G N''s n = d
A d of A n = d
A d of A N''s G G n = d
A d of A N''s G n = d
A d of A N''s n = d
A d of i G n = d
A d of i n = d
A d of m FB = d
A d of n = d
A d of n NAME = d

A d of N''s G n = d
A d of N''s n = d
A d of some m FB = d
  Sj
A G G G n has also P2 A G N''s n
A G G G n has also P2 A N''s n
A G G G n has P2 A G N''s n
A G G G n has P2 A N''s n
  Sj v Od
A G G G n of NAME
  Sj
  Od
A G G G n P1
  Sj
  Od
A G G G n P1 b v
  Sj v
A G G G n shall also v n
A G G G n shall v n
A G G G n shall also v A n
A G G G n shall also v R
A G G G n shall v A n
A G G G n shall v R
  Sj v Od
A G G G n TCv
A G G G n v
  Sj v
A G G G n v A n to v G n
A G G G n v A n to v G n of n
A G G G n v A n to v n
A G G G n v A n to v n of n
A G G G n v A n to v
A G G G n v A n to v A n
A G G G n v A n to v R
  Sj v Od Ic
A G G m n are also P2 to be less j

A G G m n are also P2 to be less P1
A G G m n are P2 to be less P1
  Sj v Ic
A G G n
  Sj
  Od
A G G n are O n
  Sj v Cs
A G G n are
  Sj v
A G G n are A G P2
A G G n are A n
A G G n are A n of A G n
A G G n are A n of A n
A G G n are also A G P2
A G G n are also A n
A G G n are also A n of A G n
A G G n are also A n of A n
A G G n are also j
A G G n are also j to v
  Sj v Cs
A G G n are also ahead
  Sj v b
A G G n are also m NAME m
  Sj v Cs
A G G n are NAME
  Sj v Cs
A G G n at n are NAME
  Sj b v Cs
A G G n has also P2 A G N''s n
A G G n has also P2 A N''s n
A G G n has P2 A G N''s n
A G G n has P2 A N''s n
  Sj v Od
A G G n shall also v A n of A n
A G G n shall also v A n of n
A G G n shall also v G n of n
A G G n shall also v n of n
A G G n shall also v A n of G n
A G G n shall also v n of G n
A G G n shall also v n
A G G n shall also v A n
A G G n shall also v A n up
A G G n shall also v R
A G G n shall also v R up
  Sj v Od

A G G n shall be j to v
  Sj v Cs Ic
A G G n shall v A n
A G G n shall v A n up
A G G n shall v A n of A n
A G G n shall v A n of G n
A G G n shall v A n of n
A G G n shall v G n of n
A G G n shall v n
A G G n shall v n of n
A G G n shall v n of G n
A G G n shall v O G G n
A G G n shall v O G n
A G G n shall v O n
A G G n shall v O less G n
  Sj v Od
A G G n shall v R
A G G n shall v R up
  Sj v Od
A G G n shall v R A n
A G G n shall v R n
  Sj v Oi Od
  Sj v Od Co
A G G n shall v R O G n
A G G n shall v R O n
  Sj v Oi Od
A G G n TCv
A G G n v
  Sj v
A G G n v A n to v G n
A G G n v A n to v G n of n
A G G n v A n to v n
A G G n v A n to v
A G G n v A n to v n of n
A G G n v A n to v R
A G G n v A n to v A n
A G G n v A n to v A n of n
A G G n v A n to v A n of A n
  Sj v Od Ic
A G m n n Pi A G n
  Sj Cs
  Od Co
A G n are also P2 to be less j
A G n are also P2 to be less P1
A G n are P2 to be less P1
  Sj v

A G n
  Sj
  Od
A G n are O n
  Sj v Cs
A G n are A n
A G n are A n of A G n
A G n are A n of A n
A G n are also j
A G n are also j to v
A G n are also ahead
A G n are also G
A G n are also up
A G n are also m NAME m
A G n are j
A G n are j to v
A G n are ahead
A G n are G
A G n are n
A G n are NAME
A G n are no less j
A G n are less j
A G n are also n of A n
A G n are also m G n to v A G n of A
G n
A G n are also m G n to v A G n
A G n are also m G n to v
A G n are also less j
A G n are also j of G n
A G n are also b n of A n
A G n are also b n
A G n are A G n Pi of A n of G n
A G n are up
  Sj v Cs
A G n also v A n of A G G n
A G n are Pi A n of n
A G n are Pi up A n of n
  Sj v Od
A G n at n are NAME
  Sj b v Cs
A G n d v to v R v are
A G n d v to v R v
  Sj Sj v Od
A G n d = d
A G n b
  Sj
  Od

A G n has also P2 A G n of R
A G n has also P2 A G N''s n
A G n has also P2 A m n
A G n has also P2 A n of G G n Pi
A G n has also P2 A n of G n Pi
A G n has also P2 A n of n Pi
A G n has also P2 A n of R
A G n has also P2 A N''s n
A G n has also P2 G n
A G n has also P2 it be P2
A G n has also P2 M n to v A n
A G n has also P2 m of R
A G n has also P2 n
  Sj v Od
A G n has also P2 n to v G n of G n
A G n has also P2 n to v G n of n
A G n has also P2 n to v n of G n
A G n has also P2 n to v n of n
  Sj v Od Ic
A G n has also P2 O n
  Sj v Od
A G n has also P2 off M n to v A n
  Sj v Od Ic
A G n has also P2 off R
A G n has also P2 R
  Sj v Od
A G n has also P2 to v A n
A G n has also P2 to v A n of d
NAME
  Sj v Od
A G n has also P2 to v G G n to v up
M n P1
A G n has also P2 to v G n to v up M
n P1
A G n has also P2 to v n to v up M n
P1
  Sj v Od
A G n has also P2 up
  Sj v
A G n has also within R A n of O G n
  Sj v b Od
A G n has been
  Sj v
A G n has been j
  Sj v Cs
A G n has been P2

A G n has been P2 up
  Sj v
A G n has been Pi G n j
A G n has been Pi n j
A G n has G G G n
A G n has G G n
A G n has G n
A G n has m NAME m
A G n has n
  Sj v Od
A G n has not
A G n has P2
  Sj v
A G n has P2 A G n of R
A G n has P2 A G N''s n
A G n has P2 A m n
A G n has P2 A n of G G n Pi
A G n has P2 A n of G n Pi
A G n has P2 A n of n Pi
A G n has P2 A n of R
A G n has P2 A N''s n
A G n has P2 G n
A G n has P2 it be P2
  Sj v Od
A G n has P2 M n to v A n
  Sj v Od Ic
A G n has P2 m of R
A G n has P2 n
A G n has P2 no n
  Sj v Od
A G n has P2 n to v G n of G n
A G n has P2 n to v G n of n
A G n has P2 n to v n of G n
A G n has P2 n to v n of n
  Sj v Od Ic

A G n has P2 O n
A G n has P2 off M n to v A n
A G n has P2 off R
A G n has P2 R
A G n has P2 to v A n
A G n has P2 to v A n of d NAME
  Sj v Od
A G n has P2 to v G G n to v up M n
P1
A G n has P2 to v G n to v to v up M
n P1
A G n has P2 to v n to v up M n P1
  Sj v Od
A G n has P2 up
A G n has to be P2
A G n has to v
  Sj v
A G n has UF b
A G n having P2 X v A S
A G n having P2 X v A n
A G n having P2 X
  Sj v Od
A G n of A n are also P2
A G n of A n are also P2
A G n of A n are also Pi
A G n of A n are P2
A G n of A n be P2 *
A G n of A n can be P2
A G n of A n has P2
A G n of A n has P2 up
  Sj v
A G n of A n of A G n
A G n of A n of A n
A G n of A n of n
etc.

3.1.3   **M**-segments

The segments starting with a Numeral Cardinal (number, plural quantifier, comparative modifier) also have one, two or three constituent parts. The first part stands for the Subject or the Object (if the segment is of one part only, without a Verbal Tense to follow). The second part is the Verbal Tense. The third part is the Object and the Complement.

    The **M**-segment usually begins with one of the following sequences of Parts of Speech:

(i)	M	(x)	M A n
(ii)	M %	(xi)	M G n
(iii)	M % of A m n	(xii)	M m G n
(iv)	M % of A m n Pl	(xiii)	M n b
(v)	M % of A n	(xiv)	M n of A G G n
(vi)	M % of A n Pl	(xv)	M of A G G n
(vii)	M % of all n	(xvi)	M of A less j
(viii)	M % of all n Pl	(xvii)	M of A m n b
(ix)	M % of G n	(xviii)	M of O G n

(G is optional, m = G)

For example:

(viii a) *10 % of all people asked*
          Sj or Od
(xviii a) *two of her children*
           Sj or Od

The most characteristic feature of the first part of the **M**-segment is the additional use of **m** and of % at the start of the segment, with % occupying the second position. Other frequent candidates for the second position are the Noun, the Adjective or yet another Numeral used as an attribute to the Noun, **are** (the paradigm of **be** without be and being) and the Preposition **of** used with the genitive of the Noun (**of** can be followed either by A or O).

In the first position, before a Noun, M is an attribute to the Noun (xiv), denoting the total number (specified or unspecified) involved.

(xiv a) M n v up (e.g. *Ten people turned up.*)
        Sj   v

When M is followed by the Preposition **of**, which in turn is followed by a Noun, then the **M**-segment means that only a certain number (specified or unspecified) are involved (xv).

(xv a)   M of A n v up (e.g. *Ten of the women came down.*)
         Sj   v
(xviii a) M of O n v (e.g. *Two of his books disappeared.*)
           Sj   v

The second and the third parts of the **M**-segments are identical to those of the **A**-segments. An interesting feature that deserves attention is the use of up to three Complements for the same Subject and the fact that here M is one of them (xvi).

(xvi)   M of A less j are A G n Pl
         Cs Sj   v Cs   Cs

This can be a sentence such as *Ten of the best-known are the watercolour portraits painted* (... *by the famous portraitist*).

Compare: *The best are ten.*
A less j are M
(In other words *The best painted portraits are ten.*)
Below the reader will find an excerpt from the Dictionary of Segments
showing the grammatical structure of the M-segments:

M % has also been P2
M % has been P2
  Sj v
m % of A m n" P1" TCv A n shall
also v
m % of A m n" P1" TCv A G n shall v
m % of A m n" P1" TCv A n shall v
  Sj v Sj v
M % of A n P1
m % of all n P1
  Od Co
m % of all n P1 v m % G n
m % of all n P1 v m % n
m % of all n P1 v G n
m % of all n P1 v n
  Sj Cs v Od
m % of G n are also j of n
m % of n are also j of n
m % of n are j of n
  Sj v Cs
m % of the n P1
  Od Co
  Sj Cs
m % of the n P1 v m % G n
m % of the n P1 v m % n
m % of the n P1 v G n
m % of the n P1 v n
  Sj Cs v Od
M % v
  Sj v
m % v A n A last FB
  Sj v Od b
M % v d can also be P2
M % v d can be P2
  Sj v Sj v
M % v d has no n
  Sj v Sj v Od
M A n
  Sj
  Od

M % has also been P2
M % has been P2
  Sj v
M % of A n P1
m % of all n P1
  Od Co
m % of all n P1 v m % G n
m % of all n P1 v m % n
m % of all n P1 v G n
m % of all n P1 v n
  Sj Cs v Od
m % of G n are also j of n
m % of n are also j of n
m % of n are j of n
  Sj v Cs
m % of the n P1
  Od
M
  Sj
M v up
  Sj v
m %
  Sj
  Od
m % of A m n" P1" TCv A G n shall
also v *
  Sj Cs v Sj v
M % has also been P2
M % has been P2
  Sj v
m % of A m n" P1" TCv A n shall
also v
m % of A m n" P1" TCv A G n shall v
m % of A m n" P1" TCv A n shall v
  Sj Cs v Sj v
M % of A n P1
m % of all n P1
  Od Co
m % of all n P1 v m % G n
m % of all n P1 v m % n

m % of all n Pl v G n
m % of all n Pl v n
  Sj Cs v Od
m % of G n are also j of n
m % of n are also j of n
m % of n are j of n
  Sj v Cs
m % of the n Pl
  Od Co
m % of the n Pl v m % G n
m % of the n Pl v m % n
m % of the n Pl v G n
m % of the n Pl v n
  Sj Cs v Od
M % v
  Sj v
m % v A n A last FB
  Sj v Od b
M % v d can also be P2
M % v d can be P2
M % v d has no n
  Sj v Sj v
M A n
  Sj
  Od
M A n are also j to v up n
M A n are also j to v n
M A n are j to v up n

M A n are j to v n
  Sj v Cs v Od
M F
m and a half = M
  Sj
  Od
M are also j
M are also G n
M are also much fun to be with
  Sj v Cs
M are also Pi to v up G n
M are also Pi to v up n
M are also Pi to v G n
M are also Pi to v n
  Sj v Od
M are also Pi of A n of G n
M are also Pi of A n of n
  Sj v
M are j
M are j of n
M are G n
M are much fun to be with
  Sj v Cs
M are n v A n can be P2
  Sj v Cs v Sj v
M v up
  Sj v
etc.

3.1.4 *n*-segments

The **n**-segments start with a Noun. They also have three constituent parts, like the previous Nominal segments.

The first part is composed mainly of the following sequences of Parts of Speech:

(i)   n
(ii)   n b
(iii) n m
(iv) n m Pl
(v)   n n
(vi) n of A b G n
(vii) n of A G G G n
(viii) n of A N''s G n
(ix) n of A N''s m G n
(x)   n of G G G n

(xi)   n of G n b
(xii)   n of i n
(xiii) n of O G G n
(xiv) n of O G n of n
(xv)   n of X
(xvi) n Pl
(xvii) n Pi G G n
(xviii) n Pi O G n
(xix) n Pi Pl
(xx)   n Pi up

The use of G is optional.

For example:

    (vii a) *brother of the former president*
            n   of A G   n

Each one of these sequences is a Subject when it is followed by a Verbal Tense. If not, it can be either a Subject or an Object. Some Subjects have Complements (xviii, xix)

    (xviii a) n Pi O G n
               Sj Cs
    (xix a)   n Pi P1 (e.g. *bottles staying opened*)
               Sj Cs

as a result of a Reduced Relative Clause.

The second and the third parts of the **n**-segment are identical to those of the previous segments.

Below the reader will find an excerpt from the Dictionary of Segments, showing the grammatical structure of the **n**-segments:

n are A G

n are A G n

n are A G n to v up

n are A G n to v

n are A less G n

n are A n

n are A n of A n

n are A n of O G n

n are A n of O n

n are A n of G G n

n are A n of G n

n are A n of n

n are A n to v up

n are A n to v

n are also A n of A n

n are also A less G n

n are also A n of O n

n are also A n of O G n

n are also A G n

n are also A n

n are also A n of G G n

n are also A n of G n

n are also A n of n

n are also another n

n are also A G n

n are also A G n to v up

n are also A G n to v

n are also A n to v up

n are also A n to v
  Sj v Cs

n are also being P2

n are also b up

n are also being P2 up
  Sj v

n are also being v to help v A n

n are also being v to v A n
  Sj v Od

n are also G

n are also G n

n are also G than n

n are also j

n are also j of n

n are also less j

n are also m of A less j

n are also m of A less G

n are also m of A less G G n j b

n are also m of A less G G n j

n are also m of A less G n j b

n are also m of A less G n j

n are also n of A n

n are also n

n are also of i n

n are also O n

n are also O G n
  Sj v Cs

n are also Pi n of less G n
  Sj v Od
n are also Pi to v up
n are also Pi to v
  Sj v
n are also Pi up A n of A N''s n
n are also Pi A n of A N''s n
n are also Pi up A n
n are also Pi A N''s G n
n are also Pi A N''s n
  Sj v Od
n are also P2
  Sj v
n are also P2 to v n
  Sj v Od
n are also P2 up
  Sj v
n are also P2 j to v M of A G n
n are also P2 j to v M of A n
  Sj v Cs v Od
n are also Pi to v A G G n
n are also Pi to v A G n
n are also Pi to v A n
n are also Pi to v n
n are also Pi to v R
n are also Pi to v A S G n
n are also Pi to v A S n
n are also Pi UF less
n are also Pi G G n
n are also Pi G n
n are also Pi n
  Sj v Od
n are also P2 to v
n are also Pi
  Sj v
n are also P2 and P2
  Sj v
n are also P2 j
n are also up
  Sj v
n are also UF n
n are another n
n are another G n
  Sj v Cs
n are being P2

n are being P2 up
  Sj v
n are being P2 to help v A n
n are being P2 to v A n
  Sj v Od
n are G
n are G G n Pi A G n
n are G G n Pi A G n of A n
n are G n
n are G than n
n are j
n are j of n
n are less j
n are m of A less j
n are m of A less G
n are m of A less G G n j b
n are m of A less G G n j
n are m of A less G n j b
n are m of A less G n j
n are n
n are n of A n
  Sj v Cs
n are not
  Sj v
n are O G n
n are O n
n are of course b G
n are of course G
n are of i n
n are O G G n
  Sj v Cs
n are P2
n are P2 and P2
  Sj v
n are P2 j
  Sj v
n are P2 j to v M of A G n
n are P2 j to v M of A n
  Sj v Cs v Od
n are P2 to v n
  Sj v Od
n are P2 to v
n are P2 up
n are Pi
  Sj v

n are Pi A n of A N''s n

n are Pi A N''s G n

n are Pi A N''s n

n are Pi A n

n are Pi G G n

n are Pi G n

n are Pi n

n are Pi R

n are Pi n of less G n
    Sj v Od

n are Pi to v up

n are Pi to v
    Sj v

n are Pi to v A S G n

n are Pi to v A G G n

n are Pi to v A G n

n are Pi to v R

n are Pi to v A S n

n are Pi to v n

n are Pi to v A n

n are Pi UF less

n are Pi up A n of A N''s n

n are Pi up A n
    Sj v Od

etc.

3.1.5   *I-segments*

(See also **such**-segments.) The **I**-segments start with an Indicative Pronoun, Article or *last, such, next*. They also have up to three parts. The most characteristic constituent elements of the first part are:

(i)	i	(xiii)	i n of n
(ii)	i G n	(xiv)	i n of Os
(iii)	i G n b	(xv)	i n of P
(iv)	i G n of m n	(xvi)	i n Pl
(v)	i G n Pi G G n	(xvii)	i n Pi
(vi)	i G P of G n	(xviii)	i n Pi G G n
(vii)	i m	(xix)	i one
(viii)	i m G n	(xx)	i one G n
(ix)	i n of A G n	(xxi)	i other n
(x)	i n of A G n j	(xxii)	i P of G n
(xi)	i n of A n	(xxiii)	i S n
(xii)	i n of m n		

(G is optional)

The sequences preceding the Verbal Tense are the Subject of the segment, but if there is no Verbal Tense to follow, they can be either Subject or Object.

The Indicative Pronoun (or the words equivalent to it) is used as a Subject (xiv), together with the Noun it specifies (xv).

     (xiv)   i   are n (e.g. *This is London.*)
            Sj v   Cs
     (xv)   i n of Os are also j (e.g. *This habit of hers is extremely annoying.*)
            Sj   v   Cs

Only the attribute (Adjective or Numeral – ii, viii, xix, xx, xxiii) or the Gerund + *of* phrase (xxii) can fill the space between the Indicative Pronoun and the Noun indicated by it. When the Indicative Pronoun is used on its own (xiv) then it replaces the Noun indicated by it, or in other words, it is equivalent to the Noun it indicates.

The second and the third parts of the **I**-segment are identical with those of the other Nominal segments.

Below the reader will find an excerpt from the Dictionary of Segments showing the grammatical structure of the **I**-segments:

I are A G n
I are A G n to v
I are A G n of n
I are A G n of G n
I are A G n of A n
  Sj v Cs
I are A G n d has P2
  Sj v Cs Sj v
I are A less G n
  Sj v Cs
I are A m n d v
  Sj v Cs Sj v
I are A m n
  Sj v Cs
I are A m n d has P2
  Sj v Cs Sj v
I are A n
  Sj v Cs
I are A n d has P2
  Sj v Cs Sj v
I are A n of EBB
I are A n of n
  Sj v Cs
I are A n of n d v
  Sj v Cs Sj v
I are A n of G n
I are A n of A G n
I are A n of A n
I are A n of I n
I are A n to v
I are A n to v up
I are all
I are all i G n
I are all too j
I are also A G n
I are also A G
I are also A n of EBB
I are also A G n

I are also A G n of n
I are also A n of n
I are also A G n of G n
I are also A n of G n
I are also A G n of A n
I are also A n of A n
I are also A G G n
I are also A n of A G n
I are also A n
I are also all i G n
I are also all i n
I are also A n of I n
I are also b j
  Sj v Cs
I are also called P
I are also called G G n
I are also called G n
I are also called n
  Sj v Od
I are also G n Pi A n
I are also G n to v
I are also G
I are also just A n
I are also j either
I are also j
I are also j up
I are also less j
I are also less G
I are also M of A n
I are also M to v
I are also n to v
I are also n
I are also O n
I are also O S G n
I are also O S n
I are also O n
  Sj v Cs
I are also Pi to be O G n

I are also Pi to be O n
  Sj v Od
I are also Pi
I are also P2 Pv
I are also P2
  Sj v
I are also Pi to be A n
  Sj v Od
I are also R
I are b all
I are b G n
  Sj v Cs
I are called P
I are called G G n
I are called G n
I are called n
  Sj v Od
I are G
I are G n Pi A n
I are G n to v
I are j
I are j either
I are j up
I are less G
I are less j
I are m b G n
  Sj v Cs
I are m n d v
  Sj v Cs Sj v
I are M of A n
I are M to v
I are n
I are n to v
I are no G n
I are no n
I are not all
I are O n
I are O S G n
I are O S n
I are Os
  Sj v Cs
I are P2
I are P2 Pv
I are Pi
  Sj v

I are Pi less of A n
  Sj v b
I are Pi to be O G n
I are Pi to be O n
I are Pi to be A n
  Sj v Od
I are Pi up less of A n
  Sj v b
I are R
  Sj v Cs
I are UF d should have P2 up
I are UF d should have P2
  Sj v Cs Sj v
I are what are b P2 n
I are what d shall also v
I are what d shall v
I are what d am Pi up
I are what d am Pi
I are what d v
I b are all
  Sj v Cs
I b
I b G
I b G n
  Sj
  Od
I b G n are also j
I b G n are j
I can also be j
  Sj v Cs
I can also be P2 up
  Sj v
I can also be A n
I can also be O G n
I can also be O n
  Sj v Cs
I can also be Pi
I can be
  Sj v
I can be A n
I can be b to v
I can be j
I can be O G n
I can be O n
I can be only A n
  Sj v Cs

I can be P2 up
I can be Pi
I can be too much to v
  Sj v
I can be why d am also j
I can be why d am j
  Sj v Sj v Cs
I d = d
  Sj
I d shall also v
I d shall v
I d v   reference to previous
segment
I d v not to v
I d v to v
  Sj v
I EAW v
  Sj b v
I FB
. . . .
I FB M of O n v
  b Sj v
I G
  Sj
  Od
I G d = d
  Sj

I G G n
  Sj
  Od
I G G n has also P2 R
I G G n has P2 R
  Sj v Od
I G n
I G n and G n
  Sj
  Od
I G n are A G G G n being P2
I G n are A G G n being P2
I G n are A G n being P2
I G n are A n being p2
  Sj v Cs
I G n are also P2
  Sj v
I G n are also Pi M n
  Sj v Od
I G n are also j
  Sj v Cs
I G n are also Pi
  Sj v
I G n are also A G G G n being P2
I G n are also A G G n being P2
I G n are also A G n being P2
I G n are also A n being P2
  Sj v Cs
etc.

3.1.6 *all-segments*

These segments start with the plural quantifier (plural indefinite determiner) **all**.

The first part (up to the Verbal Tense) of the **all**-segment looks like this:

(i)   all
(ii)   all A G n
(iii) all G n
(iv) all i
(v)   all i G n
(vi) all O n
(vii) all of i
(viii) all the n of n
(ix) all the other n
(x)   all b
(xi) all b b

The Adjective (G) and the Adverb (b) are optional.

The plural quantifier **all** means all specified objects, situations, conditions, etc., without exception.

(vi a)   all O n (e.g. *all her clothes*)

(Compare the difference between **M n, all A n** and **M of A n.**)

When the **all** part of the segment is followed by a Verbal Tense, it is the Subject of the segment (vii).

(vii a) all of i are
          Sj   v

Otherwise it can be either a Subject or an Object (vi a), depending on its relationship with the other segments within the sentence.

The second and the third parts of the **all**-segments are identical with those of the previous segments.

Below the reader will find an excerpt from the Dictionary of Segments, showing the grammatical structure of the **all**-segments:

all can be Pi up
all can be Pi
all can be up
  Sj v
all d am Pi
  Sj v
all d am Pi are also A n to v R O n
all d am Pi are A n to v R O n
  Sj Sj v   v Sj v Od Co
all d am Pi was to v R O n
  Sj Sj v   v Oi Od
  Sj Sj v   v Od Co
all day FB-BH(A-H)
all day long
all d v to v are to v up
all d v to v are v up
  Sj v
all EBN
. . . .
all except
  Sj
all FB
. . . .
all G n has to be P2
all G n shall be P2
  Sj v
all I
  Sj
  Od
all I are
  Sj v

all I are also Os
all I are also n of n
all I are also n
all I are G
all I are j
all I are j and also j
all I are n of n
all I are n
  Sj v Cs
all I are not
  Sj v
all I are Os
  Sj v Cs
all I are P2 to v
all I are P2 to v was v j
all I are P2
all I are P2 up
all I are P2 to v A n
all I are Pi
  Sj v
all I are Pi up less of A n
all I are Pi less of A n
all I are Pi up M of A n
all I are Pi M of A n
  Sj v Od
all I are up
all I can also be
all I can also be P2
all I can be
all I can be P2
  Sj v

all i b
all i n of n
all i d = d = R
  Sj
  Od
all I d v are n Pi up O n
all I d v are n Pi O n
  Sj Sj v v Cs
all I d v are n Pi
  Sj Sj v Cs
all I FB
all i G d = d = R
all I G n
all i G n
all I j
all i n
  Sj
  Od
all i n are Pi to v A n
  Sj v Od
all i n are Pi to v
  Sj v
all i n are also Pi to v R
all i n are also Pi to v A n
  Sj v Od
all i n are also Pi to v
  Sj v
all i n are Pi to v R A n
  Sj v Oi Od
  Sj v Od Co
all i n are Pi to v R
all I n v R
all I n v A n
all I n v n
  Sj v Od
all i n are also Pi to v R A n
  Sj v Oi Od
  Sj v Od Co

all i n shall also v
all i n shall v
  Sj v
all I shall v up less of A n
all I shall v less of A n
all I shall v up M of A n
all I shall v M of A n
  Sj v Od
all I sort of n
  Sj
  Od
all like A n
all like n
all like R
  Sj
all m
  Sj
  Od
all m of R = d
  Sj
all m of R shall v
all m of R should have to v
all m of R v
all m of R v to v up
  Sj v
all n
all n of n
  Sj
  Od
all n has to be P2
  Sj v
all n P1
all n Pi
  Sj Cs
all n v
  Sj v
etc.

3.1.7 *d-segments*

This is the largest body of segments and the reader will find here many new sequences of Parts of Speech.

The sign used to designate a human being (**d**) is a compound sign, representing a dozen sequences of Parts of Speech denoting a human being (see the Index at the end of the book).

The **d**-segment consists of three parts, like all Nominal segments: a) the initial part, preceding the Verbal Tense and acting as a Subject or Object; b) the Verbal Tense; c) the final part, acting as an Object or Complement.

The following sequences of Parts of Speech characterize the first part (the part preceding the Tense):

(i)   d

(ii) d all

(iii) d b

(iv) d X

As we said above, **d** is a compound sign, having sequences of its own,

A G d of A G G n	=	d
A d of i G n	=	d
A d of n	=	d
A S d of A G n	=	d
G G G d	=	d
d of A n	=	d
d of G n	=	d
M d	=	d
etc.		

which is why the first part of the **d**-segment is presented quite succinctly.

The Verbal Tenses constituting the second part are identical to those described in 3.1.1.

The third part of the **d**-segments is much more diverse than that of the other segments, therefore we will provide a more detailed list for reference:

(i)	A b G G G n	(xxi)	A n X
(ii)	A b G n	(xxii)	A n X b
(iii)	A b G n of n	(xxiii)	A only n of n
(iv)	A G G n	(xxiv)	b j
(v)	A G G n of m	(xxv)	b j X
(vi)	A G G n of m m	(xxvi)	G G n
(vii)	A G n b	(xxvii)	G n b
(viii)	A G n of A G G n	(xxviii)	G n of A M n of A G G n
(ix)	A G n of O n	(xxix)	G n of i n
(x)	A G n of P A n	(xxx)	G n of n
(xi)	A less G G n	(xxxi)	G n of O G n
(xii)	A n of A n of G n	(xxxii)	i
(xiii)	A n of A N''s n	(xxxiii)	i G n
(xiv)	A n of M G G n	(xxxiv)	j
(xv)	A n of n Pl	(xxxv)	j of A G n
(xvi)	A n of O G n	(xxxvi)	j of A N''s n
(xvii)	A n of O own	(xxxvii)	j of G n
(xviii)	A n of P A n of A G n	(xxxviii)	j of i G n
(xix)	A n of R	(xxxix)	j of O n
(xx)	A n off	(xxxx)	j of R

(xxxxi)	j of X	(lxxi)	Os
(xxxxii)	j to v	(lxxii)	P
(xxxxiii)	M	(lxxiii)	P A G G n
(xxxxiv)	M G G n	(lxxiv)	P b
(xxxxv)	M m n	(lxxv)	P G n
(xxxxvi)	M n	(lxxvi)	P X
(xxxxvii)	M n G	(lxxvii)	R
(xxxxviii)	M n of A n	(lxxviii)	R A G n
(xxxxix)	M n of G n	(lxxix)	R A G n of G n Pl
(l)	M of A G n	(lxxx)	R A n of G n
(li)	M of A less G n of G n	(lxxxi)	R A n of n Pl
(lii)	M of m n	(lxxxii)	R all
(liii)	m of O G G n	(lxxxiii)	R b n
(liv)	M of O G m G n	(lxxxiv)	R G
(lv)	n	(lxxxv)	R i n
(lvi)	n of G G n	(lxxxvi)	R i n of n
(lvii)	n of i n	(lxxxvii)	R j
(lviii)	O G G n	(lxxxviii)	R n
(lix)	O n b	(lxxxix)	R O G n
(lx)	O n b G	(lxxxx)	R Pi A G n
(lxi)	O n j	(lxxxxi)	R Pi A n of A G n
(lxii)	O n Pl	(lxxxxii)	R Pv
(lxiii)	O n Pl up	(lxxxxiii)	R up
(lxiv)	O n Pi	(lxxxxiv)	R X
(lxv)	O N''s j of M	(lxxxxv)	X
(lxvi)	O N''s n	(lxxxxvi)	X b
(lxvii)	O N''s P	(lxxxxvii)	X Pv A n
(lxviii)	of i n	(lxxxxviii)	X Pv O n
(lxix)	of P	etc.	
(lxx)	of P G n		

(G is optional; M is equal to G; N''s is also equal to G). The reader can find more information in the Dictionary of Segments.

The nominal sequences of the third part can have the following Parsing: Od (iv, ix), Od Co (xv), Oi Od or Od Co (lxxviii), Cs (xxiv, xxxiv, xxxv). Most of them can be followed by an Infinitival Complement.

Below the reader will find an excerpt from the Dictionary of Segments showing the grammatical structure of the **d**-segments:

d am A n of M G G n	d am A n to v A n
d am A n of M G n	d am A n to v n
d am A n of M n	d am A n to v up
d am A n of n	d am A N''s n
d am A n of n Pl	d am A only n of n
d am A n to v	Sj v Cs
d am A n to v R	d am about to v

d am about to v O n
d am about to v off
  Sj v
d am also A n Pi A G n of A n
d am also A n of A n
d am also A n of i n
d am also A n of m
d am also A n of M G G n
d am also A n of M G n
d am also A n of M n
d am also A n of n
d am also A n of n P1
d am also A n to v
d am also A n to v R
d am also A n to v up
d am also A n to v A n
d am also A n to v n
d am also A N''s n
d am also A only n
d am also A only n of n
  Sj v Cs
d am also about to v
  Sj v
d am also about to v O n
  Sj v Od
d am also about to v off
  Sj v
d am also after n
d am also after n b
d am also after R
d am also after n
d am also after A n
d am also after R b
d am also against A n
  Sj v b
d am also all j to v
d am also all that j
d am also b
d am also b A G n
d am also b A n
d am also b j
  Sj v Cs
d am also b P2
d am also b Pi
d am also b through P
d am also b to be P2

d am also b j
d am also b P2 A n
d am also b to v A n
d am also b to v A n of n
d am also being j
d am also being P2
d am also up
  Sj v
d both v n
d both v n to n
d both v O G n
d both v O n
  Sj v Od
d both v to v
d both v up
d can
  Sj v
d call(s)
R NAME
d called A n ''G n
  Sj v Od
d can also b be j
  Sj v Cs
d can also be
  Sj v
d can also be A G G n of O n
d can also be A G n
d can also be A G n of A n
d can also be A G n of O n
d can also be A less G G n
d can also be A less G n
d can also be A n
d can also be b
d can also be b j
  Sj v Cs
d can also be b j to v A n
d can also be b j to v A n b
  Sj v Cs v Od
d can also be G
d can also be j
d can also be j b
d can also be j of R
d can also be j to
d can also be j to v
  Sj v Cs did it also
  Sj v Od

d did just so
d did less
d did much of I
  Sj v
d did R up
  Sj v Od
d has A G G n of m m
d has A G G n of m
d has A G n of G n
d has A G n of m m
d has A G n of m
d has A G n of P A n
  Sj v Od
d has A G n to v A G G n to v
d has A G n to v A n
d has A G n to v R
  Sj v Od Ic
d has A n
d has A n b
  Sj v Od
d has P2 R Pv
d has P2 R up b
d has P2 R v to v R
d has P2 R v up b
d has P2 R v up to v R
d has P2 to v n of A n Pi n
d has P2 to v n to v A n
d has P2 to v O n
d has P2 to v up
d has P2 to v X
d has P2 to v X up
  Sj v Od
d should have P2 R A n
  Sj v Oi Od
  Sj v Od Co
d should have P2 R off A n
  Sj v Od Co
d should have P2 to v
d should have P2 to v up
  Sj v
d should have P2 to v A n
d should have P2 to v R to v
d should have P2 to v R to v S
  Sj v Od
d v A b G G G n
d v A b G G n

d v A b G n
d v A b G n
d v A b G n of A n P1 to v R
d v A G
d v A G G G n
d v A G G n
  Sj v Od
d v A G G n A n
d v A G G n b A n
d v A G G n b b A n
  Sj v Od Co
d v A G G n b has A G n of P
d v A G G n b has A G n to v A n
  Sj v Sj b v Od
d v A G G n d has P2
  Sj v Od Sj v
d v A G G n of N"'s n
d v A G G n v
d v A G less P1 n
d v A G G n of A n
d v A G G n Pi
d v A G n
d v A G n A n
  Sj v Od
d v A G n d has P2
  Sj v Od Sj v
d v A G n G
  Sj v Od Co
d v A G n of A G n of A n
d v A G n of A n of A G n
d v A G n of A n
d v A G n of A n b being P2
d v A G n of A n being P2
  Sj v Od
d v A G n of A n Pi A G n
d v A G n of m G *
d v A G n of n Pi n
  Sj v Od Co
d v A G n of N"'s n
  Sj v Od
d v A G n of n" Pi"
d v A G n of G n" Pi"
d v A G n of A G n" Pi" A n
d v A G n of A n" Pi" A n
  Sj v Od Co
d v A G n of n

d v A G n of P A n	d v A G one
d v A G n off	d v A G P of n of A n
Sj v Od	d v A HEADING
d v A G n Pl	d v A i n
d v A G n Pi	d v A less G n
d v A G n Pi A n	d v A less G n of O n
d v A G n Pi A n of A n	d v A m
d v A G n Pv O j	d v A M G G n of A G n
d v A G n Pv O n	d v A m G G n of A n
Sj v Od Co	d v A M G G n of A n
d v A G n to v R	d v A m G n
d v A G n to v R all	d v A M G n of A G n
Sj v Od Ic	d v A m G n of A n
d v A G n shall v	d v A M G n of A n
Sj v Sj v	d v A m n
d v A G n to v	d v A m n out of A n
d v A G n up	d v A m of R
d v A G n v	d v A m of R b
d v A G n v up	d v A M n of A G n
d v A G n v A n	d v A m n of A n
d v A G n v A n of n"	d v A M n of A n
d v A G n v O n	d v A n
d v A G n v off A n	d v A n A n
d v A G n v off A n of n	Sj v Od
d v A G	etc.

3.1.8 *it*-segments

The word **it** is a PPNC third person, neutral.

The **it**-segments were separated from the **d**-segments (**it** being part of PPNC is also part of **d**) for two reasons: a) to help the respective algorithm responsible for the Pronominal Reference; b) to see if the combinatorics of Parts of Speech is any different compared to that of the **d**-segments and the rest of the Nominal segments.

The only difference found was phraseological rather than syntactical. Certain phrases had to be used only with **it**, and nothing else:

(i)	it can be time	(iv)	it seems (-ed) no matter
(ii)	it hardly matters to whom	(v)	it was (high) time
(iii)	it occurred to R	etc.	

As for the algorithm, we found that it was of much help to separate the **it**-segments and to add some more specifications of the sort:

(vi)   it was A G G n itself

which is a clear indication that **itself** refers to **it**, within the boundaries of the same segment.

Below the reader will find an excerpt from the Dictionary of Segments showing the grammatical structure of the **it**-segments:

it shall v M FB to v A G n of less G n
it shall v M FB to v A n of less G n
it shall v M FB to v A G n
it shall v M FB to v A n
it shall v M n to v A G n of less G n
it shall v M n to v A n of less G n
it shall v M n to v A G n
it shall v M n to v A n
   Sj v Od Ic
it shall v so
   Sj v
it should have been just about A n of
O n
it should have been just about j
it should have been just about A n
it should have been j to v up
it should have been j to v
   Sj v Cs
it takes FB
   Sj v Od
it UM occurs to R
it v
   Sj v
it v b j to v up
it v b j to v
   Sj v Pr
it v b R to v to v
   Sj v b Od Ic
it v G
it v G and G
it v G b G
it v j
   Sj v Pr

it v n
   Sj v Od
it v O n to v n
   Sj v Od Ic
it was
   Sj v
it was A G G n itself
it was A G G n
it was A G n
it was A G n itself
it was A G n to v
it was A n
it was A n itself
it was A n of A n
it was A n to v
it was A n to v A n
it was all b to v off R
it was all b to v R
it was all b Pi
it was all b j
it was all right
it was also j to v
   Sj v Cs
it was j to be j to v O n
   Sj v Od
it was d
it was n
it shall be A G n
   Sj v Cs
it shall be A G n to v up A n
it shall be A G n to v A n
   Sj v Cs Ic
etc.

3.1.9 *G-segments*

The sign **G** was used to denote the attribute to the Noun (in some cases **G** was placed in the position of the Predicative, instead of **j**). The Adjective (G) is optional. It can be omitted if there is need for that, for example to simplify the sentence.

It was important to observe the combinatorial behaviour of G in the segments, especially in the **G**-segments. The English sentence seldom starts with an Adjective and it is quite surprising to see how often the sentence can be interrupted just before an Adjective. Sometimes this is done for enumeration. It is also worth noting that in the English sentence there could hardly be found more than four Adjectives in a row (i, ii).

(i)   G G G G n has also P2 n Pi M G G n
(ii)   G n v G G G G n

The first part of the **G**-segment (the part preceding the Verbal Tense) consists only of attributes followed by a Noun. There can be one, two, three or four attributes to the Noun. Most often there is only one. No other Part of Speech is allowed to intervene before the Noun except an Adjective.

If the first part of the **G**-segment is followed by a Verbal Tense, then it is a Subject, but if not, it can be either Subject or Object.

The only Part of Speech allowed between the first and the second part (the Verbal Tense) of the **G**-segment is the Adverb (iii):

(iii)   G n b v A G n (of n)
         Sj   b v Od

All other observations coincide with those already made for the other Nominal segments.

Below the reader will find an excerpt from the Dictionary of Segments showing the grammatical structure of the **G**-segments:

G G G G n has also P2 n Pi M G G n
G G G G n has also P2 n Pi M n
G G G G n has P2 n Pi M G G n
G G G G n has P2 n Pi M G n
G G G G n has P2 n Pi M n
    Sj v Od Co
G G G n
    Sj
    Od
G G G n has also P2 n Pi M G G n
G G G n has also P2 n Pi M G n
G G G n has also P2 n Pi M n
G G G n has P2 n Pi M G G n
G G G n has P2 n Pi M G n
G G G n has P2 n Pi M n
    Sj v Od Co
G G G n just v
    Sj v
G G G n n has also P2 n Pi M G n
    Sj v Od Co
G G G n Pl

G G G n Pi A n
    Sj Cs
    Od Co
G G G n v
    Sj v
G G n   explains Subject
    Sj
    Od
G G n has also P2 n Pi M G G n
G G n has also P2 n Pi M G n
G G n has also P2 n Pi M n
    Sj v Od Co
G G n has also P2 to v up G G G n
G G n has also P2 to v up G G n
G G n has also P2 to v up G n
G G n has also P2 to v up n
G G n has also P2 to v G G G n
G G n has also P2 to v G G n
G G n has also P2 to v G n
G G n has also P2 to v n
    Sj v Od

G G n has P2 up
G G n has P2
  Sj v
G G n has P2 n Pi M G G n
G G n has P2 n Pi M G n
G G n has P2 n Pi M n
  Sj v Od Co
G G n has P2 to v up G G G n
G G n has P2 to v up G G n
G G n has P2 to v up G n
G G n has P2 to v up n
G G n has P2 to v G G G n
G G n has P2 to v G G n
G G n has P2 to v G n
G G n has P2 to v n
G G n just v n
G G n just v n to v A n of A n
  Sj v Od
G G n just v
  Sj v
G n are also being P2 to v R
G n are also P2 to be P2 up Pi m m
G n are also P2 to be P2 up Pi m
G n are also P2 to be P2 Pi m m
G n are also P2 to be P2 Pi m
  Sj v Od
G n are also A G n
G n are also A n
G n are also n
  Sj v Cs
G n are also Pi n
  Sj v Od

G n are also P2 to v
  Sj v
G n are also A n
  Sj v Cs
G n has also P2 A G n
G n has also P2 n
G n has also P2 m n of A G n
G n has also P2 m n of A n
G n has also P2 to v up G G G n
G n has also P2 to v up G G n
G n has also P2 to v up G n
G n has also P2 to v up n
G n has also P2 to v G G G n
G n has also P2 to v G G n
G n has also P2 to v G n
G n has also P2 to v n
G n has also P2 to v G n of n
G n has also P2 to v n
  Sj v Od
G n has been Pi
G n has been Pi up
G n has P2
G n has also P2 up
G n has also P2
  Sj v
G n has P2 A G n
G n has P2 A n
G n has P2 m n of A G n
G n has P2 m n of A n
  Sj v Od
etc.

3.1.10 O-segments

The sign **O** is used to designate the Possessive Pronoun and the genitive of the Noun:

(i)   *my books*
      Jim's car
      O n

Apart from all other similarities with the Nominal segments, there is one striking similarity between the **O**-segments and **A**-segments in the use of the **b G n** sequence after O or A, as a Subject or Object (ii):

(ii)   A b G n (e.g. *the extremely high prices*)
       O b G n (e.g. *her slowly aging face*)
       Sj or Od

Here the Adverb cannot be joined to the Noun without a minimum of one and a maximum of two Adjectives to stand between. Of course the sequences **A b G (G) n** and **O b G (G) n** can be met in all other types of segments. The **b G (G) n** sequence is universal and can often be met either as a Subject or as an Object in all types of segments.

No other Part of Speech is allowed to intervene between the Possessive Pronoun or the genitive of the Noun and the Noun except the Adverb, only as part of the **b G (G) n** sequence, and the Adjective or the Numeral used as attributes. After O there can be a maximum of three Adjectives in a row used as attributes:

(iii)   O (G) (G) (G) n

(the brackets indicate that the Adjective is optional)

Everything else that could be said about the **O**-segments also applies to all Nominal segments.

Below the reader will find an excerpt from the Dictionary of Segments showing the grammatical structure of the **O**-segments:

O G G n are also of G n
O G G n are also of n
O G G n are also m m n b
O G G n are also m n b
O G G n are also m m n
O G G n are of G n
O G G n are of n
O G G n are m n b
O G G n are m n
  Sj v Cs
O G G n are also P2
O G G n are P2
O G G n are up
  Sj v
O G n can also be P2 j
  Sj v Cs
O G n can also be P2
  Sj v
O G n can also be A G n
O G n can also be A n
O G n can be P2 j
O G n can be A n
  Sj v Cs

O G n has also been A n
  Sj v Cs
O G n has also been Pi
  Sj v
O G n has also P2 A n
O G n has also P2 R
O G n has also P2 A n of A n
O G n has also been m %
  Sj v Od
O G n has been Pi
  Sj v
O G n has been m %
  Sj v Cs
O G n has P2 A n
O G n has P2 n R
O G n has P2 A n of A n
O G n has P2 A n of N''s n
  Sj v Od
O G n having been P2
O G n having P2 up
  Sj v
etc.

*3.1.11 **other**-segments*

The **other**-segments start with the Adjective (modifier), Noun, Pronoun, Determiner or Numeral (as part of M) **other**, or **another**, used as an attribute and expressing alternative (i) or addition (ii):

(i)   other n are
(ii)   another m FB (bm)

The word **another** is usually followed by an Adjective or a Numeral used as an attribute (ii) or by an 'of ' phrase (iii):

(iii)   another of N''s n v

The word **other** is connected either directly to the Noun (iv), or through the mediation of up to two attributes (v). When % is used instead of a Noun, then the whole phrase represents the Noun (vi):

(iv)   other n are P2 to v R
(v)   ther G G n v G n
(vi)   other m % v A n shall also v

The first part of the **other**-segment is always used as Subject if it is followed by a Verbal Tense, otherwise it can be either a Subject or an Object.

Like the other Nominal segments, the first part of the **other**-segment may contain a Reduced Relative Clause, used as Complement Subject (vii):

(vii)   other n Pi A G G n are n
        Sj   Cs   v   Cs

The second and the third parts of the **other**-segments are not different from the second and the third parts of the other Nominal Segments.

Below the reader will find an excerpt from the Dictionary of Segments showing the grammatical structure of the **other**-segments:

other G n are also P2 up to v A n
other G n are also P2 to v n
other G n are also P2 up to v R
other G n are also P2 to v R
other G n are P2 up to v A n
other G n are P2 up to v R
other G n are P2 to v A n
other G n are P2 to v R
  Sj / Od v Od
other G n are G G n
other G n are G n
other G n are n
  Sj v Cs
other G n are also P2
other G n are P2
  Sj v

other G n are NAME
  Sj v Cs
other G n v G n
  Sj v Od
other G n v up
  Sj v
other G n v G
  Sj v Pr
other G n v
  Sj v
other m % v A n shall also v
other m % v A n shall v
  Sj v Sj v
other n
  Sj
  Od

other n are also P2 up to v A n

other n are also P2 up to v R

other n are also P2 to v A n

other n are also P2 to v R

other n are P2 up to v A n

other n are P2 up to v R

other n are P2 to v A n

other n are P2 to v R

   Sj / Od v Od

other n

   Sj

   Od

other n also v

other n are Pi and Pi

other n are also P2 up

   Sj v

other n are G G n

   Sj v Cs

etc.

3.1.12 **both**-segments

The word **both** is a Pronoun used as a Numeral indicating a pair (the pair of). The combinatorics of the Parts of Speech (PS) following **both** is slightly different to that for the other Nominal segments.

As a matter of necessity **both** has some unique sequences of PS in the part preceding the Verbal Tense, especially (ii):

(i)   both C A n

(ii)   both d and d

(iii)   both G and G n

(iv)   both I n

(v)   both I n and next

(vi)   both n and n

(vii)   both n

(viii) both n of A n

(ix)   both n of n

(x)   both O G n

(xi)   both of I n

(xii)   both of R

(xiii) both of which

(xiv)   both

The **both**-segment, in the case when it is not followed by a Verbal Tense, is either a Subject or an Object.

The Verbal Tense and the Nominal sequence after the Tense are identical to that of the other Nominal segments.

Below the reader will find an excerpt from the Dictionary of Segments showing the grammatical structure of the **both**-segments:

both n of n v A n of A less P1

both n of n v up A n of A P1

both n of n v A n of A P1

both n of n v up A G n

both n of n v up A n

both n of n v A G n

both n of n v A G n up

both n of n v A n

both n of n v A n up

both n of n v up A G n of A less P1

both n of n v up A G n of A P1

both n of n v up A n of A less P1

both n of n v A G n of A less P1

both n v A G n of A less P1

both n v A G n of A P1

both n v A G n

both n v A G n up

both n v A n of A less P1

both n v A n of A P1

both n v A n

both n v A n up

both n v d

both n v d up

both n v O G n

both n v O n
both n v up A G n of A less Pl
both n v up A n of A less Pl
both n v up A G n of A Pl
both n v up A G n
both n v up A n of A Pl
both n v up A n
  Sj v Od
both O G n
both O G n and O less G n
both O n
both O n and O less G n
both O n and O n of n
both O n and O n
  Sj
  Od
both of I n are A n to v n
  Sj v Cs
both of R = d
  Sj
  Od
both of R Pi A G G n
  Sj Cs
  Od Co

both of which
  Sj
both of which shall v G n
  Sj v Od
both of which shall v
both of which had P2
both of which v
both of which are Pi
both of which are P2
both of which had P2
  Sj v
both Pi and Pi
  Sj Cs
both shall v
  Sj v
both shall v A G n
both shall v n
both shall v A n of A n
  Sj v Od
both shall be A S m
  Sj Cs
both shall be P2
  Sj v
etc.

3.1.13 *who*-segments

The word *who* is a Relative and Interrogative Pronoun and starts Relative or Interrogative segments (i):

(i)   (*The postman*)
    who brought the newspapers ...
    who v A n
    Sj v   Od
      Cs

(i a) *Who brought the newspapers?*

The Pronoun **who** can be replaced by the Noun defined by it (i b, ii a). Compare:

(i b) *The postman brought the newspapers.*

The Pronoun **who** acts as a Subject (Sj) in the Relative and in the Interrogative Clause (i) and (i a). The entire Relative who-Clause acts as a Complement to the previous Noun: Complement Subject to (*The postman*) in (i) and Complement Object to (*the man*) in (ii).

(ii)   *You saw the man who came last night.*
      d   v   A n   who v   b
      Sj   v   Od   Sj   v   b
                         Co

(ii a)   *The man came last night.*

The Pronoun **who** is almost always followed by a Verbal Tense (except in
Who?). No other PS can stand between it and the Verbal Tense, except an
Adverb. Compare:

(iii)   who b has M n
(iv)   who b shall also v A n

The Relative Pronoun **who** is used mostly in Defining Relative Clauses (v,
vi). Compare:

(v)   *Peter likes women who paint their faces.*
      d   v   n   who v   O   n

(vi)   *A wife is   a person who is married.*
      A n   are A n   who is P2

    The second and the third parts of **who**-segments are the same as those for
the other Nominal segments.

    Below the reader will find an excerpt from the Dictionary of Segments,
showing the grammatical structure of the **who**-segments:

who v O b G n	who v R A b G n
who v O n	Sj v Oi Od
who v O n to be n	Sj v Od Co
who v O n to v A n	who v R of P to v O N''s n
who v O n to v off A n	who v R of P to v O N''s G n
who v O n to v G n	who v R out of G n
who v O n to be G n	who v R out of n
who v O n to v n	Sj v Od
Sj v Od	who v rather like I n
who v of A G n	who v rather like I n of A n
who v of A G G n	who v rather like I n of A n of n
who v of A n	who v so b against O n
Sj v b	Sj v b
who v off Pi n	who v to be P2
Sj v Od	who v to be P2 up
who v Pi	who v to v
Sj v	Sj v
who v Pi n	who v to v A G n up A G G n
who v R	who v to v A G n up A G n
Sj v Od	who v to v A n
who v R v up	who v to v A G n up A n
Sj v Od v	who v to v A n has also P2

who v to v A n up A G n
who v to v A n up A G G n
who v to v A n has P2
who v to v A n up A n
who v to v no other n
who v to v no n
who v to v no G n
who v to v n
who v to v O n
who v to v only A n
who v to v R
  Sj v Od
who v to v up
who v up
  Sj v
who v up A G n
who v up A G G n
who v up A n
  Sj v Od
who v up b
who v up j

Sj v
who v up n
  Sj v Od
who v up of A G n
who v up of A n
who v up of A G G n
who v what
who v what A n are Pi
  Sj v
who v what d should have P2
  Sj v Sj v
who v what shall v
  Sj v
who v when d am Pi
who v where d am Pi
  Sj v Sj v
who was d NAME
  Sj v Cs
who has also P2 R v
  Sj v Od

3.1.14 *which*-segments

The determiner **which** starts Relative Clauses (defining and non-defining) and Interrogative sentences (segments). It can be followed by a Nominal segment or an Adverbial Clause, or by a Verbal Tense.

In those cases when **which** is followed by a Verbal Tense, it acts as a Subject of the Relative Clause (the segment). Otherwise, the entire **which**-segment is a Complement to the Noun it refers to. In the following case (i) it refers to a Subject and therefore is a Complement Subject:

> (*The airline*)
> *which was opened this year*
> (i)   which are P2,   bm (*was the best in Europe.*)
>   Sj   v
>   Cs

Compare:

> (i a)   *The airline was opened.*
> (i b)   *The airline was the best in Europe.*

If **which** is followed by a Nominal sequence, it can be regarded either as an Object (as in ii a, since it refers to *the airline*), or as a Subject (as in ii b, ii aa), depending on how we view the sentence. For example:

(The airline)
which   the president opened

(ii)   which A n   v *(this year was the best in Europe.)*
          Cs

Compare:

(ii a)   *The president opened the airline this year.*
          A   n   v   A   n   bm
          Sj   v   Od   bm
(ii aa)   *The airline was the best in Europe.*
(ii b)   *The airline the president opened this year was the best in Europe.*
          A   n   A n   v   I   FB are A n   in n
          Sj   Cs   bm   Cs

However, in both cases (i, ii) the **which**-segment is a Complement Subject (Cs).

If the **which**-segment refers to the Object of the previous segment, then the entire **which**-segment is a Complement Object (iii).

(iii)   *I want a computer which is   waterproof.*
          d v   A n   which are j
          Sj v   Od   Co

The second and the third parts of the **which**-segment are identical to those of the other Nominal segments.

Below the reader will find an excerpt from the Dictionary of Segments showing the grammatical structure of the **which**-segments:

which are A n
which are A n of I n
which are A n of O G n
which are A n of O n
which are A n" Pi" A n to v n
which are A very n of O G n
which are A very n of O n
which are also A G n" Pi" A n to v n
which are also A less j
which are also A n
which are also A n" Pi" A n to v n
which are also b j
which are also called NAME
which are also G
which are also G n
which are also G n of G n
which are also G n of n
which are also in n
which are also j
which are also j to v A n

which are also less j
which are also M
which are also n
which are also n of G n
which are also n of n
which are also O own
   Sj v Cs
which are also P2
   Sj v
which are also P2 G G n
   Sj v
which are also P2 less b j
which are also P2 less j
   Sj v Pr
which are also P2 to be N"s G n
which are also P2 to be N"s n
which are also P2 to v A n of G n
which are also P2 to v A n of G n j
which are also P2 to v A n of n

which are also P2 to v A n of n j
  Sj v Od
which are also Pi
  Sj v
which are also Pi A n Pi A n
which are also Pi O G n
which are also Pi O n
which are also Pi O n
which are also to v G n
which are also to v n
  Sj v Od
which are also up
  Sj v
which are P2 to be N''s G n
which are P2 to be N''s n
which are P2 to v A n of G n
which are P2 to v A n of G n j
which are P2 to v A n of n
which are P2 to v A n of n j
  Sj v Od
which b v A m n
which b v A n

which b v G n
which b v G n of G n
which b v G n of n
which b v M n to v A n
which b v M n to v A n of O own
which b v n
which b v n of G n
which b v n of n
which b v no n
which b v O n
which b v R
which b v up A n
  Sj v Od
which can also be G
which can also be j
which can also be less b P2
which can also be Os
which can also be Os b
which can also be Os by right
  Sj v Cs
etc.

3.1.15 **whose**-*segments*

The word **whose** is a Possessive Relative Pronoun (genitive case) that starts Relative (defining or non-defining) and Interrogative segments (Clauses). The pronoun **whose** is never followed directly by a Verbal Tense (except for *are, is* or *were* in Interrogative sentences). It is always followed by a Noun, or by an Adjective and Noun.

The **whose**-segment acts as a Complement Subject to the preceding Subject. Otherwise the word **whose**, within its own segment, is always a Subject. For example:

  (i) *The man, whose car had been damaged, is my uncle.*
     A   n   whose n has been P2   are O n
     Sj   Sj   v   v   Cs
     Sj   Cs

The **whose**-segment can also act as a Complement Object, if it refers to the Object of the previous segment.

The other parts of the **whose**-segments are identical to those of the other segments, described above.

Below the reader will find an excerpt from the Dictionary of Segments showing the grammatical structure of the **whose**-segments:

whose
whose G n
  Sj
whose G n are also to v
whose G n are also j
whose G n are j
whose G n are also G
whose G n are G
  Sj v Cs
whose G n are to v
whose G n are also up
whose G n are up
whose G n b are to v
  Sj v
whose G n b
  Sj
whose G n b are also to v
  Sj v
whose G n d am Pi to v
  Sj Sj v
whose G n d has also P2
whose G n d has P2
whose G n d v
  Sj Sj v
whose G n d v O G n
whose G n d v O n
  Sj Sj v Od
whose G n seemed to have been P2
whose G n seem(s) to have been P2
  Sj v
whose G n should have P2 M n
  Sj v Od
whose G n v
  Sj v
whose G n v of less j n
  Sj v
whose G n v X
  Sj v Od
whose n
  Sj
whose n are
whose n are also to v
  Sj v
whose n are A n
whose n are also j
whose n are j
whose n are also G

whose n are A G G n
  Sj v Cs
whose n are also P2 j
whose n are P2 j
  Sj v
whose n are A G n
whose n are A less j to v up
whose n are A less j to v
  Sj v Cs
whose n are up
whose n are P2
  Sj v
whose n are G
whose n are j
  Sj v Cs
whose n are also P2
  Sj v
whose n are also j
  Sj v Cs
whose n are P2
whose n are to v
whose n are also up
  Sj v
whose n b
  Sj
whose n b are also to v
whose n b are to v
whose n can also be P2
whose n can be P2
  Sj v
whose n has P2 A n of R
whose n has A G n
whose n has also P2 A n of R
whose n has also A G n
  Sj v Od
whose n of n are O n
whose n of n are also O n
whose n of n are O only n
whose n of n are also O only n
  Sj v Cs
whose n seemed to have been P2
whose n seem(s) to have been P2
whose n shall also v
whose n shall v
  Sj v
etc.

3.1.16 *whom*-segments

The Relative Pronoun **whom** is interpreted as **to whom** and as such it is related to the Adverbial **to**-segments, expressing direction and location. For example:

(i) *Was the girl whom you spoke to   a few minutes ago your sister?*
     are A n   whom d   v   up M   FB   ago O   n

Compare: *Was the girl to whom you spoke your sister?*

When used at the start of a Relative Clause, the Pronoun **whom** is usually followed by an Article or by a Noun (ii).

(ii)   whom A n are also Pi
         whom d has also P2

When used to start an Interrogative Clause, it is followed by an Auxiliary Verb (iii).

(iii)   whom shall d v up?

In all other cases it can be replaced by **who**.

The **whom**-segment can act as Complement Subject or Complement Object, depending on whether it refers to the Subject or to the Object.

Below the reader will find an excerpt from the Dictionary of Segments showing the grammatical structure of the **whom**-segments:

whom d has also been P2
whom d has also been P2 to v
whom d has also P2 only
whom d has been P2 to v
whom d has P2
whom d has P2 up
whom d has P2 only
whom d shall also v to v
whom d shall to?
whom d shall also v to v up
whom d shall v to v
whom d shall v?

whom d shall v up
whom d shall v to v up
whom d shall also v
whom d v
whom d v to v
whom d v up
whom G n v
whom G n v of
  Sj Sj v
whom shall d v up?
  Sj v Sj v
etc.

3.1.17 *such*-segments

The **such**-segments start with the Pronoun and determiner **such**. The next element after **such** can be a Conjunction as in (i), a Noun (ii), or occasionally an Indefinite Article (iii). An Adjective was recorded in one case only (iv).

(i)   such as A n
(ii) such n has P2 R
(iii) such A G G n
(iv) such G n

All other features of the **such**-segment are identical with those of the other Nominal segments.

Below the reader will find an excerpt from the Dictionary of Segments, showing the grammatical structure of the **such**-segments:

such are O G n	such as I P1 by
such are O n	Sj b
Sj v Cs	such n shall also v R to v O n
such as	such n shall v A n to v O n
such as A G G n by	such n shall v n
such as A n m	such n shall also v R to v A N''s n
such as A n	such n shall v A n to v A N''s n
such as A NAME	such n shall also v A n to v A N''s n
such as G G G n	such n shall v R to v A N''s n
such as G G n by	Sj v Od
such as G n by	such n shall also v
Sj b	Sj v
such as G n shall also P2 G n	such n shall also v A n to v O n
such as G n shall also P2 n	such n shall also v R
such as G n shall P2 G n	such n shall v R to v O n
such as G n shall P2 n	such n shall also v n
Sj v Od	such n shall v A n
such as G n v less j	Sj v Od
such as G n v less G	such n shall v
Sj v Pr	Sj v
such as I by	etc.

3.1.18 *that*-segments

When **that** is used as a Conjunction, it introduces a Subordinate Clause. The **that**-segments can be of two different types: a) referring to the Noun preceding **that** (i); b) not referring directly to the Noun preceding **that** (ii). In the Dictionary of Segments, the reader will find those referring to the preceding Noun marked as **that'**. When **that** refers to the previous Noun, it is usually followed by a Verbal Tense.

(i)   *The rumour that was spreading proved to be untrue.*
    A   n   that are Pi   v   to be j
    Sj   Sj v
    Sj   Cs

Compare:

(i a)   *A rumour was spreading.*
    Sj   v

When **that** refers to the Subject, then the whole **that**-segment is a Complement Subject (ii).

(ii)   *The rumour that   he was resigning was not   confirmed.*
         A   n   that d am Pi   are also P2
         Sj   Sj   v   v
                             Cs

The **that**-segment can also act as an Object (Od) (iii), or as a
Complement Subject (iv), or as a Complement Object (iii a).

(iii)   *The legal words are all there to   ensure*
         A   G   n   are all b   to v
         Sj   v   Cs
         that the will is   properly executed.
         that A   n   are also   P2
         Od
(iii a) *I saw the house that   was built on the hill.*
         d v   A n   that was P2 on A n
         Sj v   Od   Co
(iv)   *The truth is   that he will   not   come.*
         A   n   are that d shall also v
         Sj   v   Cs

The more common Prepositions and Conjunctions to be used after **that** as
a Conjunction are:

(v)   that for M n I are n
         that for R n are A n
(vi)   that if d am also j d can also v
         that if d am to v
         that if no n are P2
(vii)   that in A n has P2 n
         that in m v
(viii)   that instead of A n
         that instead of P n
(ix)   that what d v was also j
         that what v A n A G n are A G n
(x)   that within m n m G G n shall also v n

Below the reader will find an excerpt from the Dictionary of Segments
showing the grammatical structure of the **that**-segments:

that n are also Pi to v n   that n are P2 up
that n are also Pi to v n of n   Sj v
that n are being P2 to v R   that n are Pi to v n
  Sj v Od   that n are Pi to v n of n
that n are G   Sj v Od
that n are j   that n be P2 *
that n are n   that n can also be
  Sj v Cs   Sj v

that n can also be j
that n can also be j to v
that n can also be j to v A n
that n can also be j to v n
that n can also be j to v R
   Sj v Cs
that n can also be P2
that n can also be P2 up
that n can be
   Sj v
that n can be j
   Sj v Cs
that n can be j to to v
that n can be j to v A n
that n can be j to v n
that n can be j to v R
   Sj v Cs Ic
that n can be P2
that n can be P2 up
   Sj v
that n has also b P2 A n
that n has also P2 A n
   Sj v Od
that n has P2
   Sj v
that n has P2 A n
that n has P2 R
   Sj v Od
that n it seem(ed) has also P2
that n it seem(ed) has P2
. . . .
that n just v G n
   Sj v Od
that n not only shall v
that n of O n has P2 up
that n of M n has P2 up
   Sj v
that n of A n has also P2 i n
that n of A n has P2 i n
that n shall also v G G n
that n shall also v G n
that n shall also v m m n
that n shall also v m m n b
that n shall also v m n
that n shall also v m n b
that n shall v G G n

that n shall v G n
that n shall v m m n
that n shall v m m n b
that n shall v m n
that n shall v m n b
that n shall v to v M n
   Sj v Od
that n should have to be G
that n should have to be G up
that n should have to be j
   Sj v Cs
that n should have to be P2
that n should have to be P2 up
   Sj v
that n to v R
   Sj v Od
that n v
   Sj v
that n v A G G n are also j to v
that n v A G G n are also j to v up
that n v A G G n are j to v
that n v A G G n are j to v up
that n v A G n are also j to v
that n v A G n are also j to v up
that n v A G n are j to v
that n v A G n are j to v up
that n v A n are also j to v
that n v A n are also j to v up
that n v A n are j to v
that n v A n are j to v up
   Sj v Sj v Cs Ic
that' are Pi M n of A G n
that' are Pi M n of A n
that' are Pi O n
that' are Pi to be A G n
that' are Pi to be A n
   Sj v Od
that' are Pi up
that' are there
that' are there b
   Sj v
that' are to v A n of G n j
that' are to v A n of n j
   Sj v Od
that' b v
   Sj b v

that' b v A N''s G n Pl   that' b v R
that' b v A N''s G n Pl up   that' b v to v O n
that' b v A N''s G n right up A n   that' b v A n
that' b v A N''s n Pl   that' b v n
that' b v A N''s n Pl up   Sj v Od
that' b v A N''s n right up A n   etc.

3.2 *Verbal segments*

The Verbal segments can be divided into three main groups according to
their initial element:

a) segments starting with a Main Verb;
b) segments with an Auxiliary Verb coming first;
c) segments beginning with an Infinitive or Participle '-ing'.

The Verbal segments can also be dependent or relatively independent. The
dependent Verbal segments need to be linked to a Subject, because they were
cut off from it by a Punctuation Mark or by another segment (i):

    (i)   v n
    (i a)   *The people in the bus are German.*
           A   n   in A n v   n
           Sj   bdl   v   Cs

Compare: *The people are German.*

For more details on how to link the **v**-segment to the Subject see **Links** in
Chapter 8.

    The segments that are relatively independent need not be linked to
another part of the sentence; they can stand alone as a complete sentence or
as a clause. For example:

    (ii)   Staying upside down is a difficult matter.
           Pi   b   v A G   n

Compare: *It is a difficult matter to stay upside down.*

    (iii)   *To drink means to be thirsty.*
           to v   v   to be j
    (iv)   *Are the people German?*
           v A n   n
    (v)   *No smoking!*
           no P

In (v) there is an example of a missing Verb, substituted by the negative
Particle **no**.

    NB In the Dictionary of Segments, the Interrogative and the Imperative
segments are not marked as such (with a few exceptions). This is either
evident from the very construction of the segment (vi), or the construction of

the segment does not provide sufficient evidence for that (vii). In the latter case, the segment can be Interrogative or non-Interrogative, Imperative or non-Imperative, depending on the context. In this case, the Text Processing System will need an algorithmic procedure to find out which possibility to choose. More about this can be found in **Links**, in chapter 8.

(vi)   can A n v A G n
          v   Sj   v Od   ?
          did not d b v to be O G n
          v   Sj b v   Od   ?
(vi a)   v up A n d v
          v   Od Sj v   ?
(vii)   am A G n v up
          v   Cs
          v Sj v Pr   ?
(vii a) v up
          Pr

3.2.1 *Pi*-segments

This type of segment starts with a Participle '-ing' and most often is a Complement (Cs, Co), with some exceptions (see further).

(i)   Pi A n of A G G G n
(ii)   Pi A n of O G n
(iii)   Pi O G G n
(iv)   *The clerk came not to complain but to*
          A   n   v   also to v   but to
          Sj   v
          commiserate, asking me to pass on their regrets to
          v   Pi   R to v   on O   n   to
                        Cs
          the princess.
          A n
          bdl

Compare: *The clerk was asking me.*

(v)   *I cantered Cal down to the start trying to*
          d v   n   down to A n   Pi   to
          Sj v   Od bdl   Cs
          wind up a bit of life-force for us both.
          v   up M   n   for R both
                        br

Compare: *I was trying to wind up a bit of life-force.*

Quite often the Pi is followed by an Infinitival Complement (v, vi, vii, viii):

(vi)   Pi to v O n
        v Ic

(vii)   Pi to v R O G n
        v Ic

In some constructions, the Infinitival Complement follows after the Object (viii):

(viii)   Pi R to v A n
        v Od Ic

Constructions that start with *taking into consideration, according to, concerning, following, including, considering,* etc. are also **Pi**-segments:

(ix)   including A G G n

(x)   taking into consideration A n of O n

Here Pi acts as a Conjunction. For example:

(xi)   *He had difficulty in remembering, which wasn't surprising, considering the panic of her flight.*
    considering A n   of O n

All Conjunctions ending in '-ing' were recorded as natural language words in the Dictionary of Segments, as in example (xi), because of the existing ambiguity.

Most **Pi**-segments are dependent segments and as such they should be linked to the part of the sentence they refer to. For more details see the section **Links** in Chapter 8.

Below the reader will find an excerpt from the Dictionary of Segments, showing the grammatical structure of the **Pi**-segments:

Pi O G G n

Pi O G n

Pi O G n of n

Pi O G n v A n
  v Od

Pi O G n to v R

Pi O G n to v O n
  v Od Ic

Pi O n

Pi O n of A n

Pi O n b

Pi O n G
  v Od

Pi O n j
  v Od Co

Pi O n of G n

Pi O n of n
  v Od

Pi O n to v R

Pi O n to v O n
  v Od Ic

Pi O n up
  v Od

Pi O n" to v O" G n was less j

Pi O n" to v O" n was less j
  v Od Pr

Pi O N"s G n

Pi O N"s n
  v Od

Pi O worst
  v bp

Pi of all i n d shall also v

Pi of all i n d has not still P2
  v Od Sj v

Pi of all i n
  v Od

Pi of all i n d has also P2
Pi of all i n d shall v
Pi of all i n d has P2
    v Od Sj v
Pi of I
Pi of i n
    v Od
Pi of i n d has not still P2
Pi of i n d shall also v
Pi of i n d has also P2
Pi of i n d shall v
Pi of i n d has P2
    v Od Sj v
Pi of n of n
Pi of O G n
Pi of O n
Pi of R
Pi off A G n of G n
Pi off A G n of n
Pi off A G n
Pi off A n
    v Od
Pi off A n of O G G n are n
    v Od v Pr
Pi off A n of A n b
Pi off A n of A n
    v Od
Pi off A n of O n are n
    v Od v Pr
Pi off A n of G n
Pi off A n of G n of n
    v Od
Pi off A n of O G G G n are n

Pi off A n of O G n are n
    v Od v Pr
Pi off A n of n
Pi off A n Pi A n
Pi off A n Pi "n"
Pi off A n Pi n
Pi off A S G n
Pi off A S n
Pi off G n
Pi off I n of Os
Pi off n
Pi off n of n
    v Od
Pi off O G n to v R
    v Od Ic
Pi off O G n
Pi off O n
    v Od
Pi off O n to v R
    v Od Ic
Pi off other n of n
    v Od
Pi off to v
. . . .
Pi off to v A n of O G n
Pi off to v A n
Pi off to v A n of O n
Pi off to v out of A n to v
    v Ic
Pi other n of n
    v Od
etc.

3.2.2 *v-segments*

The **v**-segments are usually cut off from the Subject by an intervening segment. All **v**-segments start with a Main (proper) Verb.

  (i)   *The crowd, at the far end of the square, became suddenly silent.*

A	n		at	A	G	n	of	A	n		v		also		j
Sj			bl									v		Pr	

Since **became** is a linking verb, equivalent in meaning to **is** (or *am, are, was, were*), the sign for the Predicative (Pr) can be substituted for the sign for the Complement Subject (Cs).

The Verbal Tense of the Main Verb, marked as **v**, is either Present Simple or Past Simple. Both Tenses are marked with **v**. The Verbal Tense can be followed by an Object (ii) or Infinitival Complement (iii):

(ii)   v A n of n
         v Od

(iii)   v to v
         v Ic

When the **v**-segment ends with an Exclamation Mark (when it is used in Imperative Mood), then it is a stand-alone, independent sentence:

(iv)   *Come!*
        v

(v)   *Take a seat!*
        v   A n

(vi)   v up A G n!

Most **v**-segments are dependent segments and should be connected to the Subject of the sentence (see the algorithmic procedures in **Links** in Chapter 8, for how to do it).

Below the reader will find an excerpt from the Dictionary of Segments showing the grammatical structure of the **v**-segments:

v A G G n Pl
v A G G n" v"
v A G n
  v Od
v A G G n b b A n
v A G n d v
  v Od Sj v
v A G n G n
  v Od
v A G n has also been A G n
v A G n has also been A n
v A G n has been A G n
v A G n has been A n
  v Od v Cs
v A G n n
v A G n n to v A n
v A G n of A n" Pi" A G n
v A G n of A n" Pi" A n
v A G n of A HEADING
v A G n of G n
v A G n of n
v A G n of P n
v A G n" Pi"
v A G n Pi
v A G n Pl

v A G n" v"
  v Od
v A G n to v G n
v A G n to v n
v A G n to v O n
v A G n to v O n off n
v A G n to v A n
v A G n to v O n up b
v A G n to v O n up
v A G n to v R A G n
  v Od Ic
v A G n up
v A G n v
v A m m of R b
v A m of R b
v A m G G G n
v A m G G n
v A m G n
v A m n
v A n
v A n j
  v Od
v A n d v
  v Od Sj v
etc.

3.2.3 ***am****-segments*

The segments starting with the **be** paradigm (excluding *be* and *being*) can assume the role of:

a) a Complement Subject (i), where the **am** paradigm is the only Verb;
b) an Object, following after Present or Past Tense, Passive Voice, or Present and Past Continuous Tense, Active Voice (ii, iii);
c) an Infinitival Complement (iv);
d) an Independent Interrogative sentence (v).

> (i)   *is the father of ten small children*
> am A n   of M G   n
> v   Cs
>
> (ii)   *was asked to bring the two bottles (of wine)*
> am P2   to v   A M   n   (of n)
> v   Od
>
> (iii) *is singing a song*
> am Pi   A n
> v   Od
>
> (iv)   *was to go*
> am to v
> v   Ic

In all these cases, the **am**-segment is cut off from the Subject by an intervening (usually Adverbial) segment.

> (v)   *Are you ready?*
> am d   j
> v   Sj Cs

Below the reader will find an excerpt from the Dictionary of Segments, showing the grammatical structure of the **am**-segments:

am A n of A n
am A n of A n of M G n
am A n of A n of G n
am A n of A n of M n
am A n of A n of n
am A n of G n
am A n of M G n
am A n of M n
am A n of n
am A n of O N''s G n
am A n of O N''s n
am A n of O G n
am A n of O n
am A n of P
am A n v

am A n v up
 v Cs
am A S n d has also P2 R v
am A S n d has P2 R v
 v Cs Sj v Od
am about to v O n
am about to v up
am about to v
am about to v A n
am about to v R
am about to v n
 v Pr
am almost b Pi
am almost Pi
 v

am also
   v
am also A G n
am also A G n of O n
am also A G n of O G n
am also A G n of G n
am also A G n of n
am also A n of A n
am also A n of A G n
am also A n of A n
am also A n
am also A n of A n d has P2
am also A n of G n
am also A n of n
am also A n of A G G G n Pl
am also A n of A G G n Pl
am also A n of A G n Pl
am also A n of A n Pl
am also A n of A n of M G n
am also A n of A n of G n
am also A n of A n of M n
am also A n of A n of n
am also A n of M n
am also A n of O n
am also A n of O G n
am also b j
   v Cs
am also b P2 to be P2 up
am also b P2 to be P2
am also being P2
   v
am also called A n
am also called A G n
am also d Pi to v R
am also even all that j
am also G
am also G n of m
am also j
am also j of G n
   v Cs
am also j to v up
am also j to v
am also j to be
am also j to v A G N''s n
am also j to v A N''s n
am also j to be P2 up

am also j to be P2
   v Cs Ic
am also less j
am also less
am also less G
am also m
am also m % up
am also m %
am also m FB old
am also n
am also n of A n
am also n of A G n
am also n of A G G n
am also n of m
am also O less G n
am also O n P2
am also O S n
am also of A n
   v Cs
am also on the receiving end
   v b
am also P2
am also P2 j
am also P2 to v
   v
am also P2 to v A G m n b
am also P2 to v A G m n
am also P2 to v A m n b
am also P2 to v A m n
am also P2 to v
am also P2 to v up
am also P2 to be P2 up
am also P2 to be P2
am also P2 to v P
am also P2 up b to v
am also P2 up to v
   v Ic
am also P2 up
am also Pi
   v
am also Pi A b G n of n
am also Pi A n of n
am also Pi A b G n
am also Pi A b G n of G n
am also Pi A n of G n
am also Pi A n to v A n

am also Pi A n to v R

am also Pi n

am also Pi n to v to v

am also Pi O G n

am also Pi O n

am also Pi O G n of A n

am also Pi O n of A n

am also Pi O G n

  v Od

etc.

3.2.4 **to *v*-**segments

The **to v**-segment represents the Infinitive, starting with the Particle **to**. These segments are Infinitival Complements. They are either separated from the Subject by an intervening segment, or are relatively independent (iii, iv) when the Infinitive can be used as the Subject of the sentence. The Nominal sequence of Parts of Speech that follows the Infinitive can be an Object (i, ii).

(i)   *He watched her from time to time to see the*
       d v   R from n   to n   to v A
       Sj v   Od bm   Ic
       expression on her face.
       n   on O n
       Od   bl

Compare: *He watched to see the expression on her face.*
       d v   to v A n   on O n
       Sj v   Od   bl

(ii)   *She went home on time to watch television.*
       d v   n   FB   to v   n
       Sj v   Od   bm   Ic

Compare: *She went to watch television.*
       d v   to v   n
       Sj v   Od

(iii) *To spend money on horse races is   a pleasure.*
       to v   n   on G   n   are A n
       Ic   bdl   v Cs
       Sj   bdl   v Cs

Compare: *It is a pleasure to spend money.*
       Sj v   Cs   Ic
or   *I like to spend money on horse races.*
       Sj v   Od   bdl
(iv)   *To learn a computer language takes time.*
       to v   A G   n   v   n
       Sj   v Od

3.2.5   *j-segments*

The **j**-segments start with an Adjective used as a Predicative and continue either with an Adverb (i), or with a construction starting with the Preposition **of** (ii), or with an Infinitival Complement (iii). In all these cases they are a Complement Subject and are separated from the Subject by an intervening segment.

The **j** sequence following the Object as Complement Object is inseparable from the Object and is an integral part of a segment – in all such cases the **j** sequence is not a **j**-segment.

(i)	*busy now*
	j b
	Cs
(ii)	j of A n of n
	j of A P of n (e.g. *unaware of the sounding of drums*)
(ii a)	j of G n
	Cs
(iii)	*ready to wash myself*
	j to v X
	Cs

There are some exceptions, when the **j**-segment is a Verb (iv) or is an integral part of an Adverbial Clause (v):

(iv)	*Ready!* (Equivalent to *Be ready!*)
	j
(v)	right in the middle of R
	j

Below the reader will find an excerpt from the Dictionary of Segments, showing the grammatical structure of the **j**-segments:

j of A G n of n
j of A n
j of A n of n
j of A P of n
j of G n
j of n
j of O G n
j of O n
j of O n of n
j of O N''s n
j to be
j to be G
j to be j
j to be P2
j to be P2 of R

j to v
j to v A G n
j to v A G n of G n
j to v A G n of n
j to v A G n'' Pi''
j to v A n
j to v A n of A n
j to v A n of G n
j to v A n of n
j to v A n of A G n
j to v A n of O n
j to v A n'' Pi''
j to v i n
j to v n
j to v O G n

j to v O n
j to v O S n
j to v of A n
j to v of R
j to v of n
j to v R
j to v R Pl

j to v up
j to v X
j with X
   Pr
right in the middle of R
right in the middle
etc.

3.2.6 **Pl**-segments

The Participle 1st is not part of a Compound Verbal Tense and has the role of a Complement Subject (i, ii) or Complement Object (iii). When it is cut off from the Subject by an intervening segment and starts a segment of its own, it can be followed by an Adverbial Clause (i) or an Infinitival Complement (ii):

(i)   *They remained in the attic obsessed with fear.*
        d   v   in A n   Pl   with n
        Sj   v   bl   Cs   bx

Compare: *They are obsessed with fear.*

(ii)   Pl to v A n of n
       Cs Ic

(iii)   *Ann found the glass on the floor, broken.*
        d   v   A n   on A n   Pl
        Sj   v   Od   bl   Co

Note: The comma between *floor* and *broken* is often omitted.

Below the reader will find an excerpt from the Dictionary of Segments showing the grammatical structure of the **Pl**-segments:

Pl n
Pl n are m
Pl n Pi
Pl n to v i n
Pl n v O n
Pl O Pv
Pl of G n
Pl of i G n
Pl of i n
Pl of n
Pl only
Pl Pl
Pl R O n
Pl right up
Pl to v
Pl to v A G G n

Pl to v A G n
Pl to v A G G n of n
Pl to v A G n of n
Pl to v A G G n of A n
Pl to v A G n of A n
Pl to v A n
Pl to v A n of n
Pl to v A n of A n
Pl to v n
Pl to v up
Pl up
Pl up A G n
Pl up A G n are G n
Pl up A G n are n
Pl up A G n are G n of G n
Pl up A G n are n of n

Pl up A G n are G n of n
Pl up A G n are n of G n
Pl up A n
Pl up A n are G n of G n
Pl up A n are G n of n
Pl up A n are n of n
Pl up A n are n of G n
Pl up A n are G n
Pl up A n are n

Pl up are also EBO of G n
Pl up are also EBO of n
Pl up are EBO of G n
Pl up are EBO of n
Pl with G n
Pl with n
  Cs
  Co
etc.

3.2.7 *did-segments*

(**Did** represents the paradigm of **do**, with the exception of *doing*.)
  The **did**-segments can be of three types:

a) Independent Interrogative (i), ending with a Question Mark. In this case **did** is followed immediately by a Subject.
b) Independent Affirmative, followed by an Exclamation Mark (ii). In this case, the Subject is missing and **did** is followed by a Verbal Tense, which in its turn can be followed by an Object.
c) Cut off from the Subject by an intervening segment (iii). In this case **did** is followed by a Verbal Tense, which in turn can be followed by an Object.

(i)   did d has to v up i G G n ?
        Sj   v   Od
(ii)   did not v I !
        v   Od
(iii)   did v R I
        v Oi Od

Below the reader will find an excerpt from the Dictionary of Segments, showing the grammatical structure of the **did**-segments:

did also v A G n
did also v A n
did also v M
did also v R v A n
  v Od
did also v up
did b v
  v
did d
did d also v
  v Od
  v Sj
did d also v M
did d b v to be O G n

did d b v to be O n
  v Sj v Od
did d G *
did d get Pl b
did d get Pl
  v Sj v
did d v A n
did d v G G n
did d v G n
  v Sj v Od
did d v j
  v Sj v Pr
did d v M
did d v M n b

did d v M n

did d v n

did d v n of n

  v Sj v Od

did d v Pi

  v Sj v

did d v R

did d v to be O G n

did d v to be O n

  v Sj v Od

did d v to v

did d v to v up

  v Sj v

did d v to v A n of O n Pi

did d v to v A n of O n

did d v to v A n

  v Sj v Od

did d v up

  v Sj v

did I G n v R up?

did I G n v R?

did I n v R?

did I n v R up?

  Sj v Od

did I v

did n v?

  v Sj v

did not

  v

did not A n v A G n

did not A n v A n

  v Sj v Od

did not b v

  v

did not d

  v Sj

did not d b v to be O G n

did not d b v to be O n

  v Sj v Od

etc.

3.2.8 **has**-segments

The word **has** represents the paradigm of the Verb **have** (with the exception of *having*). The **has**-segments are of two types:

a) Interrogative, ending with a Question Mark (i). The Auxiliary Verb **has** is part of a Compound Verbal Tense and is followed immediately by a Subject. This is a complete segment.

b) Incomplete – part of another segment, because the **has**-segment was cut off from a previous segment by an intervening segment. In this case the Verbal Tense is usually followed by an Object (ii), or by a Complement Subject (iii).

    (i)   has d P2 O n b ?

            has d P2 A n ?

            has I been P2 ?

            has not d been b j ?

                    Sj

    (ii)   has also been Pi G n

            has also P2 A G n of G G n

            has also P2 A n of O G n

            has also P2 Z

            v   Od

(iii)   has also been j to v O G n
          has been A n of O G n
          has been j
          v   Cs

Often the Object is followed by an Infinitival Complement:

(iv)   has P2 A n to v A n
          has P2 A n to v R
          v   Od   Ic

Below the reader will find an excerpt from the Dictionary of Segments, showing the grammatical structure of the **has**-segments:

has A n Pl
  v Od Co
has also
  v
has also A G n
has also A n
  v Od
has also been n
has also been j to v O G n
has also been j to v O n
has also been A n
has also been A n of O G n
has also been A n of O n
has also been j to v R
  v Cs
has also been P2
  v
has also been up j
has also been j
has also been Pi G n
has also been Pi n
  v Cs
has also been P2 enough
has also been P2 up
  v
has also been P2 up A n
has also been P2 to v G n
has also been P2 to v n
has also been P2 to v A n
  v Od
has also M G n
has also M n

has also O G n
has also O n
has also P2 to v R
has also P2 A G n of G G n
has also P2 A G n of G n
has also P2 A G n of n
has also P2 A n of G G G n
has also P2 A n of G G n
has also P2 A n of G n
has also P2 A n of n
has also P2 A G n of n
  v Od
has also P2 A n d v up
has also P2 A n d v
  v Od Sj v
has also P2 A G n
has also P2 M G n
has also P2 M n
has also P2 O G n up
has also P2 O G n
has also P2 O n up
has also P2 R Pv
has also P2 R up
has also P2 R up to v X
has also P2 A n of O G n
has also P2 n
has also P2 up A n
has also P2 R to v X
has also P2 A n of O n
  v Od
has also P2 up
has also P2
  v

has also P2 up to v A n
   v Od
has also P2 R almost j
   v Od
has also P2 to v A n
has also P2 A n of n
has also P2 G n
has also P2 R
   v Od
has also P2 G n to v n
has also P2 n to v n
has also P2 R to v A n
has also P2 R to v n
has also P2 A n to v A n
   v Od Ic
has also P2 A n
has also P2 A n to v n
has also P2 A n of n
has also P2 A n
has also P2 R to v
has also P2 R j
has also P2 A n to v
has also P2 up G n
has also P2 G n
   v Od
has also P2 up n
has also P2 O n
has also P2 i G n
has also P2 Pv G n
has also P2 A n to v
has also P2 i n
has also P2 Pi n
has also P2 Pv A n
   v Od
has been j to v O G n
has been j to v O n
has been j to v R
has been n
   v Cs
has been P2
   v

has d been b j
   Sj v Cs
has d been b P2
   v Sj v
has d been j
   v Sj v Cs
has d been P2?
has d been up
has d just been up
   v Sj v
has d M n
   v Sj Od
has d P2?
   v Sj v
has d P2 A n
has d P2 M n b
has d P2 n
has d P2 O n b?
has d P2 O n?
has d P2 R
   v Sj v Od
has d TCv of I
   v Sj v
has d v M G G n
has d v M G n
has d v M n
   v Sj v Od
has G n
has G n of m n
   v Od
has I been P2
has I not been P2
   v Sj v
has less b P2 S
has less P2 S
has less to v up
has less to v
   v
has M G n
has M n
   v Od
etc.

3.2.9 *can*-segments

The word **can** stands for a number of Auxiliary Verbs (see the Index at the end of the book), expressing ability, condition, possibility, permission, advice, etc. For more details see Graver (1971). The **can**-segments are of two types:

a) Interrogative, complete, ending with a Question Mark. The Auxiliary Verb **can** (or any other Verb from this set) is part of a Compound Verbal Tense and is immediately followed by a Subject (i);

b) Incomplete – part of another segment, cut off as a result of an intervening segment. In this case the Auxiliary Verb (represented by **can**) or the Verbal Tense can be followed by either a Complement Subject (ii) or Object (iii).

> (i) can d v A G n ?
> can d v A n up ?
> can I all be P2 ?
> can n v ?
> can not d ?
> can A G n v ?
> v   Sj
>
> (ii) can also be A G n
> can also be j
> v   Cs
>
> (iii) can also v A G n of n
> can also v G G n
> can v up G n
> v   Od
>
> (iii a) can v R A n
> v   Oi Od
> v   Od Co

(The last example has two possible Parsings.)

Below the reader will find an excerpt from the Dictionary of Segments showing the grammatical structure of the **can**-segments:

can A S G G n v?
can A S G n v?
can A S n v?
  v Sj v
can also be
  v
can also be UI to v R up
can also be UI to v R
  v Cs
can also be P2 to v n
  v Od

can also be j to v
  v Cs
can also be P2
  v
can also be j to v R
  v Cs
can also be P2 to v
  v
can also be j to v A n
  v Cs v Od
can also be A G n

can also be A n
can also be A G
can also be out of A n
can also be out of n
   v Cs
can also have P2 I
can also have n of m m b
can also have n of m b
can also have n of m m
   v Od
can also v
   v
can also v A G n of n
can also v A n" j"
can also v A G G n
can also v A G n
can also v A n of n
can also v A n
can also v A n up
can also v A G n
can also v G n
can also v G G n
can also v i n
   v Od
can also v less G
can also v less
   v Pr
can also v M of O G n
can also v M of O n
can also v m % n
can also v M n
can also v n
can also v O n
can also v O G n
can also v of G n
can also v of n
can also v R to v
can also v R up
   v Od
can also v R A n of n
can also v R A n
can also v R M n of n
can also v R M n
   v Oi Od
   v Od Co

can d v A G n?
can d v A n
can d v A n up
can d v A n?
can d v A n of A n
   v Sj v Od
can d v any further?
can d v G
   v Sj v
can d v G n
can d v I
can d v I up
can d v M n up
can d v M n
can d v M other n
can d v n
can d v n of n?
can d v Pv?
can d v R
can d v R up?
can d v R A n of n
can d v R A n
can d v R NAME
can d v R to v up b
can d v R to v up
can d v R to v
can d v R up
can d v UF?
   v Sj v Od
can v A G G n
can v A G n of n
can v A G n
can v A n
can v A n of n
can v A n up
   v Od
can v A n" j"
   v Od Co
can v being P2
   v
can v G G n
can v G n
can v i n
   v Od
can v less

can v less G
can v little less
   v Pr
can v m % n
can v M n
can v M of O n

can v M of O G n
can v m to m n
can v m to m n of n
   v Od
etc.

3.2.10 *no*-segments

(This section also lists the segments starting with **not** and **none** – see the Dictionary of Segments for details.) The word **no** is a Particle for negation, having much wider use than its opposite for consent **yes**. The Particle **no** can be an integral part of some Adverbs (i), but it usually stands at the start of an n-segment and expresses negation (ii). It is used as a Noun when it precedes *one* or *body* (if it is separated from *body*) (iii). In one single case, when "there is" is omitted, **no** starts a shortened phrase for negation (iv).

(i)	no doubt
	no longer
	no matter
(ii)	no n are P2 to v R
	no n can be P2
	no n of G n are P2
	no n shall v A n
	no other n v G n
	no such n are P2
(iii)	no body except
	no one except d
	no one except d are P2
	no one shall v A n
(iv)	no need Pi up

The word **none** is used as a Noun in 'of' phrases (v), as a Numeral (vi), as a determiner (vii), or as a determiner with a Pronoun (viii), always expressing negation.

(v)	none of I are P2
	none of I are up
(vi)	none
	none at all (= zero)
(vii)	none of which
(viii)	none of R

The Particle for negation **not** can start a segment when it is cut off from a preceding segment by a Punctuation Mark or by another segment (ix), or when used together with an Adverb (x), or when used together with a Conjunction or Preposition (xi). Often enough it can head a stand-alone, independent segment (x, xii), if it ends with an Exclamation Mark.

(ix)   not A n
       not all G n
       not j
(x)   not again
       not always
       not just yet
(xi)   not because
       not even
       not even for
       not even with
       not merely because
       not since
       not until
(xii)   *Not today*!

Below the reader will find an excerpt from the Dictionary of Segments showing the grammatical structure of the **no**-segments:

no n are P2 to v R
no n are P2 to v A n
no n are P2 to v n
  Sj v Od
no n are to be P2
no n can be P2
  Sj v
no n of G n are P2
no n of n are P2
no n of i a(n) G n shall be P2
no n of i G n shall be P2
no n of i a(n) G n v to be P2
no n of i a(n) G n need be P2
  Sj v
no n of n
no n P1
  Sj
  Od
no n of Os shall v O n
  Sj v Od
no n Pv up A n
no n Pv A n
  Sj Cs
no n shall v O n
  Sj v Od
no n shall v
  Sj v
no n shall v R

no n shall v A n
no n shall v n
  Sj v Od
no n to v
  v Od
  v Sj v
no n v G G G n
no n v G G n
no n v G n
no n v n
  Sj v Od
no need Pv up
no need Pv
no one = d = R
  Sj
  Od
no one except
. . . .
no one except R v
no one except R
no one except d v P1
no one except d
no one except d are P2
. . . .
no one j
  Sj Cs
  Od Co
no one of R = d = R

no one P
no one Pi
  Sj
  Od
no one shall v A n
no one shall v R

no one shall v n
no one was Pi n
no one was Pi R
no one was Pi A n
  Sj v Od
etc.

3.2.11 *there*-*segments*

In this type of segment, the former Adverb **there** introduces a Verb that comes before its Subject (Hausser, 1989: 370). Some grammarians (Hornby, 1958: 60) call it 'preparatory **there**', which has no meaning. Other grammarians call it 'introductory **there**' (Leech and Svartvik, 1975: 236–8), which behaves in most cases like the Subject of the sentence, or 'anticipatory **there**' (Curme, 1955: 100), which serves as a provisional Subject.

We would prefer to regard **there** + Verb (both Auxiliary and Main, excluding the paradigm of **do** and most of the Main Verbs), as an Impersonal Verb, having singular and plural forms when used with the Auxiliary Verbs *have, has, had* and *is, are, were*.

When combined with the paradigm of **be** (excluding *be* and *being*) (i), or with the paradigm of **have** (excluding *having*) (ii), or with the set of Auxiliary Verbs represented by **can**, **shall** (iii), or with a Verb (*seem(s)*, *appear(s)*) (iv), it assumes the role of a Verb expressing presence, availability, possibility. When it is used with the Particle **no** or **not**, it expresses absence, lack of something. The **there**-segment is a self-sufficient and complete Clause or a Sentence.

The Noun (or Noun phrase) following the **there** Verb is a Subject and a Predicative to the preceding Verb (v).

(i)   there are A G n of A n
          there are also n
          there are also G n Pi M n of n
          there are also G G G n
          there are b no G n
          there are none of A n of P
          there are no n of n
          there b are A n
          v   Sj (Predicative)

(ii)   there has also been n
          there has b been no G n
          there has been R to v R
          v   Sj (Predicative)

(iii)   there can also be G n
          there can be M G n b
          there can be no n to v I
          there can be G n
          v   Sj (Predicative)

(iv)   there did v to be A n
          there v to be A n of A n
          there v to be no n of n
          v   Sj (Predicative)
(v)   *There are people who eat meat.*
          there are n   who v   n
          v   Sj   Sj   v   Od

Compare: *People eat meat.*

Below the reader will find an excerpt from the Dictionary of Segments showing the grammatical structure of the **there**-segments:

there are A G n of G n
there are A G n of G G n
there are A G n of G n j
there are A G n of n
there are A G n of n of n
there are A G n of n of A n
there are A G n of n of O n
there are A G n of n b
there are A G n of n j
there are A G n to be P2
there are A G n'' Pi''
there are A m n n b
there are A n
there are A n b
there are A n j
there are A n n shall v
there are A n of A G n
there are A n of A n
there are A n of A n to v
there are A n of G n
there are A n of G n j
there are A n of n
there are A n of n of A n
there are A n of n b
there are A n of n j
there are A n of R
there are A n of what are called n
there are A n to be P2
there are A n to v
there are A n to v up
there are A n'' Pi''
there are A N''s n
there are all A n of what are called n
   v Od
   v Sj

there are also
   v
there are also A G
there are also A G G n
there are also A G n
there are also A G n of A G n
there are also A G n of A n
there are also A G n of G n
there are also A G n of n
there are also A G n of n b
there are also A G n to be P2
there are also A G n'' Pi''
there are also A n
there are also A n b
there are also A n n shall v
there are also A n of A G n
there are also A n of A n
there are also A n of G n
there are also A n of n
there are also A n of n b
there are also A n to be P2
there are also A n'' Pi''
there are also enough n
there are also G G G n
there are also G G n
there are also G G n
there are also G n
there are also G n of n
there are also G n'' Pi'' M n
there are also G n'' Pi'' M n of n
there are also i n
there are also just so many n j
there are also less G n
there are also less n
there are also M G n

there are also M G n though
there are also M i n
there are also M n
there are also M n of n
there are also M n though
there are also n
there are also n b
there are also n enough
there are also n of A n being P2
there are also n of A n being P2 up
there are also n of n
there are also n to v
there are also n to v up
there are also n" Pi" M n
there are also n" Pi" M n of n
there are also others
there are also some sort of n
there are also UF
there are also UF Pi
there are an awful lot of n b
there are b G n
there are b no G n
there are b no n
there are b no n of n
there are d
there are d b
there are EBB
there are EBO of n
there are enough n

there are G
there are G G G n
there are G G n
there are G G n of n
there are G G n of A n
there are G G n of A n of A G n
there are G n
there are G n of A n
there are G n of n
there are G n b
there are G n b b
there are G n of P
there are G n of P up
there are G n" Pi" M n
there are G n" Pi" M n of n
there are i A n
there are i G G n
there are i n
there are indeed A G n
there are indeed A n
there are just A G n
there are just A n
there are just so many n j
　v Od
　v Sj
there are less
　v Pr
etc.

3.3 Prepositional Adverbial Clauses

The Prepositional Adverbial Clause as known traditionally and the Prepositional Segment, as defined in our study, coincide, because the Prepositional Adverbial Clause, unlike the Main and the other Subordinate Clauses of the sentence, cannot be interrupted by a Punctuation Mark or another Clause. It is always intact.

The Prepositional Adverbial Clauses start with the following Prepositions (listed in the order used by the text processing algorithm): from, over, of, at, on, with, without, within, by, into, onto, in, for, to, past, against, through, under, between, above, before, after, until, while, aboard, about, across, ahead of, along, among, around, behind, beside, beyond, down, during, inside, outside, near, prior, round, throughout, towards, upon, via, next, since, like, once. (NB This is also List No 3, used by some algorithms in Part 2.)

Most Prepositions have a number of syntactical structures (or 'syntactical words') that are common to all types of Prepositional segments. Below we will provide a list of sequences of Parts of Speech used after almost all Prepositions and an example, showing one possible word sequence, for each:

(i)   A b G n (*the extremely large table*)
(ii)   A G G G n (*the small green pepper roots*)
(iii)   A G n b (*the nice garden outside*)
(iv)   A G n of A G n (*a small garden of a big house*)
(v)   A G n of A N''s n (*the front door of the priest's house*)
(vi)   A G n of n (*a defined class of objects*)
(vii)   A G n of O G n (*the white shirt of her small sister*)
(viii)   A G n Pl (*the rain forest burnt*)
(ix)   A m n (*the ten women*)
(x)   A n of A n of A G n (*the son of the president of the United States*)
(xi)   A n of G n (*the sound of church bells*)
(xii)   A n of G n of n (*the accumulation of big grains of sand*)
(xiii)   A n of M n (*a mother of two children*)
(xiv)   A n of n of A G n (*the seat of power of the great Incas*)
(xv)   A n of O G n (*the wheels of his small car*)
(xvi)   A n of O N''s n (*the chimney of her brother's house*)
(xvii)   A N''s G n (*the car's front lights*)
(xviii)   A S (*the first*)
(xix)   A S n (*the first horse*)
(xx)   all
(xxi)   all I (*all this*)
(xxii)   both n (*both windows*)
(xxiii)   both n of A n (*both ends of the street*)
(xxiv)   both of R (*both of them*)
(xxv)   G G n (*narrow mountain pass*)
(xxvi)   G n of A n (*high peaks of the mountain*)
(xxvii)   G n of n (*big bags of sand*)
(xxviii)   I (*this*)
(xxix)   i G n (*this tall man*)
(xxx)   i n of n (*this stage of development*)
(xxxi)   m (*nine*)
(xxxii)   M G G n (*four red wine glasses*)
(xxxiii)   M n of A n (*five windows of the house*)
(xxxiv)   M n of A n of n (*two springs of the river of gold*)
(xxxv)   M n of n (*one bag of rice*)
(xxxvi)   M of A n of n (*two of the children of Israel*)
(xxxvii)   M of O G n (*several of her riding horses*)
(xxxviii) n (*people*)
(xxxix)   n of A G n (*people of the lower region*)
(xxxx)   n of G n (*people of high standing*)
(xxxxi)   n of O G n (*friends of her old parents*)

(xxxxii)   n Pl (*window broken*)
(xxxxiii) n Pi O n (*workers trying their luck*)
(xxxxiv)   O G G n (*her red silk curtains*)
(xxxxv)   O n of A n (*their side of the river*)
(xxxxvi)   O n of G n (*their system of low taxation*)
(xxxxvii) O S n (*our first position*)
(xxxxviii) P (*staying*)
(xxxxix)   R (*him*)
(l)   what
(li)   which
(lii)   whom
(liii)   X (*himself*)
(liv)   Z (*one another*)

(M = G; G is optional)

Each structure can have more than one expression in English – we have shown only one, as an example. We leave it to the students to find out how many word structures they can fit in, in any one of the above syntactical structures.

Filling such syntactical structures with words (as we have done) is a good teaching and learning practice. Students may try to fit in such words so that the whole structure, in the end, may be used with more than one Preposition (xxxxiv).

(xxxxiv) *with (for, from, against, on) her red silk curtains*

Certain word meanings fit into some structures more easily than other meanings. The Dictionary of Segments provides ample material for an exercise of this sort.

According to their meaning, the Prepositional Adverbial Clauses can be of the following types:

a)   for direction and location (bdl);
b)   for separation (bs);
c)   for reason (br);
d)   for clothing (bt) – used with the semantic group of words designating clothes;
e)   for circumstances (bc);
f)   for purpose (bp);
g)   for 'stoppage' (bg) – used with the semantic group of words denoting stopping or stoppage;
h)   for linkage or 'togetherness' (be), or joint action (bb);
i)   for location (bl);
j)   for instrument or means (bi);
k)   for time (bm);
l)   for activity (ba);
m)   for direction (bd);
n)   for manner (bn);

o)   for purpose (bo);
p)   for opposition (bz);
q)   for condition (bx);
r)   for persuasion (bw);
s)   for quantity, volume, measure (bq);
t)   for comparison (by);
u)   for concern (bu);
v)   for appearance (bj);
w)   for sequence (bv);
x)   for result (bf);
y)   for change (b change);
z)   for source or 'made of' (bk);
aa) starting point (bh).

We have compressed the traditional list of Prepositional Adverbial Clauses to help the student choose the adequate structure for a specified meaning more quickly. The compression of the list was made on the basis of generalization. For example, the meanings of the Preposition **through** as *pass through* and *pass by* were combined under one meaning, location. We have dealt similarly with some other meanings.

Table 6.1 lists the meaning of the Prepositional Adverbial Clause and the Prepositions used to express that meaning. Those Prepositions that have only one meaning were excluded from the list (for more details see Appendix 1). In the Dictionary of Segments we have marked almost all Prepositional Adverbial Clauses in accordance with the above differentiation of meaning.

The Prepositions are border markers within the sentence. Though the Prepositions are polysemous, they still serve as important guidelines in outlining the syntactical and the semantic structure of the Sentence.

Every one of the above listed Prepositions starts at least one type of Adverbial Clause, therefore we will discuss the Prepositions one by one, giving examples of the Adverbial structures involved.

3.3.1 *from*-Clauses

The Preposition **from** can start Adverbial Clauses of the following type:

(i)   For reason (br):
         (i a)   from A G n
         (i b)   from A G P
         (i c)   from O n
         (i d)   from A n of A n to v A n
         (i e)   from P

pointing to the reason why a certain action was performed or a certain result was obtained. The same meaning can be expressed by the Conjunction **because of**.

Table 6.1 Prepositions and types of Prepositional Adverbial Clauses

Meaning of the Prepositional Adverbial Clause	*Prepositions used to express that meaning*
Direction and location	from, at, in, to, against through, after
Separation	from, into
Reason	from, at, on, with, by, in, for, to, upon
Clothes, insertion	with, into, in
Circumstances	from, over, at, on, with, into, in, under
Purpose	from, at, on, with, by, in, for, to, against, about, toward(s)
Stoppage	from
Togetherness, joint action	with, along
Location	over, at, on, within, by, into, onto, in, to, past, against, under, between, above, before, after, about, across, aboard, ahead of, along, among, behind, around, beside, beyond, down, inside, near, round, throughout, toward(s), upon, next
Instrument or means	with, by, into, through, via, at
Time	from, over, at, on, by, within, in, for, to, past, through, between, before, after, prior to, until, till, while, about, ahead of, behind, around, during, inside, round, throughout, next, toward(s), since, once
Direction	at, to, via
Manner	at, on, with, by, into, in, like
Opposition	against, in, by
Source, made from	from
Starting point	from
Condition	at, in, under
Persuasion	in
Quantity, volume, measure	over, at, on, with, by, within, onto, in, for, to, under, above, about
Comparison	at, on, by, in, between, beside, like
Concern	over, on, with, in, for, about, around
Appearance	in, like
Sequence	over, at, on, in, next, once
Result	over

Compare: *The biggest losses had come, | not |*
        A G   n   had P2   not
        from wilful wrecking | but |
        from G   n   but
        from the custom of the villagers to follow a ship
        from A n   of A n   to v   A n
        | for many miles.
        for M   n

(ii)   For direction and location (bdl):
    (ii a)   from A G n P1
    (ii b)   from A n of O n
    (ii c)   from A n of G n
    (ii d)   from another n
    (ii e)   from M G n
    (ii f)   from O G n
    (ii g)   from O G n of n
    (ii h)   from R
    (ii j)   from behind A n
    (ii k)   from beneath A n
    (ii l)   from n
    (ii m) from under A G G n
    (ii n)   from under G n
    (ii o)   from above A n
    (ii p)   from amidst A G n
    (ii q)   from among G G n
    (ii r)   from afar
    (ii s)   from below A n
    (ii t)   from beyond A n
expressing the location and the direction from which certain action ensues.
    Compare: *I got a letter from him.*
              d v A n   from R

(iii)   For separation (bs):
    (iii a)   from A G n P1
    (iii b)   from A n of G n
    (iii c)   from I G n
    (iii d)   from O G n
    (iii e)   from Z
used with Verbs from the semantic group expressing separation (*break off, break, divorce, distinguish, free oneself from*, etc).
    Compare: *He was separated from his parents.*
             d am P2   from O n

(iv)   For time (bm):
    (iv a) from hence on
    (iv b) from I FB

   (iv c)   from long ago
   (iv d)   from I FB on
   (iv e)   from FB
   (iv f)   from O childhood
   (iv g)   from the beginning
   (iv h)   from the S FB
   (iv j)   from the S half of FB
   (iv k)   from the very beginning
   (iv l)   from then on
   (iv m) from A FB-BD S half
   (iv n)   from now on

used with words and phrases denoting time.

   Compare: *From the first of May.*
            from A S   of FB

(v)   For circumstances (bc):
   (v a)   from G n
   (v b)   from A G n
   (v c)   from both n of A n

describing the circumstances in which a certain activity is taking place.
Compare:
   (v a)   *They drank from big cups.*
          d   v   from G n
   (v b)   *They were suffering from the same illness.*
          d   am Pi   from A G   n
   (v c)   *They hang suspended from both ends of the rope.*
          d   v   P2   from both n of A n

(vi)   For stopping (bg):
   (vi a) from P A n
   (vi b) from P n
   (vi c) from Pi Pl
   (vi d) from G n

used with the verbs from the semantic group for stoppage or cessation or interruption of a certain activity (*prevent, avert, deter, refrain, stop, bar, ban, debar, suspend, shut,* etc.). Compare:
   (vi d) *He tried to refrain from casual remarks.*
          d v   to v   from G   n

(vii) For purpose (bp):
   (vii a) from P off n
   (vii b) from P R
   (vii c) from P n

expressing the purpose for which a certain action is being carried out.
   (vii c) *He tried to get money from cleaning cars.*

(viii) For source, material and 'made of' (bk):

(viii a) from G n

pointing out the material or source used.

(viii a) *One can   make a soup from dried vegetables.*
　　　　d   shall v   A n   from G   n

(viii b) *One can   build a house from empty beer bottles.*
　　　　d   shall v   A n   from G   G   n

(ix)   For initial starting point (bh):

(ix a)   from A G n

(ix b)   from M %

indicating the point from which a certain action has started. Compare:

(x)   *From a small child, he grew to become a strong man.*
　　　from A G   n   d v   to v   A G   n

　　Below the reader will find an excerpt from the Dictionary of Segments showing the grammatical structure of the **from**-segments:

from A n of A n	from afar
from A n of A n of n	from all I bs
from A n of A n b	from amidst
from A n of A N's n	from among
from A n of G n	from another n bdl
from A n of G n bdl bs	from any n
from A n of having P2	from b
from A n of M n	from behind A n of n
from A n of M of O G G n	from behind A n bl
from A n of M of O G n v R	from behind
from A n of n	from being j enough from being j
from A n of n of A G n	from being up b j enough
from A n of O n of n	from being up j enough
from A n of O n bdl	from below
from A n of others	from beneath A n bl
from A n UF v j	from beneath
from A N''s	from between
from A N''s G n	from between O n
from A N''s n	from beyond
from A N''s n of n	from both n and n
from A N's n Pi to v	from close to
from A S	from d
from A S n	etc.
from above	

*3.3.2   **over** – Clauses*

The Adverbial Clauses starting with **over** can be of the following types:

(i)   For location (bl):

(i a)   over A G G n
(i b)   over A G n of A n
(i c)   over A N''s n
(i d)   over G n
(i e)   over here
(i f)   over I
(i g)   over i N''s n
(i h)   over O G G G n
(i j)   over O M n
(i k)   over R
(i l)   over there
(i m)   over which

indicating the location of a certain thing or being. Compare:

(i a)   *The clouds gathered over the mountain.*
         A   n   v   over A n

(ii)   For concern (bu):
       (ii a)   over A G n
       (ii b)   over A G n of P
       (ii c)   over A n of A G n (if preceded by *to*)
       (ii d)   over G n
       (ii e)   over G N''s n to v
       (ii f)   over O G n

expressing concern. In this case **over** can be replaced by *about, concerning*. Compare:

       (ii d)   *The wrangle was about German participation.*
                A   n   are about G   n

(iii)   For result (bf):
        (iii a)   over A n (if preceded by *victory*)

specifying the result obtained after a certain action. Compare:

        (iii a)   *The army gained a brilliant victory over the enemy.*
                  A   n   v   A G   n   over A n

(iv)   For time (bm):
       (iv a)   over a(n) FB now
       (iv b)   over a period of m FB
       (iv c)   over m FB''s n
       (iv d)   over the last FB
       (iv e)   over A FB

indicating a period of time, for example:

       (iv e)   *There has been no change over the years.*
                there has been no n   over A FB

(Note that FB comprises all words denoting time, but not all can assume the position allotted for them.)

(v)   For sequence (bv):
    (v a)   over and over again
indicating a sequence or repetition of something.

(vi) For circumstances (bc):
    (vi a)   over I
    (vi b)   over many a(n) of n
    (vi c)   over many a(n) n
describing the circumstances in which a certain action takes place.

(vii) For quantity, volume or measure (bq):
    (vii a)   over m
    (vii b)   over M G G G n
    (vii c)   over m JE-D
indicating the amount or distance involved. Compare:
    (vii b) *It is over fifty miles to London.*
        it is over M   n   to n

    Below the reader will find an excerpt from the Dictionary of Segments showing the grammatical structure of the **over**-segments:

over A n   bu, bl
over A n   bf if preceded by *victory*
over A n of n   bu   bl
over A n v R j   bl
over A n are n of G n   *
over A n are n of n   *
over A n are n   *
over A n of P   bu
over A n of A n   bu if preceded by *to*
over A n of A n   bl
over A n of A G n   bu if preceded by
  to
over A N"s n   bl
over A m n
over a(n) FB now   bm
over a period of m FB   bm
over and over again   bm
over A S
over A S of M
over A S of A n
over A S of A m n
over A S of A G n
over G n   bl   bu
over G N"s n to v   bu
over here   bl
over I   bc   bl

over I FB   bm
over i N"s n   bl
over m   bq
over m FB"s n   bm
over M G G G n   bq
over M G G m   bq
over M G n   bq
over m JE-D   bq
over M n   bq
over many a(n) n of n   bc
over many a(n) n   bc
over n   bu bl
over n also Pi
over n Pi
over A N"s G n
over A N's n
over N"s n to v   bu
over NAME   bl
over O G G G n d shall v
over O G G G n   bl
over O G G n d shall v
over O G G n   bl
over O G n   bu   bl
over O G n d shall v
over O M n   bl
over O n   bu   bl

over R   bl   over the years   bm
over S n Pl   over there   bl
over the last FB   bm   over which
over the weekend   bm   etc.

3.3.3   *of*-Clauses (segments)

The sequences starting with the Preposition **of** in some cases (when **of** is
preceded by a Verb) are equivalent to a Clause (i). In others they are simply
a 'syntactical word' (ii) which is an integral part of another segment and
cannot be separated from it by another segment or a Clause, and are
equivalent to the genitive of the Noun (ii).

(i)   of A G n of O n
       of P A G n
       of P A n of G n
       of P G n
For example:
       He spoke | of his increasing popularity in the country.
       d   v   of O G   n   in A n
where **of** is equivalent to *about* or *concerning*.

(ii)   A G n of O n
(the genitive always following the governing Noun)
       He mentioned the increasing popularity of his team.
       d   v   A G   n   of O n
Compare: *He mentioned his team's popularity.*
         d   v   O N''s n

As genitive, the **of**-segment has many other different meanings –
expressing origin, possession, composition, description, gradation, etc. (for
more details see Curme, 1955: 125–9).

In some Clauses **of** is followed by the Preposition *about*, to express
approximation (iii a–iii e):

       (iii a)   of about m
       (iii b)   of about m G n
       (iii c)   of about m m n
       (iii d)   of about m m
       (iii e)   of about M n

In other Clauses it is followed by the determiners **all** or **both** to express
specified quantity (iii f–iii m), or it can express unspecified quantity (iii n).

       (iii f)   of all
       (iii g)   of all A G n
       (iii h)   of all I
       (iii j)   of all n

(iii k) of all m
(iii l)   of both n
(iii m) of both n and G n
(iii n) of b M G n
(iii n a) of some G n

and in still other Clauses it is followed by **what** or **which** to introduce a Relative Clause for proportion (iii o–iiii w):

(iii o) of what are also A n of A G n
(iii p) of what are also A G n
(iii q) of what are also n
(iii r) of what has been A G n
(iii s) of what O G n are
(iii t) of which are P2
(iii u) of which are also G n
(iii w) of which are to v

Compare:

The bookshop today received 1000 books, | ten
A   n   b   v   M   n   m
percent of which   were sold |
%   of which are P2
within   the next two hours.
within A G   M n

Below the reader will find an excerpt from the Dictionary of Segments, showing the grammatical structure of the **of**-segments:

of A n of A n
of A n of A N''s n
of A n of G n
of A n of G G n
of A n of G n of n
of A n of n
of A n of n P1
of A n of n and n
of A n of n and n P1
of A n of O n
of A n of O G G n
of A n of O G n
of A n of P O n
of A N''s G n
of A N''s m G n
of A N''s m n
of A N''s n
of A N''s n d has P2
of A N''s n of n

of A N''s P A n
of A NAME
of A P of n
of A S n
of about m
of about m G n
of about m m G n
of about m m n
of about m m
of about M n
of all
of all A G n
of all A n
of all I
of all I are also to v
of all I are to v
of all n
of all m
of all n v

of all n v up

of b G n d v

of b G G n

of b G n

of b M G n

of b M n

. . . .

of b M n d v

. . ..Sj v

of being P2

of both n

of both n and G n

of both n and n

of course

of course not

etc.

3.3.4   *at-Clauses*

The Clauses starting with the Preposition **at** are of the following types:

(i)   For time (bm):

    (i a)   at A end of I S FB

    (i b)   at A G FB

    (i c)   at A n FB-BH(A-H)

    (i d)   at A n of FB

    (i e)   at A n of P

    (i f)   at a still further stage

    (i g)   at A time

    (i h)   at a very G FB

    (i j)   at any FB

    (i k)   at I FB

    (i l)   at b A same FB

    (i m)   at different times

    (i n)   at EBL past m

    (i o)   at EBL to m

    (i p)   at FB

    (i q)   at first

    (i r)   at I early stage

    (i s)   at I FB of A FB

... etc. (See the Dictionary of Segments for more details, because very many **at**-Clauses designate time.)

(ii)   For location (bl):

    (ii a)   at A G G G n

    (ii b)   at A G G n n

    (ii c)   at A G n of G n

    (ii d)   at A G n of A n

    (ii e)   at A G n of A n Pl up

    (ii f)   at A n of A n of O G G n

... etc., denoting positioning or place of action (for more see the Dictionary of Segments, because a very large group of **at**-segments designate location).

For example (ii d) can mean: *at the upper edge of the roof*.

(iii)   For reason (br):
    (iii a)   at A n of G n
    (iii b)   at A n of A G n
    (iii c)   at being G
    (iii d)   at being j
    (iii e)   at being P2

elucidating the reason for a certain action. For example (iii b):

He shuddered at the sight of the deep precipice.
d   v   at A n   of A G n

(iv)   For manner (bn):
    (iv a)   at A n of G n
    (iv b)   at a(n) n
    (iv c)   at A G n
    (iv d)   at bay
    (iv e)   at chequers
    (iv f)   at ease
    (iv g)   at will
    (iv h)   at full length

denoting the manner in which a certain action is performed. For example (iv d):

They must be kept at bay.
d   shall be P2   at bay

(v)   For direction (bd):
    (v a)   at A G n Pi up
    (v b)   at O n (if preceded by *look* and synonyms)
    (v c)   at R
    (v d)   at Z

pointing to the direction of the action. For example (v c):

She looked at him.
d   v   at R

(vi)   For sequence (bv):
    (vi a)   at A S
    (vi b)   at A S n
    (vi c)   at first

denoting that a certain action will be repeated. Compare:

I thought at first that ...
d v   at first

(vii)   For negation:
    (vii a)   at all

used for expressing negation. Compare:

'*Do you mind?*' '*Not at all.*'

(viii) For means (b means):
    (viii a) at all events
    (viii b) at all costs

Both express certainty and are equivalent to 'by all means', or 'certainly'. The means are implicit.

(ix) For quantity, volume or measure (bq):
    (ix a) at arm's length
    (ix b) at b A same n
    (ix c) at better than M n a(n) n
    (ix d) at G n
    (ix e) at least m m
    (ix f) at m m
    (ix g) at m A n
    (ix h) at m m G n
    (ix j) at m n square
    (ix k) at m times n
    (ix l) at nearly m each
    (ix m) at S of A n
    (ix n) at the same n
    (ix o) at well below m PU a(n) n
    (ix p) at well below the n
(where the second **m** and all G are optional; PU denotes the semantic group Monetary Unit)

(x) For circumstances (bc):
    (x a) at great peril
    (x b) at I n
    (x c) at P
outlining the circumstances in which certain action is performed.

(xi) For purpose (bp):
    (ix a) at P A n
    (xi b) at P n of M of O G n
    (xi c) at P n of M of O less G n
    (xi d) at P O G n
    (xi e) at P R
used to explain the purpose or the motives for a certain action (xi a). For example:
    His entire efforts were aimed at overturning the barrel.
    O G   n   are P2 at P   A n

(xii) For comparison or evaluation (by):
    (xii a) at the most
meaning that all other options being considered, only one is the best. It is equivalent to *most of all*. Compare:
    This is | what one can hope for | at the most.
    I   is   what d shall v   up at the most

Overleaf the reader will find an excerpt from the Dictionary of Segments, showing the grammatical structure of the **at**-segments:

at A G n of A G G n

at A G n of A G G n b

at A G n of A G n

at A G n of A G n b

at A G n of A G N''s G n

at A G n of A G N''s n

at A G n of A n of n

at A G n of A n   bl

at A G n of A n are A n   bl

at A G n of A n are O G n   bl

at A G n of A n b

at A G n of A n Pl   bl

at A G n of A n Pl up   bl

at A G n of A N''s G n

at A G n of A N''s n

at A G n of G n   br

at A G n of n   bl   br

at A G n of O n   bl

at A G n of O N''s n   bl

at A G n Pl

at A G n'' Pi''   bd

at A G n'' Pi'' up   bd

at A m % n   bq

at A n   bl

at A n are also Pi

at A n are Pi

at A n S

at A n d v

at A n d v up

at A n of A G n of A G n

at A n of A G n of A n

at A n of A G N''s G n

at A n of A G N''s n

at A n of A n   bl

at A n of A n of A G n   bl

at A n of A n of n   bl

at A n of A n v A less G n

at A n of A n are A n   bl

at A n of A n are O G n

at A n of A n are O n   bl

at A n of A n b

at A n of A n of A G n

at A n of A n of A n

at A n of A n of O G G n   bl

at A n of A n of O G n   bl

at A n of A n of O n   bl

at A n of A n Pl

at A n of A n Pl up   bl

at A n of A n to v G n

at A n of A n to v n

at A n of A N''s G n

at A n of A N''s n   bl

at A n of A Name   bl

at A n of A NAME of A

NAME   bl

at A n of FB   bm

at A n of G G n

at A n of G n of n   bn

at A n of G n   bl   br   bn

at A n of G n v A G n

at A n of G n v A n

at A n of M n

at A n of M n A n

at A n of M n A n v

at A n of m N''s n

at A n of n of A n   bn

etc.

3.3.5   *on*-Clauses

The Preposition **on** starts Adverbial Clauses of the following type:

(i)   For location (bl):

(i a)   on A b G G n

(i b)   on A b G n of O G n

(i c)   on A G G n of A n of G G n

(i d)   on A G N''s n

(i e)   on A n of O N''s n

(i f)   on both n of A n

(i g)   on G n
(i h)   on I very n
(i j)   on M of A G n
(i k)   on O G n b
(i l)   on to A n of G n

... etc., indicating presence or place of action (the list is quite extensive; for more details refer to the Dictionary of Segments). For example:

(i g)   *The snow is on high ground.*
         A   n   are on G   n

(meaning: 'up in the mountain').

(ii)   For manner (bn):
        (ii a)   on A b less G n
        (ii b)   on A less G n
        (ii c)   on all fours
        (ii d)   on call
        (ii e)   on foot
        (ii f)   on G terms
        (ii g)   on M n
        (ii h)   on O own
        (ii j)   on sale
        (ii k)   on terms
        (ii l)   on the sly
        (ii m)   on O knees
        (ii n)   on purpose

showing the manner in which certain action is performed. For example:

(ii h)   *She climbed up the hill entirely on her own.*
          d   v   up A n   b   on O own

(iii)   For time (bm),
         (iii a)   on A FB of O n
         (iii b)   on A FB
         (iii c)   on end (if preceded by: FB)
         (iii d)   on FB-BE(A-L) m I year
         (iii e)   on FB-BE(A-L) m
         (iii f)   on FB-BE(A-L) m of I year
         (iii g)   on FB-BE(A-L) S
         (iii h)   on FB-BE(A-H) the S
         (iii j)   on I FB
         (iii k)   on I occasion(-s)
         (iii l)   on M occasion(-s)
         (iii m)   on O death bed
         (iii n)   on O departure
         (iii o)   on O honeymoon
         (iii p)   on O S FB
         (iii q)   on O way up

(iii r)   on O wedding
(iii s)   on other occasions
(iii t)   on the eve of the n
(iii u)   on the eve of O G n

... etc., denoting the time of action (for more details see the Dictionary of Segments). For example:

(iii r)   *It rained on his wedding.*
          it v   on O n

(iv)   For purpose (bp):
(iv a)   on A G n
(iv b)   on A N''s n
(iv c)   on P A n

expressing the purpose for which certain action is performed or will be performed. For example:

(iv c)   *It is   useless to spend the money on purchasing a house on the island.*
         it was j   to v   A n   on P   A n   on A n
                                        bp   bl

(v)   For concern (bu):
(v a)   on A G n
(v b)   on A G N''s G n
(v c)   on A n of G n Pi n
(v d)   on A n of P X
(v e)   on all m
(v f)   on G n of A n
(v g)   on how to v
(v h)   on n
(v j)   on n of G n
(v k)   on O n
(v l)   on P
(v m)   on P UF
(v n)   on R
(v o)   on whether A n shall also v A n

identical with the meaning of *about, concerning, related to.* For example:

(v h)   *Peter wrote a book on agriculture.*
        d   v   A n   on n

(vi)   For reason (br):
(vi a)   on behalf of O G n
(vi b)   on behalf of A G G n

pointing to the reason for the action. Compare:

(vi b)   *He addressed the meeting on behalf of the entire local community.*
         d   v   A n   on behalf of A G   G   n

(vii)   For circumstances (bc):
(vii a)   on I n
(vii b)   on n

expressing action or describing the circumstances in which the action occurs.
Compare:

> (vii b) *The forest is   on fire.*
>   A   n   are on n

(viii) For sequence (bv):

> (viii a) on M occasion(-s)
> (viii b) on M n

equivalent to T (*once, twice*, etc., *times*). Compare:

> (viii a) *She was absent on   two occasions.*
>   d   am j   on M n

(ix) For quantity, volume or measure (bq) (ix a), or comparison (by) (ix b):

> (ix a)   on the average of m a(n) n
> (ix b)   on the average

Compare:

> (ix b) *They are   well off on the   average*
>   d   are also up on the average

(meaning that compared to other people they are rich)

Below the reader will find an excerpt from the Dictionary of Segments,
showing the grammatical structure of the **on**-segments:

on and off		on either n of A n are A n	
on arrival	bm	on either n of A n are A n of G n	
on b G n of n	bl	on either n of A n are A n of n	
on b M G n		on either side of A n of n	
on behalf of A G G n		on either side of I	
on behalf of A G n		on if preceded by **FB**	
on behalf of A n		on n of A G n	bl
on behalf of O G n	br	on n of A n	bl, bu
on behalf of O n	br	on n of A n of n	bu
on behalf of R		on n of G n	bu
on board	bl	on n of i A n	
on both n	bl	on n of i A n of n	
on both n of A n		on n of j n	
on both n of A n	bl	on n of n of n	bl
on business	bp	on n of n	bu
on business of O own		on n of O n	
on call	bn	on n of O own	
on earth	bl	on n of Pi no n	
on earth		on n of R	bl
on EBB of A n	bu	on n Pl	
on either n of A n	bl	on n Pl b	
on either n of A n are A G n		etc.	

3.3.6   *with-Clauses*

The word **with**, as a Preposition, starts the following types of Clauses:

(i)   For togetherness (be) or joint action (bb):
    (i a)   with A d
    (i b)   with A G d Pi R
    (i c)   with A G G G n Pi A n
    (i d)   with A G G n
    (i e)   with A G G n of n
    (i f)   with A G n of O G n
    (i g)   with G G n
    (i h)   with G n of O G n
    (i j)   with i n
    (i k)   with O G n of G n
    (i l)   with other N''s n
    (i m)   with R
    (i n)   with Z

... etc. (the list is quite extensive), stressing the fact that the action is performed jointly or is accompanied by a thing or a person. For example:
    (i m)   *She came with   him.*
           d   v   with R

(ii)   For manner (bn):
    (ii a)   with n
    (ii b)   with A G n
    (ii c)   with A G n of n
    (ii d)   with G n
    (ii e)   with greater or less P
    (ii f)   with n of O G n
    (ii g)   with regret
    (ii h)   with sorrow
    (ii j)   with some n
    (ii k)   with the same n

... etc., elucidating the manner in which certain action is performed. For example:
    (ii j)   *He spoke with   some   effort*
           d   v   with some n

(iii)   For purpose (bp) (iii a–iii d), or reason (br) (iii c, iii e, iii f):
    (iii a) with n
    (iii b) with O G n
    (iii c) with O n of n
    (iii d) with A n
    (iii e) with A P
    (iii f) with n being P2

(iii g) with P R

containing, or expressing a purpose. For example:

(iii d) *She left the house with the intention to go shopping.*

      d   v   A n   with A n   to v Pv

(used with the semantic group of words meaning intention, purpose, aim, intent, motive, objective)

(iii d a) *She left the house with the hope that she will be able to find him.*

      d   v   A n   with A n   that d shall be j   to v   R

(iv)   For instrument or means (bi):

    (iv a)   with A G d Pi R
    (iv b)   with A G G n
    (iv c)   with A G n j
    (iv d)   with A G n of A G n
    (iv e)   with A G N''s n
    (iv f)   with A m m
    (iv g)   with i G G n
    (iv h)   with M G G n
    (iv j)   with n
    (iv k)   with n Pi A n

... etc., providing evidence for the means or the instrument with which certain action is performed. Compare:

(iv b) *He shaved himself with a new razor blade.*

      d   v   X   with A G   G   n

(v)   For circumstances (bc):

    (v a)   with n able to v I N''s G n
    (v b)   with d b j
    (v c)   with O G n Pi A n
    (v d)   with n

describing the circumstances in which an action occurs. For example:

(v d)   *At night the valley looked beautiful, dotted with fires.*

      at FB   A n   v   j   Pl   with n

Compare: *The valley looks beautiful when there are fires burning in it at night.*

(vi)   For clothing, or insertion (bt):

    (vi a)   with A G n
    (vi b)   with O G n

means to be wearing or have something on, or to possess something. For example:

(vi b)   *She did not part with her white coat.*

      d   shall also v   with O G   n

NB The same applies to all other objects. Compare:

I don't know what she did with her blue pencil. (meaning: where she has put it).

(vii)   For quantity, volume or measure (bq):

    (vii a)   with A G n of m n
    (vii b)   with A m m

(vii c) with T A n
(vii d) with T O n
(vii e) with up to m n
(vii f) with the average of m % P1

(viii) For concern or involvement (bu):
    (viii a) with A n
    (viii b) with G n
    (viii c) with P

meaning so far as something is concerned (viii c) or involvement (viii a). For example:

    (viii c) *We have finished with hoping.*
        d   has P2   with P

Compare: *So far as hoping is concerned, we have no more hope left.*

    (viii a) *'Some time ago and something to do*
        M   FB ago and UF   to v
      with a robbery', was all she could remember.
      with A n   are M d shall v

Below the reader will find an excerpt from the Dictionary of Segments showing the grammatical structure of the **with**-segments:

with A G n of A G G n   bb
with A G n of A G n   bb   bi
with A G n of A G n of A n bb   bi
with A G n of A G n of n   bb   bi
with A G n of A n   bb   bi   bn
with A G n of A n of A n   bb
with A G n of A n of n   bb
with A G n of G n P1   bi
with A G n of little less
with A G n of M less
with A G n of m n   bq
with A G n of n   bb   bi
with A G n of n of n   bi   bn
with A G n of n of A n   bi   bn
with A G n of n of A G n   bi   bn
with A G n of n P1   bi
with A G n of O G n
with A G n of O n
with A G n P1
with A G n P1 up b
with A G n Pi A n   bb
with A G n Pi n   bi
with A G n Pi up
with A G N''s G n   bb

with A G N''s n   bb   bi
with A n of n
with A n of i G n
with A n of Pi A G n
with A n Pi b
with A n to v O n
with A S n
with A S n of A n
with both n
with M n Pi R
with M of A N''s n
with M of A N''s n Pi
with M of A N''s n Pi up
with M of G n   bb
with M of G n P1   bi
with M of G n P1 up   bi
with M of i n
with M of n   bb
with M of n P1   bi
with M of n P1 up   bi
with M of O G n
with M other G n
with M other n
etc.

3.3.7   *without-Clauses*

The Preposition **without** is, in some cases, more like a Conjunction, because it can be interpreted as an **if**-clause (*if something or somebody is absent ...*, *if there is no ...*, *if there is not a single ...*). Here are some examples:

(i)   without A G n of A G n
(ii)   without O n
(iii) without P A n of A n of A n
(iv)   without P O n

... etc. Otherwise, as Preposition, it means absence of something. Compare:

They were left without water for three days.

d   am P2 without n   for M   FB

Below the reader will find an excerpt from the Dictionary of Segments showing the grammatical structure of the **without**-segments:

without O n A n v
without O n
without O n A n v up
without P
without P A n
without P A n of A n of A n
without P A n of A n
without P O n off A n
without P O n
without P O n off R
without P R any sort of n
without P R
without P R any kind of n
without P to v X
without Pi

without Pi up
without Pi A n
without Pi A G n of R
without Pi A n v
without Pi n j
without Pi n up
without O Pi R
without R Pi R S
without Pi to v
without Pi to v A n
without Pi UF j
without Pi up O n
without Pi O n
without R
etc.

3.3.8   *within-Clauses*

The Preposition **within** means that the action does not exceed certain defined boundaries of time or space. There are only two major types of Clauses, for time (i) and for space (ii), as the latter includes such notions as ability, strength, etc. as well as several individual phrases expressing distance (iii).

(i)   For time (bm):
    (i a)   within A FB
    (i b)   within FB
    (i c)   within FB of O n
    (i d)   within FB of O Pi
    (i e)   within I FB

(i f)   within M FB
(i g)   within M FB of O n
(i h)   within O n
... etc. For example:
(i a)   *Everything will be decided within a month.*
          UF   shall be P2   within A FB

(ii)   For location (and strength, ability, etc.) (bl):
(ii a)   within A G n of G n
(ii b)   within A n of A n
(ii c)   within A n of n
(ii d)   within n of A n
(ii e)   within G n
... etc. For example:
(ii e)   *The companies are within greater London*
          A n   are within G   n

(iii)   For distance (bq):
(iii a)   within reach
(iii b)   within sight of Z

Below the reader will find an excerpt from the Dictionary of Segments showing the grammatical structure of the **within**-segments:

within A FB   bm
within A G n of G n
within A G n of n
within A n
within A n of A n
within A n of n
within A n of A G n
within A n of G n
within a(n) FB   bm
within b of Z
within FB   bm
within FB of Z
within FB of O Pi up   bm

within FB of O n   bm
within FB of O Pi
within FB of O Pi up   bm
within FB of O Pi   bm
within I FB   bm
within I n
within j G n
within j n
within M FB   bm
within M FB of A n   bm
within M FB of O n   bm
etc.

3.3.9 **by**-*Clauses*

The Preposition **by** starts the following types of Adverbial Clauses:

(i)   For instrument or means (bi) or (b means):
(i a)   by A b G n of O G n
(i b)   by A G G G n
(i c)   by A G G n Pi
(i d)   by A G n of i G n

(i e)   by A G n of A n of A n
(i f)   by A G n of A n
(i g)   by A G P of A n
(i h)   by G P
(i j)   by M n of A G n
(i k)   by M of A n
(i l)   by M of O G n of n
(i m)   by n
(i n)   by O n
(i o)   by P
(i p)   by P n
(i r)   by P O n to v G n
(i s)   by P R
(i t)   by virtue of I G n
... etc. (G is optional as usual)

(NB We've tried always to select the most characteristic structures to represent a particular meaning encompassed in them. For more structures see the Dictionary of Segments.)

The predominant meaning of **by** is to state what instrument or means were employed to carry out a certain action. For example:

(i m)   *They arrived by train.*
        d   v   by n
(i f)   *She fell into a deep sleep, lulled by the pounding gallop of the train.*
        d   v into A G   n   Pl   by A G   n   of A n

(ii)   For location (bl):
        (ii a)   by A G n
        (ii b)   by A n of A n
        (ii c)   by O n
designating the place of action. For example:
        (ii a)   *A minute later he had joined Ann at her post by the window.*
                 A FB   b   d has P2   n   at O n   by A n

(iii)   For manner (bn):
        (iii a)   by A G G n
        (iii b)   by chance
        (iii c)   by coincidence
        (iii d)   by G P
        (iii e)   by hand   (can be also bi)
        (iii f)   by n
        (iii g)   by P
        (iii h)   by P A G G G n
        (iii j)   by P O own n of n
        (iii k)   by X   (also bi)
specifying the manner in which certain action is performed. For example:

(iii h)   *The breaking away in the course of time*
 A   P   up   in A n   of n
 of great lumps of rock and loose
 of G   n   of n   and G
 earth had obliterated any semblance of track, and
 n   has P2   G   n   of n   and
 it was necessary to progress
 it was j   to v
 by bracing the feet on hassocks of grass and
 by P   A n   on n   of n   and
 outcroppings of stone.
 n   of n

(iv)   For time (bm):
   (iv a)   by A n of A FB
   (iv b)   by early FB-BD
   (iv c)   by early yesterday EBN
   (iv d)   by EBP (by EBS, by EBT, by FB)
   (iv e)   by I FB
   (iv f)   by late yesterday EBN
   (iv g)   by m o'clock
   (iv h)   by the close of the FB
   (iv j)   by the end of last FB
   (iv k)   by the end of FB
   (iv l)   by the end of the FB
   (iv m) by the end of I FB
   (iv n)   by the FB
   (iv o)   by which FB
... etc., determining the time of action.

(v)   For reason (br):
   (v a)   by A n of O n
   (v b)   by dint of n
   (v c)   by M of O n
   (v d)   by M of O n of n
   (v e)   by n of A n even to v R
   (v f)   by P up
   (v g)   by the same n
explaining the reason for a certain result. For example:
   (v f)   *By playing idly, they lost the game.*
          by Pi   up   d   v A n
Compare: *The reason why they lost the game was because they played idly.*

(vi)   For quantity, volume or measure (bq):
   (vi a)   by A m
   (vi b)   by A n
   (vi c)   by as much as m n
   (vi d)   by EBK m n

(vi e)   by just m n
(vi f)   by m   (used also for time)
(vi g)   by m EBL
(vi h)   by m G n
(vi j)   by M m n
(vi k)   by n
... etc. For example:
(vi b)   *The rice is   sold by the pound.*
         A   n   are P2 by A n

(vii) For opposition (b opposition), or comparison (by):
       (vii a) by contrast

(viii) For purpose (bp):
       (viii a) by P A n
expressing the purpose or goal of a certain action. For example:
       (viii a) *By watering the plants, one can increase production.*
       by P   A n   d shall v   n

(ix) For comparison (by):
      (ix a) by far the G (G in superlative)
      (ix a) *Mount Everest is by far the highest in the world.*
      n   are by far A G   in A n

Below the reader will find an excerpt from the Dictionary of Segments showing the grammatical structure of the **by**-segments:

by A G n of A n   bi
by A G n of A n NAME   bi
by A G n of A n of A n
by A G n of i G
by A G n of i G n of n
by A G n of i G n   bi
by A G n of i n of n
by A G n of i n   bi
by A G n of n   bi
by A G n of n" Pi" A G n
by A G n of n" Pi" A n
by A G n of O G n   bi
by A G n of O G n v R v j bi
by A G n of O G n v R v n   bi
by A G n of O n v R v j   bi
by A G n of O n v R v n   bi
by A G n Pl
by A G n Pi
by A G n X
by A n of A n of A n
by A n of A n Pi   b means

by A n of A n Pi up   b means
by A n of A n v
by A n of b G n   bi
by A n of G G n
by A n of G n   bi
by A n of G n b
by A n of G n Pl
by A n of i G n
by A n of I G n   bi
by A n of i n   bi
by A n of M G n
by A n of M G n b
by A n of M n
by A n of M n of n   bi
by A n of M n b
by A n of M N"s n
by A n of n   bi
by A n of n b
by A n of n Pl
by A n of n to v   bi
etc.

3.3.10 *into-Clauses*

The Clauses starting with the Preposition **into** can be of the following types:

(i)   For time (bm):
       (i a)   into A G FB (e.g. *into the New Year*)

(ii)   For location (bl):
       (ii a)   into A G n
       (ii b)   into A N''s G n
       (ii c)   into G n
       (ii d)   into m G n
       (ii e)   into n of A G n of O n
       (ii f)   into P O G n
designating the place of action or the whereabouts of a thing. For example:
       (ii a)   *She walked into the bedroom.*
              d   v   into A n

(iii) For clothes (bt), or for a position inside a thing:
       (iii a) into A G n
       (iii b) into O n

(iv)   For manner (bn):
       (iv a)   into A n
       (iv b)   into A n of G n
       (iv c)   into A N''s G n
       (iv d)   into play
expressing the manner in which the action is performed, or the result of the action. For example:
       (iv d)   *He brought it into play.*
              d   v   R into play

(v)   For circumstances (bc):
       (v a)   into A n of n
       (v b)   into G n
       (v c)   into M G n
       (v d)   into P
       (v e)   into P n b
providing information about the circumstances in which something or somebody can be found. For example:
       (v e)   *He went into playing football again.*
              d   v   into P   n   b

(vi)   For separation (bs):
       (vi a)   into m G n
meaning that something is divided into smaller parts. For example:
       (vi a)   *She divided the melon into ten equal parts.*
              d   v   A n   into m G   n

Below the reader will find an excerpt from the Dictionary of Segments showing the grammatical structure of the **into**-segments:

into A G n of G n

into A G n of n

into A G n of A G n

into A G n of A n

into A G n Pl

into A n   bl   bn

into A n   bl   bt

into all i

into A n of M n

into A n of A n of n

into A n of i n

into A n of n   bc

into A n of A n

into A n of n b

into A n of O n

into A n of A n

into A n of O G n

into A n of A G n

into A n of n

into A n of G n   bn

into A n of A n of G n

into A n of n   bn

into A n of i G n

into A n v A n Pi b G G n

into A n v A n Pi b G n

into A n v A n Pi b n

into A n v A n Pi G G n

into A n v A n Pi G n

into A n v A n Pi n

into A n G with n

into A n Pi

into A n Pl

into A N''s G n   bl   bn

into A N''s n

etc.

3.3.11   **onto**-*Clauses*

The preposition **onto** is used to designate location (i) or awareness, with an abstract meaning of location (ii).

(i a)   onto A G n

(i b)   onto A G n Pl

(i c)   onto O G n

(i d)   onto R

(i e)   onto UF else

(ii)   onto O G n

For example:

(i a)   *He got onto   the motorbike.*

       d   v   onto A n

(ii)   *She is   onto   your secret games.*

       d   am onto O   G   n

Below the reader will find an excerpt from the Dictionary of Segments showing the grammatical structure of the **onto**-segments:

onto A G n

onto A G n Pl

onto A n

onto A n Pl

onto O G n

onto O n

onto R

etc.

3.3.12 *in*-Clauses

The preposition **in** starts the following types of Adverbial Clauses:

(i)   For time (bm):
    (i a)   in A FB
    (i b)   in A FB of FB-BD
    (i c)   in A FB of M FB
    (i d)   in A FB S
    (i e)   in A G n of FB-BD
    (i f)   in A M FB
    (i g)   in A n of FB-BD
    (i h)   in A S EBL of FB-BD
    (i j)   in A S m FB of i FB
    (i k)   in A S m to m FB
    (i l)   in as many FB
    (i m)   in a while
    (i n)   in about M FB
    (i o)   in about M FB time
    (i p)   in all A FB since then
    (i q)   in FB
    (i r)   in I FB
    (i s)   in O life time
    (i t)   in O spare time
... etc., designating the time of action (see Dictionary of Segments).

(ii)   For manner (bn):
    (ii a)   in A b G G n
    (ii b)   in A G n
    (ii c)   in a line
    (ii d)   in A n of n
    (ii e)   in G n
    (ii f)   in G P
    (ii g)   in kind
    (ii h)   in M G n
    (ii j)   in M ways
    (ii k)   in O G n
    (ii l)   in P
    (ii m) in silence
... etc., expressing the manner in which the action is performed. For example:
    (ii m) *They stood in silence.*
            d   v   in silence

(iii)   For location (bl), or direction and location (bdl):
    (iii a) in A b G G n
    (iii b) in A G G G n
    (iii c) in A G G n of A G n
    (iii d) in A n of G n

(iii e)   in A n of i n
(iii f)   in A n of O G n
(iii g)   in all O n
(iii h)   in I N''s n of A G n
... etc., denoting a place. For example:
   (iii g)   *She has mirrors in all her rooms.*
         d   v   n   in all O n

(iv)   For clothes (bt), or insertion, inclusion:
   (iv a)   in A b G G n
   (iv b)   in A G G G n
   (iv c)   in G
   (iv d)   in G n Pi n
   (iv e)   in n
   (iv f)   in O G G n
... etc., meaning dressed in or inserted in. For example:
   (iv e)   *She is all in fur.* (meaning she is wearing fur clothes)
         d   am b in n

(v)   For circumstances (bc):
   (v a)   in A G n
   (v b)   in A n of G n
   (v c)   in A n of P A n
   (v d)   in A N''s n
   (v e)   in all O n
   (v f)   in b G n
   (v g)   in between n   (also bm or bl)
   (v h)   in M n of G n
   (v j)   in n
   (v k)   in O n
... etc., describing the circumstances in which the action is performed. For example:
   (v c)   *They were in the process of buying the car, when they detected a small defect.*
         d   am in A n   of P   A n when d v   A G   n

(vi)   For purpose (bp or bo):
   (vi a)   in A G n to v A G n
   (vi b)   in A n of G n
   (vi c)   in favour of n
   (vi d)   in P G G n
   (vi e)   in P R v G N''s G G n
   (vi f)   in P v n
   (vi g)   in quest of A n
   (vi h)   in return for G n
... etc., clarifying the purpose behind a certain action. For example:
   (vi g)   *They set off in quest of a new land.*
         d   v   up in n   of A G   n

(vii) For opposition (bz), contrast, or denial:
    (vii a) in b G n
    (vii b) in spite of A G n
    (vii c) in spite of A G n of m n
    (vii d) in spite of all O n
    (vii e) in spite of n
    (vii f) in spite of O G n
where *in spite of* is equivalent to *despite*. For example:
    (vii b) *They came in spite of the heavy rain.*
           d   v   in spite of A G   n

(viii) For language (b lang.), or means (b means):
    (viii a) in n
    (viii b) in O N''s G G n
For example:
    (viii a) *The letter was written in ink.*
          A   n   are P2   in n
    (viii a) *The book was in German.*
          A   n   are in n

(ix) For sequence (bv):
    (ix a) in O n
    (ix b) in the S n
denoting sequence of events. For example:
    (ix a) *She smiled, in her turn.*
          d   v   in O   n

(x) For quantity, volume, measure (bq):
    (x a) in n of n
    (x b) in M n

    Below the reader will find an excerpt from the Dictionary of Segments showing the grammatical structure of the **in**-segments:

in A G n of i G n	in A G N''s n
in A G n of i n	in A G of n
in A G n of m n	in a hurry
in A G n of n bl	in a line bn
in A G n of NAME	in A M FB bm
in A G n of O n	in A n of A G n
in A G n of P A n bc	in A n of A n bl
in A G n P1	in A n of n FB-BH (A-H) v n
in A G n Pi off	in A n of n of Gn
in A G n Pi	in A n of A n
in A G n to v A G n bp	in A n of A n Pi R
in A G n to v A n bp	in A n of A n of n
in A G n'' Pi'' R	in A n of A n P1 b
in A G N''s n of n	in A n of A n P1

in A n of A N''s n	in the name of A G n
in A n of A N''s n of n	in the name of A n
in the least	in the name of O n
in the long run bm	in the near future bm
in the meantime bm	in the offhand way bn
in the morning bm	in the offing bm
in the name of	etc.

3.3.13 *for*-*Clauses*

The preposition **for** starts Adverbial Clauses of the following type:

(i)   For purpose (bp) or for reason (br):

For purpose:
- (i a)   for a bit of P
- (i b)   for a change
- (i c)   for A G G G n only
- (i d)   for A G G G n
- (i e)   for A G n of A n
- (i f)   for G G N''s G G n
- (i g)   for having P2 O G n
- (i h)   for I
- (i j)   for I G n
- (i k)   for M G n
- (i l)   for M of O G n
- (i m)   for O n
- ... etc.

For reason:
- (i a)   for a certain n
- (i b)   for A G n of n
- (i c)   for A G n
- (i d)   for A G n of A n
- (i e)   for d has also P2 G G n
- (i f)   for G G n of M n
- (i g)   for G n to v O n
- (i h)   for having P2 A n
- (i j)   for I n
- ... etc.

defining the aim to be achieved through the action (bp), or the motives that have inspired the action (br). For example:

(i m)   *She came for her book.* (bp)

        d   v   for O n

(i j)   *He paid thousands for this horse.* (br)

        d   v   M   for I   n

Compare: *The reason why he paid thousands was to have this horse.*

(ii)   For time (bm):
   (ii a)   for A last FB
   (ii b)   for a little while
   (ii c)   for a little more than a FB
   (ii d)   for EBK m FB
   (ii e)   for even a single FB
   (ii f)   for FB
   (ii g)   for FB on end
   (ii h)   for A S FB in FB
   (ii j)   for I FB
... etc., specifying the time of action. For example:
   (ii f)   *It was going on for years.*
       it was Pi   up for FB

(iii) For quantity, volume or measure (bq):
   (iii a)   for EBK half of all n
   (iii b)   for m
   (iii c)   for M G n
... etc. For example:
   (iii b)   *He bought it for ten.*
       d   v   R for m
Compare: *It has cost him ten pounds.*

(iv)   For concern (bu):
   (iv a)   for A G n
   (iv b)   for A G n of G n are also j to v
   (iv c)   for each m n d v
   (iv d)   for G G n
   (iv e)   for I are A G G n
   (iv f)   for i n
... etc., meaning *concerning* (*so far as something is concerned*). For example:
   (iv f)   *There is no place for this table.*
       there are no n   for I   n
Compare: *So far as this table is concerned, there is no place for it in the room.*

(v)   For explanation:
   (v a)   for example
   (v b)   for instance

(vi)   Used as Conjunction:
   (vi a)   for A G n of n has P2 up
   (vi b)   for A n are also Pi G n to v
   (vi c)   for d am also n
   (vi d)   for d has also been j
... etc., starting a Nominal segment, followed by a Verbal Tense and having the meaning of *because*. For example:
   (vi a)   *The river was very high, for a great deal of snow had melted lately.*
       A   n   are also G   for A G   n   of n   has P2   up

Compare: *The water level of the river was high, because much snow had melted lately.*

Below the reader will find an excerpt from the Dictionary of Segments showing the grammatical structure of the **for**-segments:

for a little less	for having P2 O G n bp
for a little more than a FB bm	for having P2 O n bp
for a little while bm	for having P2 R
for a long time bm	for I bu bp
for A m bq	for Pi A n
for both A n and A n	for Pi G G G n
for both n	for Pi n
for both n and n	for Pi R
for both of R	for Pi R j br
for d has P2 A n	for Pi R up
for d has P2 G G n br	for Pi to v
for d has P2 G n br	for Pi to v A n
for d has P2 n br	for Pi X
for d shall also v O n	for R
for d shall also v O n UI	for R all
for d shall also v Pi M	for R also to v
for d shall v O n	for R both
for d shall v O n UI	for R to be
for d shall v Pi M	for R to v
Sj v Od	for R to v O G n bp
for d shall v to v	for R to v R
for d shall v up	for R to v up
Sj v	for R to v up to
for each m n d v bu	for R to v X
for each one refer to last n	for reasons beyond O control br
for each one of R	for the rest of O FB bm
for each one P1	for the rest of O life
for having been j	for the rest of O n
for having been so j	for the rest of the FB bm
for having P2 A n	for the time being
for having P2 A n of n br	etc.

3.3.14 *to*-Clauses

The preposition **to** can start the following types of Adverbial Clauses:

(i) For direction and location (bdl), or for location only (bl) or for direction only (bd):
   (i a)   to A b G n of A G n   (bdl)
   (i b)   to A G G G n   (bdl, bd)

(i c)   to A G n of G G n   (bdl)
(i d)   to A less G n of n   (bd)
(i e)   to A less G n
(i f)   to A less j of G n
(i g)   to A N''s G n
(i h)   to i n of G n
(i j)   to n
(i k)   to O n   (bl)
(i l)   to O N''s G n   (bdl)

... etc., expressing either the direction or the location of the action, or both. For example:

(i b)   *He came to the church.*
          d   v   to A n

(ii)   For reason (br):
       (ii a)   to A G n of such a(n) n
       (ii b)   to all n
       (ii c)   to O n

explaining the reason for a certain action. For example:

(ii c)   *We drank to his health.*
           d   v   to O n

(iii)   For time (bm):
        (iii a)   to A G G FB
        (iii b)   to FB
        (iii c)   to the FB-BD S half
        (iii d)   to the last FB
        (iii e)   to the S of FB

denoting a point of limit in time. For example:

(iii d)   *Your permit is valid to the first of January.*
          O   n   are j to A S   of FB

(iv)   For addition (b addition):
       (iv a)   to A G G n
       (iv b)   to I n
       (iv c)   to I n of n

used with the verbs *add, apply, put, complement,* etc. to express addition. For example:

(iv a)   *The cook added some salt to the soup.*
         d   v   M   n   to A n

(NB The meaning of addition is a subgroup of a more general meaning, that for direction and location.)

(v)   For quantity, volume, or measure (bq):
      (v a)   to A G n of m m
      (v b)   to M G n
      (v c)   to just below m %
      (v d)   to less than m %

(v e)   to M
(v f)   to m %
(v g)   to m % of n

... etc., setting a limit to a measurement, amount, volume, quantity, etc. For example:

(v c)   *The unemployment figures fell to just below 10 %.*
           A   G   n   v   to just below m %

(vi)   For purpose (bp or bo):
(vi a)   to A n
(vi b)   to n of O n
(vi c)   to O P
(vi d)   to P A G n
(vi e)   to P A n j of n
(vi f)   to the very n of n

explaining the purpose behind a certain action. For example:

(vi a)   *The helicopter came to the rescue.*
            A   n   v   to A n

Below the reader will find an excerpt from the Dictionary of Segments showing the grammatical structure of the **to**-segments:

to A G G n   b addition   bd   to A G n of m m   bd   bq
to A G G n of A n   bdl   to A G n of m
to A G G n of A n b Pi G n   to A G n'' Pi'' n   bd
to A G G n of A n b Pi n   to A G n' j' A n
to A G G n of A n Pi G n   to A G n' Pi'
to A G G n of A n Pi n   to a great extent   b
to A G n j of Pi   to A JE
to A G n j of Pi G n   to a large degree
to A G n of m of N''s G n   to a large extent
to A G n of n of N''s G n   to A less G n of n   bd
to A G n of n   bd   to A less G n
to A G n of A n Pi G n   to A less j of G n   bd
to A G n of A n Pi n   to A less j of n   bd
to A G n of A n b Pi G n   to A M n
to A G n of A n b Pi n   to A M of R
to A G n of such a(n) n   br   to A n
to A G n of n   ....
to A G n of A n   to A n A n of A n
to A G n of G G n   bdl   to A n A n
to A G n of G n   bdl   etc.

3.3.15 *past-Clauses*

The preposition **past** is used to denote:

(i)   Location (bl):
   (i a)   past A G n
   (i b)   past n of n
... etc., meaning near, near by or beyond something. For example:
   (i a)   *They went past the village*
         d   v   past A   n

(ii)   Time (bm):
   (ii a)   past m
   (ii b)   past P n
meaning that a certain limit in time is exceeded. For example:
   (ii a)   *It is ten past eleven.*
        it is m past m
   (ii b)   *He is long past driving age.*
        d   am also past P   n

3.3.16 *next-Clauses*

The preposition **next** is used to start Adverbial Clauses denoting time (i), sequence (i and ii) and location (only when it is followed by **to**) (iii). For example:

(i)   next FB
(ii a)   next n
(ii b)   next n to v
(ii c)   next v G n
(iii a)   next to A n
(iii b)   next to R

Below the reader will find an excerpt from the Dictionary of Segments showing the grammatical structure of the **next**-segments:

next FB
next n
next n to v
next time round
next to A n   bl
next to R   bl
next v A G n

next v A G n of n
next v A G n of n P1
next v A G n of n P1 are m
next v G n
next v n
etc.

3.3.17 *against-Clauses*

The Adverbial Clauses starting with the Preposition **against** express direction and location (bdl or bl) (i), contrast or opposition (ii) and purpose or reason (iii). For example:

(i a) against A G n of A n (bl)
(i b) against A n of I n (bdl)
(i c) against A n (bdl)
(i c) *He propped his stick against the wall.*
     d   v   O   n   against A n

(ii a) against A n
(ii b) against G G n
(ii c) against O G n
(ii a) *There was a big demonstration against the regime.*
     there are A G   n   against A n

(iii a) against n
(iii a) *She saved from her salary against retirement.*
     d   v   from O n   against n

Below the reader will find an excerpt from the Dictionary of Segments showing the grammatical structure of the **against**-segments:

against A G n of A n bl	against I
against A G n of G n bl	against M n
against A G n of n	against n b opposition
against A G n	against n v
....	against n to v A n Pl
against A n shall v G G n	against O G n b opposition
against A n shall v G n	against O G n of n bdl
against A n shall v n	against O n bdl b opposition
v Od	against O N''s bl
against A n	against P
against A n of A n	against P A n b b
against A n of I n bdl	against P A n b
against A n of G n	against P A G n b
against A n of n	against P A G n
against A n b opposition	against P A n
against both of R	against P A G n b b
against G	against P b
against G G n	against P n
against G G n of n b opposition	against P R
against G n b opposition	against R
against G n v	against which
against i n	etc.

3.3.18 *through*-*Clauses*

The preposition **through** starts Adverbial Clauses of the following type:

(i)   For time (bm):
        (i a)   through A FB
        (i b)   through A G n of A FB-BL
        (i c)   through FB

For example:
        (i c)   *We have enough supplies to carry us from 1994 through 1999.*
                  d   has also   n   to v   R from FB   through FB

(ii)   For direction and location (bdl), which is a very general meaning and
        can substitute a number of other meanings, for example (iii, iv).
        (ii a)   through A n
        (ii b)   through G n
        (ii c)   through G n of A n

For example:
        (ii a)   *We passed through the town.*
                  d   v   through A n

(iii)   For means (bi, b means), or source:
        (iii a)   through A n
        (iii b)   through G n
        (iii c)   through G n of A n
        (iii d)   through O n
        (iii e)   through P

... etc., elucidating the means used to perform the action. For example:
        (iii a)   *I got it through a friend.*
                  d v R through A n

Compare: *A friend helped me to get it.*

(iv)   To finish or reach the end of something:
        (iv a)   *I went through the book.*
                  d   v   through A n

Compare: *I perused the book from one end to the other.*

Below the reader will find an excerpt from the Dictionary of Segments
showing the grammatical structure of the **through**-segments:

through A G n of n		b means		through A n	bl	b means
through A G n of A FB-BL	bl			through A n of n Pi n		
through A G n of A n	bl			through A n Pi n		
through A G n of n	bl	b means		through A n of n	bl	b means
through A G FB	bm			through A n are n of G n		*
through A G n	bl	b means		through A n of G n Pl		
through A G n	bi			through A n are n of n		
through A last M FB	bm			through A n of n Pl		
through A m n Pl	bl	b means		through A n of P n		

through A n of G n	through O N''s n
through NAME bk	through P b means
through O G b means	through R
through O n b means	etc.

3.3.19 *under-Clauses*

The prepositions **under** and **beneath**, at the start of an Adverbial Clause, express the following types of meaning:

(i)   For quantity, volume or measure (bq):
    (i a)   under m
    (i b)   under m %
    ... etc.
For example:
    (i b)   *The inflation rate is   under   10 %.*
        A   G   n   are under m %

(ii)   For location (bl):
    (ii a)   under A b G n
    (ii b)   under A G n of A N''s n
    (ii c)   under n
... etc., providing information about the place of action or the whereabouts of a thing. This is also a very general meaning that can substitute a number of other meanings (see (i)). For example:
    (ii d)   *The cat is under   the table.*
        A   n are under A n

(iii)   For circumstances (bc) or condition (bx):
    (iii a)   under n
For example:
    (iii a)   *The boiler is   under   pressure.*
        A   n   are under n
    (iii ab)   *The project is   under   development.*
        A   n   are under n
    (iii ac)   *Your proposal is   under   consideration.*
        O   n   are under n

(iv)   When **under** is used in the construction:
    (iv a)   under i circumstances
it acts as a Conjunction, meaning *then, thus, therefore.*

Below the reader will find an excerpt from the Dictionary of Segments showing the grammatical structure of the **under**-segments:

under A G n of A G n Pl	under A G n of A n'' Pi O G n''
under A G n of A G n'' Pi O G n''	under A G n of A G G G n'' Pi O n''
under A G n of A n Pl	under A G n of A G G n'' Pi O n''

under A G n of A G n'' Pi O n''
under A G n of A G G n
under A G n of A G n
under A G n of A G G n   bl
under A G n
under A G n of A n'' Pi O n''
under A G n of A n
under A n NAME
under A n of A G n
under A n of A G n'' Pi O n''
under A n of EBO of G n
under A n of EBO of n
under A n of A n'' Pi O n''
under A n of A G n   b means
under A n of FB-BD
under A n of G n Pl
under A n of n Pl
under A n of A G n Pl
under A n of A G n   bl
under A n of A n Pl
under A n of A n   bl
under A n of others
under A n of others b j to v
under A n of A N''s n   bl
under A n of A G G n
under A n of A G G G n'' Pi O G n''
under A n of A G G n'' Pi O G n''
under A n of A G n'' Pi O G n''
under A n of A n'' Pi O G n''
under A n of A G G n
under A n of A G G G n'' Pi O n''
under A n of A G G n'' Pi O n''

under A n Pl
under A N''s n
under A NAME NAME
under A TITLE HEADING
under consideration
under G n   b means
under G n Pl
under i G n of A G G n
under i G n of A G n
under i G n of A n
under i n of A n
under i n of A G G n
under i n of A G n
under m G n NAME
under m n NAME
under n   bq   b means
under n m of G n
under n m of G G n
under n m of n
under n n
under n Pl
under n subject to n
under O
....
under O A G n v up
under O A G n v
under O A n v up
under O A n v
     Sj v
under O G n
etc.

3.3.20 *between-Clauses*

At the start of an Adverbial Clause, **between** is used to indicate location (i), time (ii) and comparison (iii), both in the abstract and in the concrete sense. In some cases it is used with the Conjunction **and**, in others without it.

(i a) between A n and A G n
(i b) between A G G n Pl
(i c) between A G n are n of G n
(i d) between O G G n
(i e) between R and A G n
... etc. For example:

(i a)   *The village is situated between   a river and a   mountain lake.*
         A   n   are P2   between A n   and A G   n

(ii a) between the intervals
(ii b) between m and m o'clock
For example:
         (ii b) *I'll   be here between   four and five o'clock.*
                 d shall be up between m   and m o'clock

(iii)   between n and n
For example:
         (iii a) *There   isn't   a big difference between   pink and red*
                  there are also A G   n   between n   and n

Below the reader will find an excerpt from the Dictionary of Segments
showing the grammatical structure of the **between**-segments:

between A G n	between A n and A G n
between A G n and A n	between A n and A n
between A G n and A G n	between A n of A G G n
between A G n of A G n	between A n d shall
between A G	between A n P1
between A G n P1	between A n of A m G n
between A G and G n	between A n of A m n
between A G and G n can be P2	between A n and O n
between A G G n P1	between A n of n
between A G n and	between A n are n of G n
between A G n P1	between A n of A n
between A G n of A n	between A n are n of n
between A G n of A G n	between A n are n
between A G n are n of G n	between A n and A G G n
between A G n are n of n	between A n and A G n
between A G n are n	between A n and A n
between A m n	between b
between A M n	between A G n and A G n of A G G n
between A m of R	between G and G n
between A m G n	between G n there v
between A n and	between G n
between A n and O G n	between G n P1
between A n	between i
between A n of A G n	etc.
between A n and R	

3.3.21 *above*-Clauses

When used at the beginning of an Adverbial Clause, the preposition **above**
means positioning or location (i), or sets a limit to quantity, measure and
volume (ii).

(i a) above A n
(i b) above G n
For example:

    (i a)   *We were flying above the ocean.*
         d   am Pi   above A n

(ii a) above m
(ii b) above m FB of age
For example:

    (ii b) *All children above five years of age must go to school.*
        M n   above m FB of age shall v to n

When used with **all** it can be a Conjunction, **above all** (meaning *all things considered, everything taken into consideration, first of all*).

Below the reader will find an excerpt from the Dictionary of Segments showing the grammatical structure of the **above**-segments:

above A n of O n	above M n
above A n of A G n	above n
above A n of A n	above O G n
above all	above O n
above board n	above O n A G G n
above G n	above O N''s n
above I are G n	above R
above I are n	etc.
above m	

3.3.22 *since*-Clauses

Apart from being a Conjunction, **since** is used as a Preposition at the start of the Adverbial Clauses denoting time (i).

(i a) since FB
(i b) since i FB
(i c) since P A n
(i d) since O N''s n
(i e) since then

Below the reader will find an excerpt from the Dictionary of Segments showing the grammatical structure of the **since**-segments:

since A G n	since A n of G n
since A G n of n	since A n v P
since A n of n	etc.

3.3.23 *before*-Clauses

At the start of an Adverbial Clause, the preposition **before** is characterized by two meanings: time (i) and location (ii).

(i a) before A G n
(i b) before FB
(i c) before long
(i d) before m
(i e) before m o'clock
(i f) before next FB
... etc. For example:

    (i b)   *The decision must be taken before February.*
        A   n   shall be P2   before FB

(ii a) before A G n
(ii b) before R
... etc. For example:

    (ii b)   *Two of the guards were walking before him. The other two were behind.*
        M of A d   are Pi   before R   A other m am up

Below the reader will find an excerpt from the Dictionary of Segments showing the grammatical structure of the **before**-segments:

before A n   bl   bm
before A n did
before A n of n
before A n of n Pi P1
before A n of G G n
before A n of G n
before A n of n of n
....
before A n shall v R up
before A n shall v R
before A n shall v A n
before A n shall v A n up
  Sj v Od
before A n to be P2
before A n v up
....
before A n v to v R
  Sj v Od
before A n v
....
before A n v to v A n
  Sj v Od
before A n v to v
....

before A n v to v n
  Sj v Od
before A n v
....
before A n v A n of A n
before A n v A n
before A n v A n up
before A n v R
before A n v R up
  Sj v Od
before A n X
before all i G n
before all i n
before being P2
....
before d all v O G n
before d all v O n
  Sj v Od
before d am P2
before d b v
  Sj v
before d b v M n of O n

before d b v M n

  Sj v Od

before P

before P A G n

before P A n

before P n

before P O G n

before P O n

before P O S n

before P R

before P up

before P up b

before R   bl

before Pi A n

before Pi O n

before Pi O n for R to v

before Pi O n to v

before Pi X

before R to v

before too long   bm

etc.

3.3.24 *after-Clauses*

In its function as a Preposition heading the Adverbial Clause, **after** has two meanings (both implying sequence): for time (i) and for location (ii), including an expression for direction and location (iii).

(i a) after A FB

(i b) after A FB of P

(i c) after A FB of P A n of n

(i d) after A G G n

(i e) after a while

(i f) after a great interval of time

(i g) after FB

(i h) after FB S

... etc. For example:

    (i h) *She is   expected to arrive after January 1st.*

          d am P2   to v   after FB   S

(ii a) after A n

(ii b) after O n

... etc. For example:

    (ii a) *The bank is in this direction, after the Post Office.*

          A   n   are in i   n   after A   n

(iii a) after R

For example:

    (iii a) *The pack of wolves followed after him.*

          A   n   of n   v   after R

Below the reader will find an excerpt from the Dictionary of Segments showing the grammatical structure of the **after**-segments:

after A FB   bm

after A FB of P   bm

after A FB of P A n of n

after A FB of P A n

after A FB''s n

after A FB''s P

after A G G n   bm

after A G n

after A G n of n
after A G n b
after A G n   bm
after A G n of Pi
after A n   bm
after A n of n
....
after A n are also P2
after A n are P2
  Sj v
after A n b
after A n Pi A N''s G n   .
after A n Pi A N''s n
after A n Pi O G n
after A n Pi O n
after A n v A n
  Sj v Od

after A n v X
  Sj v Cs
after A n' Pi A n of A n v'
after A n' Pi A n of A G n v'
  Sj Cs v
after A Pl m m n
after A Pl m n
after A P has P2
after A P has P2 n
after A S
after A S of O G n
after A S of O n
after a while   bm
after a great interval of time   bm
after about m n
after about m A n
etc.

3.3.25 *until, till, while, once, prior to, during*-Clauses

The Adverbial Clauses and all other Dependent Clauses starting with any of these Prepositions denote time (bm). Slightly different is *once*, because it can also mean repetition or sequence (v d).

(i a)   until A n v Pv
(i b)   until d has also P2
(i c)   until FB
(i d)   until M of R v
(ii a) till there are G n (*prior to, until* and *till* set a limit in time for the action)
(iii a) while A G G n v up
(iii b) while d am P2 up to v A n
(iii c) while on A G n v n of n
(iii d) while P O G n
(iv a) during A FB
(iv b) during A n
(iv c) during A n of A n
(iv d) during P (*while* and *during* specify the duration of concurrent action(s))
(v a)   once d has P2 to v R
(v b)   once d v A n
(v c)   once for all
(v d)   once in a while
... etc.

3.3.26 *like*-Clauses

The preposition **like** starts Adverbial Clauses for comparison, or appearance (i) or for manner (ii). There is no apparent difference between (i) and (ii).

(i a) like A G G n
(i b) like A G n of A G n
(i c) like A n of n
(i d) like G n Pi to be P2
(i e) like n Pi A n out of A n
(i f) like O n
... etc.
For example:
     (i f)   *He is like his father.*
            d am like O n
(ii a) like A G n
(ii b) like A n of n
(ii c) like G n Pi to be P2
(ii d) like I of G n
... etc.
For example:
     (ii a)   *She was dressed like an old man.*
            d am P2   like A G n

3.3.27 *about*-Clauses

The Adverbial Clause starting with the Preposition **about** can have the following meanings:

(i)   For concern (bu):
     (i a)   about A n of A G n
     (i b)   about A n of G n
     (i c)   about A n of O G n
     (i d)   about G n
     (i e)   about I
     (i f)   about O G G n
... etc., meaning *concerning, so far as something is concerned.*
For example:
     (i e)   *We must talk more about this.*
            d shall v more about I

(ii)   For location (bl):
     (ii a)   about A n
     (ii b)   about m JE-Dn JD of n
... etc.
For example:
     (ii a)   *She must be about the house.*
            d shall be about A n

(iii)   For quantity, volume, measure (bq):
     (iii a) about m m
     (iii b) about M n
... etc., meaning *approximately.*

(iv)   For purpose (bp or bo):
       (iv a)   about n
... etc., only if immediately preceded by certain Verbs (*ask, enquire, come,* etc.).
For example:
       (iv a)   *He asked about money.*
                d   v   about n

(v)   For time (bm):
       (v a)   about now
       (v b)   about m o'clock
... etc.

3.3.28   **aboard, across**-*Clauses*

The Adverbial Clauses starting with the Prepositions **aboard** or **across** designate the place of action or location of something (bl).
For example:

(i a)   aboard A G G G n
(ii a) across A G n of n
(ii b) across A n
(ii c) across O n
... etc.
For example:
       (i a)   *The customs inspector came aboard the ship.*
                d   v   aboard A n
       (ii b)   *The tree fell across the road.*
                A   n v   across A n

3.3.29   **along**-*Clauses*

The Adverbial Clauses starting with the Preposition **along** can designate (parallel) location (bl) and togetherness (be). For example:

(i a)   along A G G n
(i b)   along A G n of A G G n
(i c)   along G n
(i d)   along i n
... etc., also covering the abstract meaning *in conformity with.*

(ii a) along with A G n
(ii b) along with M G n
(ii c) along with O G one
(ii d) along with O n
(ii e) along with R
... etc.
For example:

(ii d)   *She planned the trip along with her companions.*
d   v   A n   along with O n

3.3.30   among-*Clauses*

The preposition **among** (or **amongst**) is used with the Adverbial Clause to designate location (bl):

(i a)   among A G G n of n
(i b)   among A G n of I b G n
(i c)   among A n
(i d)   among n of G n
(i e)   among O G n
... etc. For example:

(i c)   *A word was spread among the people, that ...*
A n   are P2   among A n

3.3.31   around-*Clauses*

As part of an Adverbial Clause the Preposition **around** can designate time (i) or location (ii). For example:

(i a)   around m o'clock
(i b)   around the age of m
meaning *approximately.*

(ii a) around A n
(ii b) around O G n
... etc.
For example:

(ii a)   *They walked all day around the town.*
d   v   M FB around A n

3.3.32   behind-*Clauses*

The Adverbial Clauses starting with the Preposition **behind** designate location (i) (in the abstract sense, meaning *support*), and only in a few cases denote time (ii). For example:

(i a)   behind A n of A n
(i b)   behind A n of n
(i c)   behind A n of n Pl
(i d)   behind A n of O N''s n
(i e)   behind b G G n
... etc.

(ii a) behind schedule
(ii b) behind time

3.3.33 *beside*-*Clauses*

The Adverbial Clause starting with **beside** can mean location (i) and comparison (by) (ii). For example:

(i a) beside A G G n
(i b) beside n

> (i a)   *He likes to sit beside   the fireplace.*
>   d   v   to v   beside A   n

(ii)   beside R
. . . etc.

> (ii a)   *There is   no one beside him, who can sing so well.*
>   there are no n   beside R   who can v   b

(in the latter case assuming the meaning of the Conjunction *except.*)

3.3.34 *beyond*-*Clauses*

The Adverbial Clauses starting with the Preposition **beyond** designate location (bl) in the concrete and in the abstract sense, meaning further than a certain location or limit. For example:

(i a) beyond A G n
(i b) beyond A m G n
(i c) beyond A n of G n
(i d) beyond I
. . . etc.

> (i a)   *There are some more   villages beyond   the hill.*
>   there are M   more n   beyond A   n

3.3.35 *down*-*Clauses*

The Adverbial Clauses starting with the Preposition **down** designate location (bl). For example:

(i a) down A G n
(i b) down here
. . . etc.

> (i a)   *They are swimming down the river.*
>   d   am Pi   down A n

3.3.36 *inside*-*Clauses*

The Adverbial Clauses starting with the Preposition **inside** designate location (i) and, in one case only, time (ii). For example:

(i a) inside A G G n
(i b) inside A n n

(i c) inside A n of A n
(i d) inside n
(i e) inside O G n
(i f) inside R
... etc.

(ii)   inside A FB (e.g. *inside an hour*)

3.3.37 **near**-*Clauses*

The Adverbial Clauses starting with the Preposition **near** designate location
(meaning *in the close proximity of*). For example:

(i a) near A G n
(i b) near A G n of A G n
(i c) near A n Pi n
(i d) near R
... etc.
> (i a)   *They have a house near the lake.*
>   d   v   A n   near A n

3.3.38 **round** *and* **throughout**-*Clauses*

The Adverbial Clauses starting with the Prepositions **round** or **throughout**
designate location (i) or time (ii). For example:

(i a) round A G G n
(i b) round A n of n
(i c) round A N''s n
(i d) round here
(i e) round O G n
(i f)   throughout I G n
... etc.
In this particular meaning **round** is identical with **around** (discussed in
3.3.31).

(ii a) round m o'clock
(ii b) round the clock
(ii c) throughout O G n
(ii d) throughout the m hour clock
... etc.
> (ii b)   *They work on shifts, round the clock.*
>   d   v   on n   round the clock

3.3.39 **towards**-*Clauses*

The Adverbial Clauses starting with the Preposition **toward(s)** express
purpose (i), time (ii) and direction and location (iii). For example:

(i a) towards n
(i b) towards P A G n
... etc.

    (i b) *I am putting aside money towards buying a new car.*
        d am Pi   up n   towards P   A G n

(ii)   towards FB
... etc.

    (ii a) *It gets colder towards evening.*
        it v   G   towards FB

(iii a) towards A G G n
(iii b) towards A G n of A G n
(iii c) towards G n
(iii d) towards O G n
... etc.

    (iii a) *They were heading towards the sea.*
        d   am Pi   towards A n

3.3.40 **upon**-*Clauses*

The Adverbial Clauses starting with the Preposition **upon** denote reason (i) and location (ii). For example:

(i a) upon P O n v O S n
(i b) upon P A n
(equivalent to the Conjunction *because*)
    (i b) *They were rejoicing upon hearing the news that they had won.*
        d   am Pi   upon P   A n   that d   has P2

(ii a) upon A n of A G n
(ii b) upon A n
(ii c) upon n
(ii d) upon O G n
... etc.

    (ii b) *When he saw the wolf, he climbed upon a tree.*
        when d v   A n   d v   upon A n

3.3.41 **via**-*Clauses*

The Adverbial Clauses starting with the Preposition **via** designate direction (i) or means (ii). For example:

(i a) via A G G n
(i b) via A G n of n
(i c) via n
... etc.

    (i c) *They came via London.*
        d   v   via n
(meaning *through*)

(ii a) via n

    (ii a)   *They came via British Airways.*
             d   v   via G   n

7 Parsing algorithm

The algorithm presented in this chapter serves to identify a portion of text (not longer than a sentence) with a segment from the Dictionary of Segments (DS). Since the segments have a pre-recorded Parsing, the text is parsed automatically. If there is more than one possible Parsing (there are not more than two), the user is alerted to this fact and asked for help.

The algorithms presented below have a much deeper significance for the user – for example, if a portion of the text cannot be identified with a segment, this is yet another cause for concern, because it can mean that a) either the segment corresponding to that portion of text is not registered in the Dictionary of Segments, or b) that portion of text is syntactically incorrect.

In the former case the user adds (registers) the new segment, in the latter she (or he) corrects the text. If the user is an English student, our advice is to try to paraphrase that portion of text in such a way that it matches a segment from the Dictionary of Segments.

Some of the part of speech disambiguation algorithms and the parsing method described in this book are already available (Georgiev, 1993a) as a computer software program called SYNTPARSE. Syntparse is able to parse any English sentence or text. At the output the program displays the actual part of speech of every word in the sentence and the parts of the sentence: subject, object (direct, indirect), complement (subject, object, infinitival), verb and verbal tense, type of clause, etc. A variant of Syntparse, called SEMPARSE, displays, in addition, the semantic group to which a particular word belongs.

(Note that a commercial copy of SYNTPARSE is available for free download on the Internet – see Internet Downloads at the end of the book.) The program saves much time and effort, because there is no need to locate the segment in the Dictionary of Segments and to look for its Parsing there – this is done by the computer automatically.

1 Identification of the segment

Here we will discuss the identification of a Syntactic Structure (a segment) within the sentence.

The segments are arranged in alphabetical order and presented as a Dictionary of Segments (DS), available on the Internet (see Internet Downloads at the end of the book). The segments are read by the algorithm (computer program), one after the other, in the sequence shown in the Dictionary.

The text to be parsed should be grammatically correct and semantically meaningful. The text is read from the beginning to the end, running word by running word, as they flow naturally in the formation of the text. Each consecutive running word is sent to the Dictionary of Wordforms (DW) to collect all grammatical (and semantic) information stored for it there. For example:

Running word	Grammatical Information
car	G, n
break	G, n, v
reading	G, Pi, n, P, Pv
elected	G, P1, P2, j, v
they	d, PPNC (plural)
she	d, PPNC (feminine singular)
etc.	

The running words from the sentence *The pianist, sitting down to play, gave her a brief look* will have the following grammatical choice registered in the Dictionary of Wordforms:

Wordform	Choice (grammatical information)
the	A, the
pianist	d, n, R
sitting	G, Pi, n, P, Pv
down	C, up, off
to	to
play	G, n, v
gave	v
her	R, O
a	A, a(n)
brief	G, v, n
look	n, v

Naturally the computer will have to choose only one alternative where there are several (as for *sitting, play, brief, look*). In order to do this, the computer runs the grammatical information of the first word of the sentence through the first members of the Syntactic Structures (the segments), marks those segments where the grammatical information of the first word matches the first element of the segment and then starts running the grammatical information of the second word of the text through the second members of those segments whose first elements were already identified, etc., till it reaches the end of the segment as registered in the DS.

The matching of a portion of the text with a segment from the DS is performed in the manner described below. Let's consider the same sentence as above. Horizontally, the numbers show the steps of the sequence of identification and choice, depending on the continuation of the segment(s). Vertically, the abbreviations show the choice(s) made at each step.

The	pianist	sitting	down	to	play	gave	her	a	brief	look.
1	2	1	2	3	4	1	2	3	4	5
A	d	G	up	to	G	v	R	A	G	n
	d	Pi	up	to	v	v	R	A	G	n
	d	Pi	off	to	n	v	O	A	n	v
	n	Pv	down			v	O	A	G	n

Chosen alternatives (matching existing segments):

The	pianist	sitting	down	to	play	gave	her	a	brief	look.
1		1	2	3	4	1	2	3	4	5
d		Pi	off	to	v	v	R	A	G	n

The choice of an alternative at each step is made on the condition that the segment can find a continuation for its next step:

    1 links to 2
    1 and 2 link to 3
    1 and 2 and 3 link to 4
    ... etc.

(i.e. the 2nd member is sought only if the 1st member of the sequence is already matched, the 3rd is sought only if the 1st and 2nd members match, etc., to the end of the segment, then a new segment is started and the same conditions applied.)

The above sentence will match the following segments from the Dictionary of Segments:

(i)   d
       Sj (pre-recorded Parsing – Subject)
(ii)   Pi up to v
       v (pre-recorded Parsing – Verb)
(iii) v R A G n
       v Oi Od (pre-recorded Parsing – Verb, Object Indirect, Object Direct)
       v Od Co (pre-recorded Parsing – Verb, Object Direct, Complement Object)

(the computer does not know yet whether R is Oi or Od)

If a shorter segment is identical with the initial part of a longer segment the shorter segment is disregarded and the longer segment is accepted. For example:

(1)   d v R   *I bought him.*
(2)   d v R A n   *I bought him a car.*

If the sentence from the text reads *I bought him a car*, then segment (1) is ignored and segment (2) is identified as the right one to match that particular portion of the text. Here is another example:

(2)   d v R A n   *I bought him a car.*
(3)   d v R A n b   *I bought him a car yesterday.*

If the portion of the text is *I bought him a car yesterday*, then segment (2) is discarded and segment (3) is considered to be identical to that particular portion of the text.

Thus the identification is carried out portion after portion, segment after segment, till the end of the sentence. In the case of two or more identical segments (when the initial parts coincide, as in the above examples) only the longest one to match the portion of text will be accepted. For example, the identification of the sentence below will be performed in the following order:

> *They want to believe | that they are going to be discovered | looking their best | behind closed doors, | just when | they thought | that all was lost, | by a man | who has battled | across continents.*

and the resulting segments will be as follows (the Parsing is shown below, in bold):

d v to v
Sj v
that d am Pi to be P2
that Sj **v**
Pi O best
v Od
behind G n   bl
just when
d TCv
Sj v
that M are j
that **Sj v Cs**
by A n   bi
who has P2
Sj v
across n   bl

When two (or more) segments of equal length happen to be identified with the same portion of text, then we are met with ambiguity on the syntactic level which can possibly be resolved on the semantic level. In this case both (or all) the segments are stored in the memory to await the respective semantic algorithm to process them, or the user is asked for help. For example:

(4)   d v R n Pi = *I found him home reading.* (Compare: *He was at home, reading.*)
(5)   d v R G n = *I found him home reading.* (Compare: *I found home reading for him.*)

since *home* can be G, n, etc., *reading* can be Pi, P, n, etc.
Or:

(6)   d v O n n = *John gave his baby money.* (Compare: *John gave money to his baby.*)

(7)   d v O G n = *John gave his baby money.* (Compare: *money he was given as a baby.*)

since *baby* can be G, n, etc.

   If the identification of (6) or (7) continues, because the portion of the text has not ended; e.g. in *John gave his baby money to buy a doll*, then the ambiguity will remain for the computer so long as there are two identical segments,

(6a)   d v O n n to v A n
(7a)   d v O G n to v A n

though for the humans the ambiguity has now ceased to exist. Compare for contrast:

(8)   *John gave his baby money to Richard the second.*
      d   v   O G   n   to n   A n

In such cases there are two alternatives:

a) the program alerts the user and asks him (her) to intervene and choose the correct option;
b) the program automatically switches on the respective algorithm for semantic disambiguation.

   The algorithmic procedure for identification of a portion of text with a segment from the Dictionary of Segments will be as follows below.

1.1 Algorithmic notation of Algorithm No 7

Algorithm No 7 uses two dictionaries: the Dictionary of Wordforms and the Dictionary of Segments.

   NB The Dictionary of Wordforms contains both running words and phrases. The phrases are not placed in a separate dictionary for greater convenience. Each phrase is registered with its grammatical information. For example:

United States of America	= n
too well	= b
for a certain period of time	= b
for a change	= b
take place	= v
take over	= v
bring down	= v
... etc.	

Most phrases are compound Adverbs and phrasal (separable compound) Verbs.

The wordforms of the text are read one by one in the sequence they follow and are compared with the wordforms (or phrases) in the Dictionary of Wordforms. The reader can use any English Language (especially Pronouncing) Dictionary, if he (she) complies with the abbreviations for Parts of Speech adopted in this study (see Chapter 5 and the General Index of Abbreviations).

The Punctuation Marks to be reckoned with are presented below as List No 2. These Punctuation Marks interrupt the segment and the algorithm starts to identify the next segment in sequence (this is also done by the Auxiliary words, see List No 1 in section 3 of Chapter 6). The Punctuation Marks ignored by the program are shown below in List No 4, with one exception – when ' is used to designate the genitive of the Noun. The Inverted Commas used to emphasize a word, phrase or sentence are ignored.

List No 2 ; : , . ! ? ( ) -
List No 4 " '

The identification of the sentence with a segment or segments is carried out according to the following algorithmic procedure. The block-scheme of the procedure is shown in Figure 7.1.

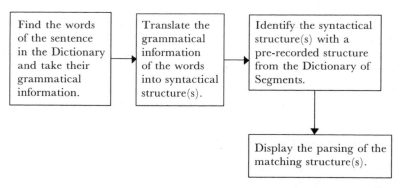

Figure 7.1   Block-scheme of the procedure

Here is the flow-chart notation of the same procedure:

1. Read the wordforms of the sentence (from full stop to full stop) one by one; has the sentence (or the text) ended?
2. Yes. Go to 1 to read the wordforms of the next sentence. If the text has ended, stop and end operation.
3. No. Take each individual wordform of the sentence (starting with the first) and compare it with the List presented in the Dictionary of Wordforms (DW). In those cases where the wordform from the text coincides with the first word of a phrase (or first words of more than one phrase) in the DW, take, consecutively, the next word(s) of the sentence and compare them with the phrase(s) in the DW to see if a phrase can be matched. If a phrase is

matched, take the grammatical information registered for the phrase and store it. Otherwise, take the grammatical information registered for that particular individual wordform and store it. If a wordform from the sentence cannot be matched with a wordform from the DW, display the wordform and ask the operator to register it in the DW together with its grammatical information. Then repeat the operation of identification.

The grammatical information of each wordform of the sentence is stored and presented as shown above (see the example with *The pianist, siting down to play, gave her a brief look.*). The words of the sentence are arranged in a horizontal sequence (as they follow), and the grammatical information is arranged vertically under each word (as shown above, p. 179).

NB A segment cannot be interrupted or cut to make it fit. Only a complete segment can be fitted into the whole sentence or part of it. The segments are fitted from left to right, one after the other, up to the end of the sentence. The next segment cannot begin before the previous one has ended. If several segments fit up to a certain length of the sentence, only the longest of them is accepted. The last segment should fit exactly into the place left between the end of the previous segment and the full stop (the end of sentence); if not, the operator is asked to intervene.

The procedure described above is similar to the identification procedures used in Text Processing, for example to match a word from the text with a word in the dictionary. In that case, a particular word from the text can match the initial parts of many other words in the dictionary, but finally, it has only one real match – the word that is absolutely identical to it from the first letter to the last. Similarly, being a fixed sequence of elements and having a fixed length, the segment, like the word, can match only an absolutely identical sequence contained in the sentence. Then the segments follow in sequence to form a sentence in the same way as the natural language words follow each other to form a sentence.

When a portion of the text is identified with a segment from the Dictionary of Segments, the computer checks if there is a long interval left indicating an instruction concerning that particular segment, and if there is such an instruction, carries it out. For example:

> *He is a tall one*
> d am A G one   Refer 'one' to the last **d** as Sj.
> Sj v Cs

Then, the program finds the last **d** used as Subject and refers *one* to it (replaces *one* with it). The parsing of the segment is shown under it. If several (or more) structures, following in alphabetical sequence, have the same parsing, the parsing is shown at the end of this sequence. A blank row (or dots) is left where no parsing is provided. For example:

> I m n are also Pi to v R
> I m n are also P2 G n
>   Sj v Od

all at once
all b Pi
all because
....

When a segment has more than one parsing it is marked as ambiguous and is stored to await further instructions to solve this ambiguity on a semantic level, or the operator is asked to intervene. For example, the two segments shown below have two possible parsings:

d has also P2 R b A n
d has also P2 R G n
Sj v Oi Od
Sj v Od Co

The segment and the sentence (each constituent element of it) always go together with their parsing, since the instructions of the algorithms can refer to either the segment or its parsing when decisions are to be made. For example:

She bought a nice house near London.
d   v   A G n   near   n
Sj   v   Od   bl

2 Parsing of the segment

There is no Text Processing (verification of the grammatical correctness of the Sentence, Machine Translation or Information Retrieval) without parsing.

The reader can find a definition of a Parse in Gazdar and Mellish (1989: 149) or McEnery (1992: 80). In principle, Parsing is synonymous with identifying the grammatical and syntactical structure of the sentence. In Text Processing, the outstanding problem is **what** structure, **how** it is structured and **with what rate of success**. There are different views and approaches to these questions, therefore the best thing would be to leave this to the critics and to the users to decide.

When we write, or speak, what we say is called *meaning*. The way we say it is called *grammar, syntax, style*. What we say and how we say it is a universal dilemma and a cherished subject of many schools of thought. Some (schools) recognize that **what** comes first and then they find a way **how** to express it. Others think that **what** and **how** are inseparable and they should be dealt with simultaneously.

We have taken the view that syntax, for the purposes of study and description, can be separated from the lexical and other semantic meaning, acknowledging the fact that then we deal only with the frame, not with the substance. In our case, the frame is the segment, understood most generally as a syntactically correct sequence of Parts of Speech.

However, in the segment we have introduced enough semantic information to make the Parsing a reality. This includes the differentiation between the Noun as a Subject (d) and as an Object (n, R), and the preservation of the Verbal Tenses, the Infinitive and the Adverb in their actual positions in the sentence, which has enabled us to determine the Complement and the Object in the Predicate (in the Verbal Phrase). In other words, the segment was born with its Parsing. The Parsing was predetermined by the internal structure of the segment. There was no need for lengthy algorithms to describe how to recognize the Parts of Speech (as we have done in Part 1) and, consequently, how to recognize the Parts of the Sentence.

The Parsing of the segment depends on the type and composition of the segment. The latter was discussed in Chapter 6, Section 3. In this section, in order to help the reader understand our Parsing method, we will provide examples to cover all possible varieties of segments and Parsings.

The most important element of the Sentence is the Subject (the doer) and then comes the Verb (the Predicate denoting action). For example:

(i)   *Teresa came.*
       d   v
       Sj   v

The Verb (as Tense) describes what the Subject does, did or will do.

Third in importance is the Object (Od) – the object of the action. Then the Subject and the Object (of the action) are placed in a relationship, described by a Verb (Verbal Tense). For example:

(ii)   *Peter asked Mary.*
       d   v   n
       Sj   v   Od
(iii) *Mary has bought a book.*
       d   has P2   A n
       Sj   v   Od

There are two varieties of Objects – Direct (Od) and Indirect (Oi). Examples (ii) and (iii) are for a Direct Object. This means that the connection, or the relationship between the Subject and the Object is direct. There is nothing to intervene to stand in between.

The Indirect Object (Oi) intervenes between the Subject and the Object. For example:

(iv)   *Mary has bought him a book.*
       d   has P2   R   A n
       Sj   v   Oi   Od

Compare:

(iv a) *Mary has bought a book for him.*
       Sj   v   Od   bp

All other elements (or parts) of the Sentence are Complements (or modifiers) either to the Subject, or the Verb, or the Object Direct. The

Complement explains, clarifies, brings additional information. Below we discuss the complements one by one.

1. Complement to the Subject (Cs). The Complement Subject can assume two positions in the segment.
   a) It can follow after an Auxiliary Verb from the **be** paradigm or after a modal verb (*shall*, etc.) plus **be** (*shall be*) (v, vi, vii), or after a linking Verb (*become, seem, feel*, etc.). What is usually meant by a Predicate Complement (Curme, 1955: 113), or by a Nominative Agreement (Hausser, 1989: 370) (as in examples v, vi, vii), we would prefer to call a Complement Subject, accepting that it is a Nominative Agreement when the Complement Subject contains a Noun. For example:

   (v)   *Mary is a housewife.*
          d   v A n
          Sj   v Cs

or

   (vi) *He must be the owner.*
          d shall be A n
          Sj v   Cs

Compare:

   (vii) *The girl on the chair is my sister.*
           A   d   on A n   are O n
           Sj   bl   v Cs
   (vii a) *My sister is on the chair.*
   (vii b) *My sister is the girl on the chair.*
   (vii c) *The girl is my sister.*

When the Adjective is used as a Second Argument (Hausser, 1989: 370) it is a Complement Subject. For example:

   (viii) *The man is hungry.*
            A   d am j
            Sj   v Cs

Compare:

   (viii a) *The hungry man (eats a cake).*
             A   G   d   v A n

showing that *hungry* can be used as an attribute to the Noun, without substantially changing the meaning of the sentence.

   b) It can follow immediately after the Subject, as part of an abridged Relative Clause. For example:

   (ix)   *The man eating the cake is hungry.*
           A   d Pi   A n   are j
           Sj   Cs   v Cs

Compare:

    (ix a)   *The man who eats the cake is hungry.*
           A   d   who v A n are j
           Sj   Sj v Od   Cs
           Sj   Cs

    (x)   *The man overboard is a pirate.*
           A   d   b   are A n
           Sj   Cs   v Cs

2. Complement to the Object (Co). The Complement Object always follows immediately after the Object Direct. For example:

    (xi)   *She called him a liar.*
           d   v   R A n
           Sj v   Od Co
    (xii)   *You must now say something funny.*
           d   shall also v UF   j
           Sj v   Od   Co

Some authors (Graver, 1971: 146) point out that the Infinitive can also be used as an Object to the Verb. Compare:

    (xiii)   *I want to stay.*
           d v   to v

However, we would prefer to call the Infinitive in this and in other cases an Infinitival Complement (Ic), because of its varied use (xiv, xv). For example:

    (xiv)   *She asked him to wait.*
           d   v   R to v
           Sj v   Od Ic
           Sj v   Od Co

In (xiv) the Subject of the Infinitive is also the Object of the Main Verb, the Infinitive playing the role of a Complement Object.

    (xiv a) *He was the first man to go.*
           d am A G   n   to v
           Sj v   Cs   Ic
           Sj v   Cs   Cs

In (xiv a) the Subject of the Infinitive is a Complement Subject, the Infinitive is also a Complement Subject.

    (xiv b) *The crowd watched the procession pass.*
           A   n   v   A n   v
           Sj   v   Od   Ic
           Sj   v   Od   Co

Note the ambiguity:

    A n   v   A G n
    Sj   v   Od

In (xiv b) the Infinitive is used without the Particle *to*.

    (xiv c)   *To read is to know.*

    to   v   are to v
    Sj   v
    Sj   v   Cs

In (xiv c) the Infinitive *to read* is used as a Subject.

    (xv)   *I went with them to drink a beer.*

    d v   with R   to v   A n
    Sj v   be   v   Od
    Sj v   be   Ic

In (xv) the Main Verb and the Infinitive form a single unit. Compare:

    (xv a)   *I went to drink a beer.*

    Sj   v Od

According to Curme (1955: 108) the Infinitival Complement in example (xv) will be an instance of Predicate Appositive used instead of a Clause of Purpose.

3. Complement to the Verb. The Adverb, the adverbial phrase, the Prepositional Adverbial Clause and the Infinitival Complement are used to elucidate the meaning of the Verb. For example:

    (xvi)   *We went to the town by car.*

    d   v   to A n   by n
    Sj   v   bdl   bi

The Adverbial Clauses in (xvi) explain further the meaning of the Verb (the action denoted by the Verb): towards what location (bdl) and by what instrument or means (bi).

    (xvii)   *Today it rained the whole day.*

    b   it v   A G   FB
    b   Sj v   bm

In (xvii) the Adverb (b) and the adverbial phrase (bm) add more information to the meaning of the Verb, pointing out the time of action.

    (xviii) *It has started to grow.*

    it has P2   to v
    Sj v   Ic

In (xviii) the Infinitival Complement explains what has started. In this case, the Infinitival Complement refers only to the action of the Verb.

However, in (xiv d) below the Infinitival Complement refers indirectly to the Verb and directly to the Object, if we consider the entire **that**-clause to be the Object of the Verb *said* (xivd b). Compare:

(xiv d) *She said that he should have to wait.*
         d   v   that d should have to v
(xiv da) Sj   v   that Sj v   Ic
(xiv db) Sj   v   Od

The fact that the abridged form of the Infinitival Complement can be used as a Complement Object (xix) suggests that the Infinitival Complement in such cases as (xix a) plays the same role.

(xix)   *He deemed him an honest man.*
          d v   R   A G   n
          Sj v   Od Co

(xix a) *He deemed him to be an honest man.*
          d v   R to be A G   n
          Sj v   Od Ic

It seems that the Parsing of the segments starting with **there** (*there are, there has, there can, there shall, there v*) is somewhat controversial. In some languages 'there + Verb' is recognized as an impersonal Verb. In English, Curme (1955: 100) calls it 'anticipatory' *there* and terms it a provisional Subject to the real Subject (xx).

(xx)   *In this building there lived an interesting woman.*
        in i   n   there v A G   n
        Sj   v Sj

So far as the real Subject is concerned, all English language dictionaries and Hausser (1989: 370) confirm this, saying that the Subject is used as Predicate of Auxiliaries (xxi).

(xxi)   *There are people ...*
      v   Sj

However, if we take the view point that 'there + Verb' is an impersonal Verb, then we can also assume that the real Subject is missing (xxi) or unspecified (xxii) and that what follows after it is either a Complement Subject (xxi a, xxi b), a Subject (xxi c) or an Object (xxii). Through a transformation, the Prepositional Adverbial Clause can also become a Subject (xxii b).

(xxi)   *There are people ...*
(xxi a) *I am one of them.*
(xxi b) *You are one of them.*
... etc. Sj   v   Cs
(xxi c) *There are people, who eat bananas.*
            Sj   Sj   v Od

(xxii)   *There are two apple trees in my garden.*
    v   Od   bl

(xxii a) *I have two apple trees in my garden.*
    Sj v Od   bl

(xxii b) *My garden contains two apple trees.*
    Sj   v   Od

Below there is a list of the most common Parsing sequences met in the English sentence (the Adverb and the Prepositional Adverbial Phrase are excluded – for details concerning their position in these Parsing sequences see the Dictionary of Segments):

(xxiii)   Sj
(xxiv)   Sj v
(xxv)   Sj v Cs
(xxvi)   Sj v Od
(xxvii)   Sj v Od Co
(xxviii)   Sj v Oi Od
(xxix)   Sj v Od Ic
(xxx)   Sj v Od Co Ic
(xxxi)   Sj v Ic
(xxxii)   Sj v Cs Ic
(xxxiii)   Sj Cs v Cs

For more information see the Dictionary of Segments.

The Parsing terminology used in this study closely follows that used by Quirk *et al.* (1972).

2.1 Parsing ambiguities

No parsing system can be perfect for two reasons:

a) many ambiguities inherent in the language cannot be resolved;
b) the Parsing System is not powerful enough to parse what to our human minds is unambiguous. In other words, the ambiguity does not exist in the text (in the sentence), it is created by the inability of the Parsing System to cope efficiently with the text.

We will concentrate our attention on the latter problem, since the former is well documented in the literature.

The ambiguities that could arise using our Parsing System are of the following types:

a) ambiguities that may occur within the segment – when a certain portion of text matches more than one segment;
b) ambiguities that may arise at the juncture of the segments – when the same sentence can have two (or more) presentations in view of the uncertain boundaries between the constituent segments (when it is not clear where the previous segment should end and the next should begin);

c) ambiguities inherent in detached (or incomplete) segments, when a segment is split by an intervening segment and therefore its pre-recorded parsing allows for more than one possibility.

Algorithm No 7 matches the segments by using a deterministic approach. One can improve the algorithm by making it display the different options, so that the operator can intervene and choose the right option.

2.1.1 Ambiguities within the segment

This type of ambiguity can be subdivided into three groups:

a) when a portion of a text matches more than one segment and all these segments have the same pre-recorded Parsing. This type of ambiguity is due mainly to the fact that some Parts of Speech are regarded as equal in function and marked so respectively in the Dictionary of Wordforms (m = G, m = n, S = G, S = n, Pi = n, P = n, etc.). For example:

(i)	*They have money.*			
(i a)	d	has	n	
(i b)	d	v	n	
	Sj	v	Od	
(ii)	*The first man came.*			
(ii a)	A	S	n	v
(ii b)	A	G	n	v
	Sj			v

In this case, the ambiguity is ignored and the analysis of the sentence continues uninterrupted.

b) when a portion of the text matches one segment, but this segment happens to have two possible parsings (iii, iv). For example:

(iii)	*She bought him flowers.*			
	d	v	R	n
	Sj	v	Oi	Od
	Sj	v	Od	Co

The above segment has two parsings because it can match such sentences as iii a and iii b:

(iii a) *She thought him rich.*
   d v R n
   Sj v Od Co
(*rich* can be a Noun or an Adjective)

(iii b) *She gave him money.*
   d v R n
   Sj v Oi Od

(iv)   *a big house*
        A G n
          Sj
          Od

Compare:

(iv a)   *A big house | on the lake |costs much.*
         Sj
(iv b)   *They bought | a big house | in Paris.*
                         Od

Example (iv) serves to illustrate the problem with the incomplete (detached) segments (see 2.1.3).

If in example (iii) we use *her*, instead of *him*, the ambiguity will be different:

She bought her flowers.
d   v   R n
d   v   O n
Sj   v   Oi Od
Sj   v   Od Co
Sj   v   Od

Since the so called 'linking Verbs' (Curme, 1955: 106) are not taken into separate account, only one Parsing is provided instead of the two possible (v and v a). For example:

(v)   *She became a mother.*
        d   v   A n
        Sj   v   Od

is also equivalent to

(v a)   *She is a mother.*
        d   am A n
        Sj v   Cs

If, however, this phenomenon is seen from a different angle, it may no longer be considered as a Parsing problem.

In the case where the computer software program is faced with two options, there are two possibilities: either to switch on a subroutine to select the right alternative (say by checking whether *flowers* can be used as an Adjective and see that it cannot be used as an Adjective because it is in the plural, or to check what Verbs, after the Subject, can be used with the Object and what with the Complement Object) or to interrupt the analysis of the sentence and ask the user for help.

Below we present an efficient algorithm (Algorithm No 21) to facilitate the choice when we have two alternatives: a segment that can be either a Subject or an Object (see example (iv) above).

Algorithm No 21 to choose between Subject and Object (for appositional segments marked as Subject or Object).

1. Is Sj/Od segment preceded by a full stop?
2. Yes. Record: a Sj. Go to the next segment marked Sj or Od. Go to 1. (For brevity we will use: Go to 1).
3. No. Is Sj/Od immediately preceded by Sj/Od, which in turn is preceded by a full stop?
4. Yes. Same as 2.
5. No. Is Sj/Od preceded by:
   Sj v Oi Od
   Sj v Od
   Sj am Pi Oi Od
   Sj am Pi Od
   Sj has P2 Oi Od
   Sj has P2 Od   ?
6. Yes. Record: Od. Go to the next Sj/Od. Go to 1.
7. No. Is Sj/Od followed by **b**-clause(s)?
8. Yes. Same as 2.
9. No. Is Sj/Od followed by a segment that starts with v (Verb) or by a segment that starts with **am** (**was, were, are**)?
10. Yes. Same as 2.
11. No. Is Sj/Od followed by another Sj/Od (or up to 3 other Sj/Od segments), in turn followed by a **v**-segment or by an **am** (**was, were, are**)-segment?
12. Yes. Same as 2.
13. No. Is Sj/Od segment followed by **and** + Sj/Od segment, which in turn is followed by a **b**-clause or by a **v**-segment or by an **am**-segment?
14. Yes. Same as 2.
15. No. Unrecognized. Ask operator for help. Go to the next Sj/Od. Go to 1.

c) when a portion of the text matches two segments, both of which have different Parsing. For example:

(vi)	*They took the Earl prisoner.*			
(vi a)	d	v	A n	n
	Sj	v	Od	Co
(vi b)	d	v	A G	n
	Sj	v	Od	

(On the condition that in the Dictionary of Wordforms *Earl* is marked both as an Adjective and as a Noun.) This type of ambiguity can be seen in yet another example:

(vii)	*Her worst vice is smoking.*			
(vii a)	O	G	n are Pi	
	Sj		v	

(vii b) O   G   n   are n
         Sj   v   Cs

(of which only **vi a** and **vii b** are correct). At this stage, the only solution would be to ask the user to intervene and to choose the correct alternative.

2.1.2   Ambiguities arising at the juncture of the segments

One of the main reasons for this kind of ambiguity is that some Verbs can be used both with and without Prepositions or Adverbial Adjuncts (*bring, bring in; look, look after*, etc.) and the computer program would not know if the Preposition is used with the Verb or belongs to the Adverbial Clause that follows next. We have tried to nip this ambiguity in the bud by listing those Prepositional Verbal Phrases that are almost idiomatic as one-word entries in the Dictionary of Wordforms. Another thing that could be done in this case would be to check if at the juncture there are two consecutive Prepositions. If so, this is an indication that the first Preposition is part of the Verb and the second is part of the Adverbial Clause (i).

(i)   *They went on with their work.*
        d   v   up with O   n

Selecting the longest segment is no solution in (iii), although it works in (ii).

(ii)   *I passed on the messages of sympathy.*
        d v   up A n   of n
        Sj v   Od
(iii)   *I landed on a heap of stones.*
        d v   up A n   of n
        Sj v   Od

The correct parsing for (iii) is:

(iii a) *I landed on a heap of stones.*
         d v   on A n   of n
         Sj v   bl

The two sentences are absolutely identical, but their sequences of Parts of Speech are not, and hence their Parsing is also different: (ii) is one sentence that is equal to one segment; (iii) is one sentence that is composed of two segments, the second of which is an Adverbial Clause. There is no conceivable way to resolve this problem on purely formal syntactical grounds, though we can suggest the following amendment to Algorithm No 7: when the identification of the segment reaches a Preposition, the software program should offer two alternatives. The first alternative will be to continue, as in (ii), and to identify the longest segment (available in the Dictionary of Segments). The second alternative will be to interrupt the previous segment before the Preposition, assuming that the Preposition starts a Prepositional

Adverbial Clause, and to try to identify it with an existing segment. At the output, examples (ii) and (iii) will be presented as (ii) and (ii a) and (iii) and (iii aa), and the user will be asked to intervene to make the correct choice.

(ii a)   *on the messages of sympathy*
(iii aa) *on a heap of stones*

Yet another example of the same sort is presented in (iii b, iii c, iii d):

(iii b) *She clumsily knocked over a chair.*
        d   also   v   A n
        Sj   v   Od
(where *knock over* = v)

(iii c) *She clumsily knocked over a chair.*
        d   also   v   up A n
        Sj   v   Od
(where *knock over* = v up)

(iii d) *She clumsily knocked over a chair.*
        d   also   v   over A n
        Sj   v   bdl

where (iii b) and (iii c) match two different segments having the same Parsing (*knocked over* is presented in the DW as one word, therefore the resulting structure in (iii b), but a great number of other Verbs filling this position will give rise to (iii c) and (iii d)).

Another reason for an ambiguity at the borderline of the segments is the fact that the Indicative Pronoun **that** and the Conjunction **that** coincide. When a sentence encompasses **I** or **i** (signs for an Indicative Pronoun), the computer software program using this method would not know if **that** is used as an Indicative Pronoun and therefore is part of the previous segment, or if it is used as a Conjunction and is the first element of a new segment (a Subordinate Clause). Following the rule that the longer segment has precedence, the program may come up at the output with a wrong Parsing (iv a). For example:

(iv)   *We can no longer say that within the current structure this is so.*
(iv a) d shall also v I   within A G n I are b
        Sj v   Od bl   Sj v Pr
(iv b) d shall also v that within A G n I are b
        Sj v   that bl   Sj v Pr

where *that* in (iv a) is identified as Object, instead of being identified as a Conjunction as in (iv b). To remedy this problem, we would have to amend Algorithm No 7 in the same way as we would do for the Prepositions (examples (ii) and (iii)): the computer program will provide two versions at the output (iv a) and (iv b) and the user will be asked to choose one of them.

2.1.3   Ambiguities inherent in the incomplete segments

Let's consider the following sentences:

   (i)   *'You have acted bravely', was his answer.*
           d   has P2   up   are O n
           Sj   v   b   v   Sj

Compare:

   (i a)   *His answer was 'You have acted bravely'.*
           Sj   v   Sj   v   Pr
   (ii)   *This, without any   doubt, was his answer.*
           I   without any n   are O n
           Sj   Prep. Adv. Clause v Cs

where the incomplete segment **are O n** will have two parsings (i, ii), depending on the context.

Other factors that may affect the overall performance of the computer software program developed on this basis are the choice of the programming language and the ingenuity of the programmer.

8   Links of predicates and incomplete segments

All links, before being syntactic, are logical links as well as semantic links. In Text Processing, there is a need to establish (also algorithmically) the link of a) Predicative appositive (as part of a segment, or as interrupted segment) and b) Interrupted segment, where a segment is interrupted by another segment (the intervening segments are usually adverbial or appositional) and its two parts are cut off from one another.

This is a very common practice in English and no computational grammar can avoid it, because of its significance. Compare, for example:

(i)   *He rose to   his feet to greet us.*
         d   v   to O n   to v   R
         Sj   v   bn   v   Od
                                  Ic

(i a)   *He rose to greet us.*

NB The links of the predicates and of the incomplete segments described below do not have the strength of algorithms. They should be used only as general guidelines.

1 Links of P1

The Participle 1st (P1) represents the Past Participle forms of the regular (*-ed*) and the irregular Verbs. There are two possibilities for the P1.

a) To be an integral part of a segment, positioned before a Noun (as an attribute to the Noun, marked as G), after the Subject (as Complement Subject, marked as P1), after the Auxiliary Verb or Verbal Tense used as a Linking Verb (as Complement Subject, marked as P1), or after the Object (as Complement Object, marked as P1).

If the segment ends with P1 this means that:

1.   The P1 is a Complement Object if preceded by the Object. If not, it is a Complement Subject when preceded by a linking verb and should be linked to the Subject of the same segment, to its left, according to the formulae:

Sj is P1 (1)
Od is P1 (2)

2. The P1 should also be put at the beginning of the next segment (i da, ii da below).

These algorithmic operations start immediately after the appearance of P1 at the end of the segment. For example:

(i)   *He remained seated on the sofa.*
        d   v   P1   on A n
        Sj v   Cs   bl
(ii)   *I found her dressed for the party.*
        d   v   R P1   for A n
        Sj v   Od Co   bp

The above sentences consist of two segments:

(i a)   *He remained seated*   = d v P1
(i b)   *on the sofa.*   = on A n
(ii a)   *I found her dressed*   = d v R P1
(ii b)   *for the party.*   = for A n

Since the first segments end with P1, in accordance with the above instructions (1) and (2) the computer will make the following arrangements for further clarification of the links of the P1 and of the meaning of the sentence as a whole:

(i c)   *He is seated.*
(i d)   *He remained seated*
(i da)   *seated on the sofa.*
(ii c)   *She is dressed.* (since *her = she*)
(ii d)   *I found her dressed*
(ii da)   *dressed for the party.*

Or in another example:

(iii)   *The method employed in measuring the pressure in the renal vessels was one based upon the general principle employed in human blood pressure estimations.*

When processed by Algorithm No 7 this sentence will yield the following segments:

(iii a)   *The method employed*   = A n P1
(iii b)   *in measuring the pressure*   = in P A n
(iii c)   *in the renal vessels*   = in A G n
(iii d)   *was one based*   = was one P1
(iii e)   *upon the general principle employed* = upon A G n P1
(iii f)   *in human blood pressure estimations.* = in G G G n

Following the instruction concerning P1, the computer will 'know' that the following links must be made:

(iii g)   *The method is employed*
                        employed in measuring the pressure
(iii h)   *in renal vessels.*
(iii j)   *The method was one based*
                        based upon the general principle employed
(iii k)   *employed in human blood pressure estimations.*

Before linking the P1, check first to see if the P1 is at the end of an Adverbial Prepositional Segment. If so, do not link it to the Subject! If the P1 is at the end of an Adverbial Prepositional segment, link it to the Noun immediately preceding it, using the formula (see iii j, iii k):

n are P1 (3)

(iii l)   *the general principle is employed in ...*

b) To start its own segment (**P1**-segment). In this case the **P1**-segment (being cut off) is an integral part of another segment within the sentence, and should be linked to its Subject. All segments beginning with P1 are Cs (Complement Subject). There are some exceptions to this rule.

If the **P1**-segment starts the sentence or is not preceded by a Subject (to the left till full stop) then it should be linked to the first Subject to the right. For example (in (iv) the **P1**-segment *surprised* is cut off by a Prepositional Adverbial Segment, the **by**-segment):

(iv)   *Surprised by this turn of events she remained hidden behind the door.*
         P1   by I   n   of n   d   v   P1   behind A n
         Cs   br   Sj   v   Cs   bl
(iv a)   *She is surprised.*
(iv b)   *She is hidden.*

The above instruction is also applied to all segments starting with 'not P1'. The formula then will read:

Sj am not P1 (4)

However, when the **P1**-segment consists only of P1 and does not start the sentence, then a more elaborate algorithmic procedure is needed to decide how it should be linked. Then it is more likely to link the **P1**-segment to the **d** (the Noun designating a human being) of the preceding Adverbial segment than to the Subject of the sentence.

2 Links of Pi

The Participle '-ing' can be used either as an integral part of a segment or to start a segment of its own, and depending on this it can have the following links.

If the segment ends in Pi, this means that Pi should remain at the end of this segment as it is, but it should also be put at the beginning of the next segment. This algorithmic operation starts with the appearance of Pi at the end of the segment. For example:

(i) *She saw him practising in the yard.*
d   v   R Pi   in A n
Sj   v   Od Co   bl

(i a) *She saw him practising*
(i b)   *practising in the yard.*

When Pi is Complement Object to R (as in (i)), then the logical link to be used by the computer should be made according to the formula:

1. Find the reference of R (if the reference of R is a PPNC find its reference).
2. Replace R with its reference. Then use the reference of R in the formula

R are Pi (1)
R is Pi
(R was Pi)
(R were Pi)

Using the above formula the computer will 'know' that:

(i c) *He is practising.*

because the reference of *him* is *he*. If the reference of *He* is *John*, then we will have:

(i d) *John is practising in the yard.*

When Pi is a Complement Object to a Noun, no reference of the Noun is needed. Simply use the formula:

n are Pi (2)
Co

For example:

(i e) *He watched the water streaming through a hole.*
d v   A n   Pi   through A n
Sj v   Od   Co   bl
(i ea) *the water is streaming*

When Pi is a Complement Subject, then link it to the Subject using the formula

Sj are Pi (3)
Sj is Pi

For example:

(i f) *The girl sitting on the chair is my sister.*
d   Pi   on A n   are O n
Sj   Cs   bl   v Cs

Using formula (3) the computer will know that:

(i fa)   *The girl is sitting on the chair.*

When Pi is an integral part of a segment and is used in the Predicative immediately after the Verbal Tense, then it should be linked to the Subject of the same segment using formula (3):

(i g)   *She started singing at the age of five.*
          d   v   Pi   at A n of n
          Sj   v   bm
(i ga)   *She is singing.*

In the case of a **Pi**-segment where Pi starts the segment and is followed by a sequence that includes a Possessive Pronoun (Pi + O + ...), then use the following formula to link Pi:

(the referent of O) + was + (Pi + O + ...) (4)

For example, if we have the segment:

(i h)   Pi O n = *taking his coat*
          and if the referent of *his* is *Leon*, then we will have
(i j)   *Leon was taking his coat.*

(NB Remember that **was** stands for *is*, *were* and *are* as well.)

If the **Pi**-segment is followed by a **like**-segment, then link the **Pi**-segment to the last Noun to the left (no matter whether Subject or Object) – excluding the Nouns in the Adverbial Clauses – using the formula:

Noun are Pi (5)

(i k)   *He stayed at home all day singing like mad.*
          d   v   at n   M FB Pi   like n
          Sj   v   bl   bm   bn
(i ka)   *He is singing.*

In (i k) the **Pi**-segment (*singing*) is cut off by intervening Prepositional Adverbial segments (bl) and (bm).

If the **Pi**-segment is preceded by a **which**-segment, link it to the Noun preceding *which* (the referent of *which*) using formula (5).

If Pi is part of a **not**-segment (*not Pi*), or part of an **as if**-segment (*as if Pi*), then connect the **not Pi** or **as if Pi** segment to the last Subject using the formula:

Sj am Pi (6)

If Pi is part of a **without**-segment (*without Pi*) then link the **without Pi** segment to the last Subject using the formula:

Sj am not Pi (7)

The above instructions should follow in the presented order. Having completed the instructions shown above, then follow the instructions presented below.

In the case of a **Pi**-segment, link the **Pi**-segment to the Subject of the same sentence (to the last Subject if the **Pi**-segment is preceded by a Subject (i l), or to the next Subject if the **Pi**-segment starts the sentence (i m)). If, however, there is no Subject either to the left or to the right within the same sentence, then the Participle '-ing' (Pi) is a Gerund and, if followed by a Verbal Tense, is the Subject of the segment (i n) and need not be linked to another segment (in other cases, when the Verbal Tense is an Auxiliary Verb only from the **be** paradigm, it is a Complement Subject (i na)). For example:

(i l)   *The glomerular membrane plays a passive role performing no work.*
          A G   n   v   A G   n Pi   no n
          Sj   v   Od   v   Cs

Hence:

(i la)   *The glomerular membrane is performing no work.*
(i m)   *Trying to escape from the thorny grasp of the bush, she tore her blouse.*
          Pi   to v   from A G   n   of A n   d v   O n
                         bl (bp, bs)   Sj v   Od
(i ma)   *She is trying to escape.*
(i n)   *Reading came last on his agenda.*
          P   v   up on O n
          Sj   v   bm
(i na)   *Reading is   his favourite pastime.*
          P   are O G   n
          Cs   v Sj
  or: Sj   v Cs

If the first Subject to the left is *who*, link the **Pi**-segment to *who* and after that link it to the referent of *who*. For example:

(i o)   *The man, who came to the office asking questions . . .*
          d   who v   to A n   Pi   n
          Sj   Sj v   bl
(i oa)   *The man was asking questions.*

If, however, the **Pi**-segment extends from full stop to full stop do not touch it. Leave it as it is.

In the case where a **Pi**-segment starts with *not* one should use formula (7).

If the **Pi**-segment consists only of one word, the Participle '-ing', then link it to the last Object to the left if it does not start the sentence.

3 Links of the j-segment

If the **j**-segment extends from full stop to full stop, leave it as it is. Otherwise, if the **j**-segment starts the sentence, link it to the first Subject to the right; if not, link it to the last Subject (to the left). For example:

(i)   *Aware of her presence he remained silent.*
       j   of O n   d v   j
                              Sj v   Pr
                              Sj v   Cs

(i a)   *He is aware of her presence.*
       d am j   of O n
       Sj v Cs

(ii)   *She packed her suitcase, in haste, ready to leave.*
       d   v   O n   in n   j   to v
       Sj v   Od   bn

(ii a) *She is ready to leave.*
       d am j   to v
       Sj v Cs Ic

The linkage was made according to the following formula:

    Sj am **j**-segment   (1)

If **j** is alone, between commas, and to the left there is no Subject, then link it to the first Noun to the right:

(iii)   *Near her, silent, stood a man I knew.*
       b   R j   v   A n   d v
       bl   v   Od Sj v

(iii a) *A man was silent.*

If **j** is alone in the sentence, between commas, and to the right there is no Noun to follow till the end of the sentence, then connect it to the last Noun to the left excluding the Noun in a **b**-clause, using the formula:

    n was j   (2)

4 Links of the G-segment

When G is alone in the sentence, between commas, and to the right there is no Noun to follow till the end of the sentence, then connect it to the last Noun to the left, but not to a Noun in a **b**-clause, using the formula:

    n was G   (1)

If the **G**-segment consists of a G and a Noun or of several G (in sequence) and a Noun and is positioned between commas, then connect the **G**-segment to the first Subject to the left, within the same sentence, using the formula:

    Sj am G-segment   (2)

If the Subject is a PPNC find its referent and use it instead.

5 Links of the v-segment

Verbal segments cannot usually exist on their own without a Subject, therefore they should always be linked to the first Subject to the left, except when the **v**-segment:

a) extends from full stop to full stop;
b) begins with *let, let's*;
c) ends with an Exclamation Mark;
d) is preceded by:

> d TCv
> Sj v

e) is preceded by an Adverbial segment.

The other verbal segments – all those beginning with *am, are, did, has, can, should, may,* etc. – should also be linked to a Subject, except when they end with a Question Mark or are preceded by an Adverbial segment. Other exceptions include *may* and *should* after a full stop (at the start of a sentence) (iv, below), and *was, is* or *are* when they are separated from the Interrogative Pronoun (*what, why, how, where, when, which*) (vi) or predicate a Subject (on their right) (vii).

When the **v**-segment does not start the sentence and there is no Subject to the left, or when between the Subject and the **v**-segment there is a Prepositional Adverbial Clause containing R or a **b**-segment, then link the **v**-segment to the Prepositional Adverbial Segment or Adverbial segment (**b**-segment) positioned to the left (i), (ii), (iii):

> C R
> until A n

> (i)   *Near her, silent, stood a man I didn't know.*
> (i a)   *Near her stood a man.*
> (ii)   *Until the man on the horse was able to see him …*
> (ii a)   *Until the man was able to see him …*
> (iii)   *When the bus comes for you, get these men to help you.*
> (iii a) *When the bus comes get these men to help you.*
> (iii b) *You get these men to help.*

For the link in (iii b) we need an additional specification.

Modal Verbs like *may, should,* etc. at the start of a sentence, need no linking (iv):

> (iv)   *May you live happily for ever.*
> (v)   *Should you see him, tell him that I am here.*

The segments starting with an Auxiliary Verb, in direct and reported speech, are also a special case (vi, vii):

> (vi)   *'And what', Ann said flatly, 'is a solution?'*

(vii)   *'You have acted bravely', was her answer.*
$$\text{Sj}$$

Compare:

(vi a)   *She said, you have acted bravely.*

6 Links of the and-segment

The **and**-segment should always be linked to the previous segment. When the **and**-segment is followed by a **v**-segment, separate the **v**-segment and link it according to the instructions in Section 5.

7 Links of the Infinitive

The Infinitive, when cut off from a segment, should be linked (jumping the intervening segment) to the preceding segment starting with a Subject (Sj v, Sj v Cs) within the same sentence (i), with the exception of

d   TCv
(*John said*)
Sj   v

In other cases, the Infinitive should be linked to the Object, to its left (ii).

(i)   *It is dishonourable do you understand, to trade nowadays in weapons of war.*
it was j   did d v   to v   b   in   n   of n
Sj v Cs   v Sj v   Ic   ba (br)

(i a)   *It is dishonourable to trade nowadays ...*

(ii)   *She requested them, at my suggestion, to stay with her.*
d   v   R   at O n   to v   with R
Sj   v   Od br   Ic   be

(ii a)   *She requested them to stay with her.*
d   v   R   to v   with R
Sj   v   Od Ic   be

(ii ab)   *They should stay with her.*

(In ii a the Infinitival Complement acts as a Complement Object.)

When the Infinitive starts the sentence and is used as its Subject (iii), then we need a transformational procedure.

(iii)   *To ride a bicycle on such a wet day is   awful.*
to v   A n   on I a(n) G n   am j
Sj   bm   v   Cs

Compare:

(iii a)   *It must be awful to ride a bicycle on such a wet day.*
it shall be j   to v   A n   on i   A G n
Sj   v Cs Ic   bm

8 Other links and discussion of the links

8.1 Links marked with two or three blank spaces left within a segment

When the computer matches a portion of the text with a segment from the Dictionary of Segments, the program will ignore the space left within the segment (this space is one or sometimes two intervals longer than the accepted space of one interval between the constituent elements of a segment). For example:

(i)   *The people in the bus are German*
          d   in A n   are n

will be marked as

(i a)   in A n   are n

(two intervals are left between **n** and **are**)

During the identification procedure the interval left before **are** will be ignored, but it will serve as an indication that the part that follows after **are** should be linked to the previous segment. If three spaces are left, the part that follows should be linked to the first Subject to the left, before the full stop.

NB The two and three spaces left in a segment, to indicate that what follows is not part of the same segment, duplicate the situation where the disconnected part was separated as an incomplete segment (compare the segments starting with an Auxiliary Verb). In example (i) *are German* will be a separate segment and will obey the links specified in Section 5 above. It will not be linked to *in the bus* as above (i a).

NB We have preferred to separate the detached part of a segment and to register it as a separate, incomplete segment, rather than to link it to the segment it does not belong to and leave blank spaces.

8.2 Discussion of the links

Let's consider the following sentence:

(i)   *The girl sitting on the chair is my sister.*
          d   Pi   on A n   are O n
          Sj   Cs   bl   v   Cs

The constituent segments of this sentence are:

    d Pi
    on A n
    are O n

hence, according to the rules specified in Links (governing the Nominative

Agreement by using the paradigm of **be**), the computer software program will be able to produce the following true statements:

(i a)   *The girl sitting is my sister.*
(i b)   *The girl is sitting.*
(i c)   *The girl is sitting on the chair.*
(i d)   *The girl is my sister.*
(i e)   *My sister is the girl sitting.*
(i f)   *My sister is the girl sitting on the chair.*
(i g)   *My sister is sitting.*
(i h)   *My sister is sitting on the chair.*

9 Reference

1 Reference within the segment

The references within the segments are marked with the signs '' and '.

When the segment is being identified, the signs '' (except in N''s) and ' should be ignored. They are used to indicate the word links within a segment. In the following segments

    (i)   G n shall v n'' to v n of A n of O'' n
    (ii)   d v up R'' n up X''
    (iii)   A n'' Pi'' A n of O N''s n

the links indicate that in (i) the Possessive Pronoun marked with O'' refers to the Noun marked with n''; in (ii) the Reflexive Pronoun marked with X'' refers to the Personal Pronoun Objective Case, marked with R'' (and not to **d**!); in (iii) the Pi'' refers to the previous Noun.

The references within the segment are dealt with by Algorithm No 8.

1.1 Algorithm No 8 for the references within the segment

NB In this algorithm, the word *letter* means the abbreviation of a Part of Speech or a natural language word used in the segment.

1.   Read the segment letter by letter. Is the letter marked with the sign '' – except in N''s – (right top side of the letter)? (letter = Part of Speech which in turn = a wordform in the text).
2.   Yes. Remember it temporarily. Go on reading the segment to the end. Is there another letter marked with the same sign ''?
2a.   Yes. This letter (i.e. wordform) refers to the previous one also marked '' (the one that was remembered temporarily).
2b.   No. There is a mistake. Ask for help. Go to 1 to read the next segment.
3.   No. Is the letter marked with the sign ' – except when used with a natural language word to mark the Genitive of the Noun – (right top side of the letter)?
4.   Yes. Remember it temporarily. Go on reading the segment to the end. Is there another letter marked with the same sign '?

4a.   Yes. This letter (i.e. wordform) refers to the previous one marked ' (the one that was remembered temporarily).

4b.   No. There is a mistake. Ask the operator for help. Go to 1 to read the next segment.

5.   No. Is the letter marked with the sign '" (right top side of the letter)?

6.   Yes. Remember it temporarily. Go on reading the segment to the end. Is there another letter marked with the sign " or with the sign '?

6a.   Yes. Refer this letter (the one marked " or ') to the one marked '" (the one that was remembered temporarily).

6b.   No. There is a mistake. Ask the operator for help. Go to 1 to read the next segment.

7.   No. Is there a letter marked with the sign " then another letter, after it, marked with the sign ' or vice versa?

8.   Yes. Remember them temporarily. Go on reading the segment to the end. Is there another letter marked with the sign " "?

8a.   Yes. This letter refers to both previous letters marked respectively " and '.

8b.   No. There is a mistake. Ask the operator for help. Go to 1 to read the next segment.

9.   Go to 1 to read the next segment.

2 Pronominal Reference

The reference of a Pronoun to a particular Noun in the text is called Pronominal Reference. The Pronoun acts as a substitute for the Noun.

Pronominal Reference is based on meaning. Since meaning cannot function without syntax, it is possible to establish the Pronominal Reference using syntactical procedures. The syntactical procedures will be stated algorithmically (so that, eventually, they can be turned into computer software programs) for each Pronoun.

The algorithms dealing with Pronominal Reference use, as a database, the Dictionary of Wordforms, the Dictionary of Segments and the results of Algorithm No 7.

2.1 Identification of the Pronouns. Algorithm No 9

The segment, after identification with a portion from the text, is read letter by letter according to the procedure presented in Algorithm No 9 (*letter* stands for Part of Speech, which in turn represents a particular word from the text; *letter* also stands for a natural language word used in the segment):

1.   Is this O or Os? (the genitive of the Noun is excluded from O)
2.   Yes. Go to Algorithm No 10.
3.   No. Is this R? (names are excluded from R)
4.   Yes. Go to Algorithm No 11.
5.   No. Is this X?

6.   Yes. Go to Algorithm No 12.
7.   No. Is this PPNC (Personal Pronoun Nominal Case)?
8.   Yes. Go to Algorithm No 13.
9.   No. Is this Z?
10.   Yes. Go to Algorithm No 14.
11.   No. Is this **who**?
12.   Yes. Go to Algorithm No 15.
13.   No. Is this **which**?
14.   Yes. Go to Algorithm No 16.
15.   No. Is this **whom**?
16.   Yes. Go to Algorithm No 17.
17.   No. Is this **both**?
18.   Yes. Go to Algorithm No 18.
19.   No. Start to read the next segment. Go to 1.

At this stage one particular type of word reference is omitted. Here is an example of such word reference:

> *The missionary widows tittered still unsure of Jim's sense of humour and pushed their wooden cart. The iron wheels rang on the stony track shaking the body which the two women were about to bury.*

It will not be difficult to devise a procedure to find the referent of *The two women* which, in this case, is *the missionary widows*.

2.1.1   *Reference of the Possessive Pronoun. Algorithm No 10*

The Possessive Pronoun is marked as O or Os (the genitive of the Noun, marked as N''s, is excluded from O). The block-scheme of the algorithm is shown in Figure 9.1. The full flow-chart notation is available on the Internet (see Internet Downloads at the end of the book).

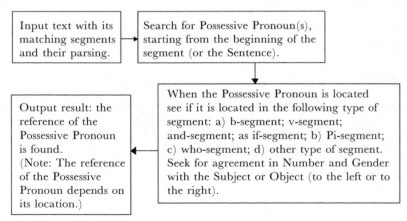

Figure 9.1   Block-scheme of Algorithm No 10

NB This algorithm is not perfect. On every 100 Possessive Pronouns processed, up to 2 per cent errors can be expected for various reasons. The main fault is that the computer program does not have sufficient knowledge yet, since we have given it only some grammatical and syntactical information and a very limited amount of semantic information, namely the knowledge of **d**. We hope that later, with the introduction of semantics, the computer will become more intelligent. But even then, if grammarians do not decide to introduce certain norms governing the use of Pronouns, it is doubtful whether Pronominal Reference can be made 100 per cent accurate. See the ambiguity in the following sentence(s):

(i)   *Monica (woman No 1), she (she No 2) reflected later, as they (woman No 1 and she No 2) strolled slowly along the lake shore, knows far more than I (I = she No 2) do; it is right that she (i.e. Mme de Lanneui, mentioned earlier in the text, she No 3) resembles a sphinx. The morning had passed quite pleasantly in her (Monica's) company.*

(ii) *Jim dipped a finger in the hot water but Dr Ransome brusquely waved him away. Clearly his (Ransome's) conversation with the camp commandant had upset him – he was preparing for the winter as if trying to convince himself that they would all be there when it arrived.*

In (i) the reference is very complicated. *Mme de Lanneui* (*she* No 3) is far back in the text, mentioned in a previous conversation between woman No 1 and *she* No 2. The Possessive Pronoun *her* in the last sentence can be erroneously referred to either *she* No 2 or *she* No 3, if the reference is not based on meaning.

In (ii) the reference is found correctly by the algorithm (Algorithm No 10), but it may well be *Jim* who might have talked to the commandant. Let us see, step by step, how Algorithm No 10 will find the reference of the Possessive Pronoun *his*.

Instruction 3 finds out that *his* is in a **b**-clause (after the full stop the segment starts with the Adverb *clearly* and ends with the appearance of the Preposition *with*) and proceeds with the analysis in 18. The main clause of the same sentence (*he was preparing*) does not have an Object. The analysis is passed on to 20, where it is seen that *his* does agree with the Subject *he* of the same sentence (see Table 9.1). We have to use Algorithm No 13 to find the referent of *he*. Instruction 17 of Algorithm No 13 requires an agreement with a **d**, as Subject, to the left in this paragraph (the first **d** as Subject to the left is considered first, excluding the **d** which is Subject of the Pronoun under analysis) and finds that *Ransome* (**d**, Subject, 3rd person singular – this information is taken from the Dictionary of Wordforms) agrees in gender and number with *he*. The referent of *his* is found – it is *Ransome*. Then the algorithm starts a search for the next Possessive Pronoun.

Table 9.1   Reference of O (Os)

O (Os)	Agrees with
I, d (masculine or feminine)	my, mine
you, d (masculine or feminine n)	your, yours
he, d (masculine)	his
she, d (feminine)	her, hers
it, n (d excluded) singular	its
we, d (plural)	our, ours
you, d (plural)	your, yours
they, d plural, n plural	their, theirs

2.1.2   Reference of PPOC. Algorithm No 11

Reference of the Personal Pronoun Objective Case marked R. The block-scheme of the algorithm is shown in Figure 9.2. The full flow-chart notation is available on the Internet (see Internet Downloads at the end of the book). On the Internet, Algorithm No 11 uses the information shown in Table 9.2.

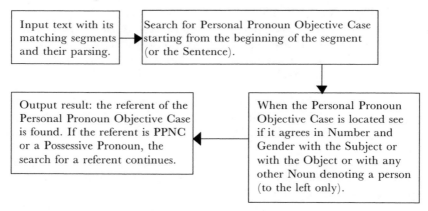

Figure 9.2   Block-scheme of Algorithm No 11

Table 9.2   Reference of PPOC

PPOC is marked as R.

R	Agrees with
I, d (masc. or fem.), N''s (d's)	me
d (masc. or fem.), N''s (d's)	your you yours
he, his, d (masculine)	him
she, her, d (feminine)	her
it, its, n (singular)	it
we, our, d and d, d and O d, d (plural)	us
you, your	you
they, their, d and d, d and O d, d (plural)	them

The reference of R is not 100 per cent accurate. It will be ambiguous in segments like

d v O m n = *I gave her 10 pounds.*
d v R m n = *I gave her 10 pounds.*

where R coincides with O, if that error is not corrected beforehand. The user should expect up to 2 per cent errors when the above procedure is implemented.

If we want to improve the reference of PPOC, we will have to introduce strict grammatical regulations governing their use – the same as those for spelling.

In order to illustrate the performance of Algorithm No 11, let us consider again the last sentence.

(i) *Jim dipped a finger in the hot water but Dr Ransome brusquely waved him away. Clearly his conversation with the camp commandant had upset him – he was preparing for the winter as if trying to convince himself that they would all be there when it arrived.*

The analysis of the first *him* (*waved him away*) starts with instruction 1 (where it is seen that *him* is not equal to *me*) and proceeds, without result, to instruction 7, where the algorithm finds out that *him* agrees with *Jim* in number and gender (*Ransome* is excluded from consideration, being the Subject of the same segment), and instruction 8b decrees to replace *him* with *Jim* (i a).

(i a) ... *but Dr Ransome brusquely waved Jim away.*

The analysis of the second *him* (*the camp commandant had upset him*) begins with instruction 1 and goes further, unsuccessfully, until it reaches instruction 7, where the procedure establishes the fact that *him* agrees with *his* as the Subject of a previous segment in number and gender (note that the **with-**segment separates this particular segment into two parts, functioning now as independent segments). Since the referent is a Possessive Pronoun, Algorithm No 10 must find the referent of the Possessive Pronoun and then *him* can be replaced with it (i b).

(i b) *Clearly Dr Ransome's conversation with the camp commandant had upset Dr Ransome ...*

2.1.3 Reference of the Reflexive Pronoun. Algorithm No 12

The Reflexive Pronoun is marked with X.

1. Is X in the plural?
2. Yes. Go to 8.
3. No. Does X agree with the d in the previous segment (see Table 9.3)?
4. Yes. Refer X to that **d**. Take next X and go to 1.
5. No. Does X agree with the last **d** (to be understood the first to the left) from the same sentence till a full stop?

6.   Yes. Refer X to that **d**. Take next **d** and go to 1.
7.   No. Is X preceded by: **d** and **d**, **d** and O **d**, d in plural, to the left till a full stop?
8.   Yes. Refer X to them. Take next X and go to 1.
9.   No. The reference of X is not found. Ask for help.

Table 9.3   Reference of the Reflexive Pronoun

X	Agrees with
I	myself
you	yourself
he, d (masculine)	himself
she, d (feminine)	herself
it, n (singular)	itself
we	ourselves
you	yourselves
they, d and d, d and O d, d (plural), n (plural)	themselves

As an example, we'll use the same sentence as above:

(i)   *Jim dipped a finger in the hot water but Dr Ransome brusquely waved him away. Clearly his conversation with the camp commandant had upset him — he was preparing for the winter as if trying to convince <u>himself</u> that they would all be there when it arrived.*

If the reader takes the Reflexive Pronoun *himself* and follows carefully the instructions of the algorithm, a point will be reached, at instruction 5, when *himself* will be compared to *he* (**d**) — the first **d** to the left within the same sentence. Table 9.3 shows that there is an agreement between the two. Then, Algorithm No 13 will be triggered to find the referent of *he*.

This algorithm yields 99 per cent correct results when hand checked on randomly chosen texts.

2.1.4   *Reference of PPNC. Algorithm No 13*

The referent of the Personal Pronoun Nominal Case (**PPNC** is a subclass of **d**) can be found using the block-scheme shown in Figure 9.3. The full flow-chart notation is available on the Internet (see Internet Downloads at the end of the book). On the Internet, Algorithm No 13 uses the information shown in Table 9.4.

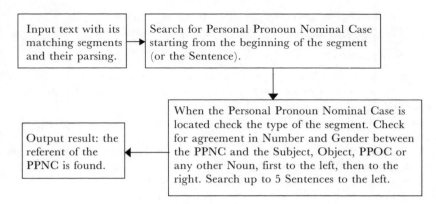

Figure 9.3   Block-scheme of Algorithm No 13

Table 9.4   Reference of PPNC

PPNC	Agrees with
d, name	I
d, name	you
he, name (masculine), d	he
she, name (feminine), d	she
it, n (singular)	it
we, d and d, d and O d	we
you, d and d, d and O d	you
they, d and d, d and O d, d (plural), n (plural)	they

To exemplify the performance of the algorithm we will use the following text:

> *Aunt Beatrice, Roland's sister, spoke with a slight French accent heavily overlaid with American. She had a mass of cloudy hair, not dark and long like Monica's, but white going on pale orange.*

The initial procedures of the algorithm check the identity and the typical surroundings of the Pronoun and when it is seen that no match is found, this clears the way for the next steps. Finally, instructions 17 and 18 find out that *she* agrees in number and gender with the Subject of the previous sentence, *Aunt Beatrice* (provided that all feminine and masculine proper names are also registered in the Dictionary of Wordforms and codemarked respectively), and this settles satisfactorily the identification and reference problem.

(NB The reference of PPNC is less accurate – up to 4 per cent errors can be expected using the present procedure. The errors are mainly connected with the uncertain attribution of **I** and **you**).

2.1.5   Reference of the Reciprocal Pronoun. Algorithm No 14

The Reciprocal Pronoun is marked as Z. The analysis of the sentence is performed according to the following procedure:

1. Z in the text (also in the segment) is found. Go left to find the 1st **d** in the plural (left up to 5 sentences back, jump to previous paragraphs if necessary). Have you found it?
2. Yes. Replace Z with it (or remember that Z refers to it). Take the next Z and go to 1.
3. No. Go left up to 5 sentences back and find the 1st (the 1st to appear): **d** and **d**, **d** and O **d**. Have you found it?
4. Yes. Replace Z with it. Take next Z and go to 1.
5. No. The reference of Z is not found. Ask for help.

Let's go through the algorithm with the following sentence and try to find the reference of the Reciprocal Pronoun:

> *They looked at each other and smiled.*
> d   v   at Z   and v

The algorithm locates (instruction 1) the first occurrence of Z (the abbreviation for a Reciprocal Pronoun in the segment) and goes left in search of a doer in the plural. The first doer in the plural to be found is the **PPNC** *they*. This satisfies the conditions and if the user (or the program) wants to know who *they* are, the reference of *they* can be found further back in the text (see Algorithm No 13).

The algorithm yields 99 per cent correct results.

*2.1.6   Reference of **who**. Algorithm No 15*

1. **Who** is located. Is **who** immediately preceded by a full stop, then immediately followed by a **v** and at the same time does the **who**-segment end in a question mark?
2. Yes. **Who** starts an interrogative sentence and does not refer. Take the next **who** and go to 1.
3. No. Is **who** immediately preceded by a **b**-segment or by a Prepositional Adverbial segment?
4. Yes. Jump the **b**-segment or the Prepositional Adverbial segment(s). Refer **who** to the **d** ending the last but one segment (the segment before the **b**-segment). Take the next **who** and go to 1.
5. No. Refer **who** to the **d** (Noun) ending the last segment. Take the next **who** and go to 1.

The sentence below will serve as an example showing how the algorithm finds the reference of the Relative and Interrogative Pronoun **who**.

> *Three or four times we had known what the other was thinking, in the sort of telepathic jump that sometimes occurred between people who knew each other well, but not on a regular basis, and not lately.*

The conditions laid down by the first and the third steps of the algorithm are not met and the way is paved for a final decision in (5) – to refer *who* to the preceding doer (d, n), in this case to *people*.

The present algorithm yields 99.3 per cent correct results.

2.1.7 Reference of **which**. Algorithm No 16

1. **Which** is located. Is **which** preceded by a full stop and does the **which**-segment end with a question mark?
2. Yes. **Which** starts an interrogative sentence and therefore does not refer. Take next **which** and go to 1.
3. No. Is **which** immediately preceded by **b**-segment(s)?
4. Yes. Jump **b**-segment(s). Refer **which** to the last **n** (or **n** + **v**) preceding the **b**-segment(s), left only till a full stop is reached. Take next **which** and go to 1.
5. No. Refer **which** to the last **n** in the previous segment.

Below are shown some examples of the reference of the Determiner and Pronoun **which**.

  (i)   *Pollution is   a problem which   must concern us all.*
         n   are A n   which shall v   R all
  (ii)   *She behaved with   the gaiety sometimes*
         d   v   with A n   b
         induced by risk-taking, which   to Peter
         v   by n   which to n
         and Danielle at least   proved infectious.
         and n   at least v   j
  (ii)   *The channel tunnel, which the Queen opened in May, was Britain's first road link with the Continent.*

In (i) the reference of *which* is found by instruction 5 – *which* is referred to the last Noun (*problem*) of the previous segment. Earlier it was made clear that *which* can be referred also to *pollution*, since *problem* is a Complement Subject of *pollution* and in Nominative agreement with it.

In (ii), instruction 4 ignores the preceding Adverbial segments (starting with *by* and *with*) and refers *which* to *she behaved*. Since the Adverbial Clauses modify the Verb, *which*, indirectly, refers to the whole predicate. However, the algorithm fails to refer *which* directly to *gaiety*.

In (iii), the reference of *which* is found by instruction 5 – *which* is referred to *tunnel*.

The reference of *which* is 99.3 per cent accurate.

2.1.8 Reference of **whom**. Algorithm No 17

1. The first occurrence of **whom** is located in the text. Is **whom** preceded by a full stop and does the **whom**-segment end with a question mark?

2. Yes. **Whom** starts an interrogative sentence and as such does not refer. Take next **whom** and go to 1.
3. No. Refer **whom** to the last **d**. Take next **whom** and go to 1.

As is seen, the reference of **whom** is quite straightforward. It is always referred to the last Noun as **d**.

The reference of the Relative Pronoun **whom** is similar to that of the other Relative Pronouns.

2.1.9   *Reference of* **both**. *Algorithm No 18*

Refer **both** to the last PPNC (plural), R (plural) or to the next **d** in the plural or to the next (immediately following): **d** and **d**, **d** and O **d**, **n** and **n**, **n** and O **n**. For example:

> *Instantly both John and Raymond were wide awake.*

2.1.10   *Reference of PPNC with subsequent logical inference. Algorithm No 19*

The reference of PPNC is based on the results obtained by Algorithm No 13 and then the analysis of the sentence is carried out according to the following procedure:

1. Does PPNC refer to the Subject of the previous segment or (if not) of the previous sentence?
2. Yes. Is the previous segment (or sentence) of the type: Sj v Cs? (where Sj = d; v = am (*is, are, were*); Cs = O n (where O n = O d)).
2a. Yes. Since PPNC refers to the **d** as Subject it also refers to the **d** as Complement Subject (Cs = O d). Therefore replace PPNC with the **d** in O d (Cs). Replace also the referent of PPNC with O d. Go right to find the next PPNC then go with it to 1.
2b. No. Proceed further till you find the next PPNC and when you find it go with it to 1.
3. No. Proceed further till you find the next PPNC and when you find it go to 1 with it.

Let us consider the following example:

> (i)   *The girl sitting on the chair is my sister.*
> d   Pi   on A n   am O n
> Sj   Cs   bl   v   Cs
> *She is eating a cake.*
> d am Pi   A n
> Sj v   Od

In the text, the referent of *my* will be determined by Algorithm No 10. Let's say that the referent is *John* (therefore *John's*). The referent of *she* is *the girl* – determined by Algorithm No 13. The word *sister* is Complement Subject to the *girl* and both the Subject and its complement (Cs) are **d** (doers) and there is a Nominative agreement between them. Therefore they can substitute each other since they denote the same person (or the same thing, in other examples).

Using the algorithmic procedure of Algorithm No 19 (the algorithmic notation of Algorithm No 19 is available on the Internet – see Internet Downloads at the end of the book) the computer can generate the following statements (sentences about the sentence) preserving the meaning of the sentence and, in fact, making a logical inference (i b, i c):

(i a) *My sister sitting on the chair is my sister.*
(i b) *My sister is eating a cake.*
(i c) *My sister is sitting on the chair.*
(i d) *My sister is sitting.*
(i e) *My sister is my sister* (a repetition which can be wiped out).

(i b) and (i c) are examples of 'logical inference' based on syntax.

10 Recognition of the Independent and Dependent Clauses

In this chapter, we present an algorithmic procedure to determine the structure of the sentence: Independent and Dependent Clauses, including Adverbial Clauses. This procedure is based on the Dictionary of Segments.

To this end, we remind the reader that:

a) the sentence is viewed as a sequence of segments;
b) the next segment in sequence cannot start before the previous one has ended;
c) there must be a segment in the Dictionary of Segments for every part of the sentence, for any sentence;
d) the segments are the building blocks of the sentence – they assume an intermediate role in the sentence and they can be either a sentence, a clause, a wordform or a phrase;
e) the segments determine the internal structure of the sentence.

The relationship between the constituent members of the segment (Parts of Speech, natural language wordforms, semantic groups) and their position within the segment is fixed (predetermined). The relationship between the segments in the sentence and their position within the sentence is not fixed: it has to be established using the algorithmic procedure described below.

1 Algorithm No 20

(NB Algorithm No 20 is to be run after Algorithm No 7. It uses the results obtained by Algorithm No 7. Algorithm No 7 establishes the boundaries between the segments in a sentence. List No 1 is a List of all Auxiliary words that are used as a first word of a segment – see Dictionary of Segments, or Section 3 of the Chapter 6. *Bearing the meaning expressed by the word from List No 1* refers to the meaning of the Prepositional Adverbial Clause – for details concerning the meaning of the Prepositional Adverbial Clauses see Section 3.3. in Chapter 6.)

The block-scheme of the algorithm is shown in Figure 10.1. The flow chart, 375 instructions, is available on the Internet (see Internet Downloads at the end of the book).

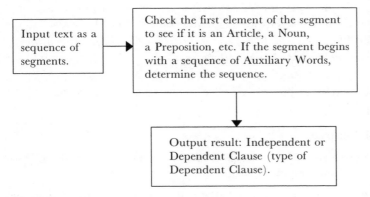

Figure 10.1 Block-scheme of Algorithm No 20

1.1 Examples of the performance of Algorithm No 20

Let's take as an example the following sentence and analyse it with Algorithm No 20 (the boundaries between the segments are already established by Algorithm No 7 and here they are marked with /).

(i)   *Alex was an enormous man, | weighing | around three hundred | and fifty pounds | with a beer belly | on him | that rested | like a balloon | on his knees | when he sat down.*

The algorithm checks and identifies the first word of the first segment (*Alex*) and passes, gradually, through the operations until operation 255 is reached. The first word *Alex* is identified as a name (d) and the first segment is declared to be an Independent Clause:

(i a)   *Alex was an enormous man,* (= Independent Clause)

Then the algorithm proceeds with the identification of the first word of the second segment, *weighing*, starting again from operation 1 and going through the operations unsuccessfully, almost to the end of the procedures. Finally, operation 297 ascertains that *weighing* is a detached **Pi**-segment (used as a Complement Subject) and instructs the computer program to link it to a Noun from the previous segment, as specified in **Links** in Chapter 8:

(i b)   *Alex was an enormous man, weighing*
(i ba) *Alex is weighing*
(i bb) *Man is weighing*

After that, the algorithm starts to identify the first word of the third segment, *around*. The same procedure is followed as described above.

Instructions 169–170 identify *around* and its pre-recorded meaning as a Prepositional Adverbial Clause for quantity, volume or measure:

(i c)   *around three hundred*

Operation 13 identifies the first word of the fourth segment, *and*, and examines its surroundings. Then, in 14d, a decision is taken to link *and* to the previous segment:

(i d)   *around three hundred and fifty pounds*

The first word of the fifth segment is *with*. The algorithm identifies it in operation 101 and takes the pre-recorded information for the segment

with A G n   bn   bb   bi

bn   bb   bi and prints:

(i e)   *with a beer belly* (Adverbial Clause for manner, or togetherness, or instrument and means)

The Preposition *on* comes next. It is the first word of the sixth segment and is recognized as such by operation 99. As a result, the computer is instructed to take the pre-recorded meaning of the segment:

on R   bl bu

bl bu and to print:

(i f)   *on him* (Adverbial Clause for location or concern)

Next, as first word of the seventh segment, comes the Conjunction *that*. Operation 19 identifies it and states that it introduces a Dependent Clause to explain the meaning of the previous Noun. Since *belly* is the last Noun to be used:

(i g)   *that rested* (Dependent Clause)
(i ga)   *belly rested*

The first word of the eighth segment is *like*. It is spotted by operation 135 and the following statement is issued:

(i h)   *like a balloon* (Dependent Clause for comparison)

The first word of the ninth segment comes next. This is again the Preposition *on* and it is dealt with by operation 99:

(i j)   *on his knees* (Adverbial Clause for location or time)

The tenth (the last) segment starts with *when*:

when d v up

The word *when* is identified by operation 37 and since the segment does not end with a Question Mark, operation 38b issues the following statement:

(i k)   *when he sat down* (Dependent Clause for time)

2 Role and meaning of Conjunctions

The Conjunctions serve to connect Subordinate (Dependent) Clauses and most of them have a logical function, expressing comparison (cy), reason (cr), time (cm), condition (cx), alternative or option (ct), addition (cq), exclusion (cs), antithesis or adverseness (cz), circumstances (cc) or manner (cn), as well as serving to start Interrogative or Relative Clauses.

Most of the Conjunctions are used together with a Preposition, connecting the Prepositional Adverbial Clauses.

In order to study the Conjunctions better, we have divided them into groups, according to their underlying meaning:

(i)   Comparison (cy): as, inasmuch as, how, so, according to, somehow, thus.

(ii)   Reason (cr): because, as, since, why, hence, that's why, therefore, lest.

(iii)   Time (cm): as, then, since, when, as yet, hence, whenever, so far.

(iv)   Condition (cx): as, since, though, if, unless, or, even if, so, on condition that, albeit, depending on, given.

(v)   Alternative, option (ct): than, rather than, otherwise, else, though, in spite of, but, yet, notwithstanding that, although, even though, or, then, since, therefore, nevertheless, even, in order that, albeit, anyway, besides, either or, instead, in lieu of, nonetheless, otherwise, whether.

(vi)   Addition (cq): and, also, besides, moreover, even.

(vii)   Exclusion (cs): but, except, yet, lest, apart from, far from, instead, neither, neither nor, in lieu of, nor, unless.

(viii) Adverseness or counterpoising (cz): but, yet, otherwise, whatever, even, else, despite, in spite of, either or, far from, however, irrespective of, neither nor, nevertheless, nonetheless, otherwise, therefore, unless, whereas, though, notwithstanding that, although, even though, since, besides, than.

(ix)   Circumstances (cc): that, so, according to, regarding, thereby, what, as to, so far as.

(x)   Manner (cn): how.

(xi)   Pronouns used at the start of Interrogative or Relative Clauses as determiners and Conjunctions: whom, whose, who, which, whoever, when, what, where, why, how.

Table 10.1 illustrates the meaning of the Conjunctions. There it can be seen how many different meanings a particular Conjunction may have and how this Conjunction relates, in meaning, to the other Conjunctions. The sign + is used to indicate the presence of a particular meaning; the sign - indicates its absence.

NB Compare the meaning of the Conjunctions with the meaning of the Prepositions (for details see Appendix 1).

Table 10.1 Meaning of Conjunctions

(+ marks the presence of a particular meaning, the dash (-) marks its absence)

Conjunction	cy	cr	cm	cx	cq	cs	cz	cc	cn	ct
No	1	2	3	4	5	6	7	8	9	10
according to	+	-	-	-	-	-	-	-	-	-
albeit	-	-	-	+	-	-	-	-	-	+
also	-	-	-	-	+	-	-	-	-	+
although	-	-	-	-	-	-	+	-	-	+
and	-	-	-	-	+	-	-	-	-	-
anyway	+	-	-	-	-	-	-	+	-	-
apart from	-	-	-	-	-	-	-	+	-	-
as	+	+	+	+	-	-	-	-	-	-
as yet	-	-	+	-	-	-	-	-	-	-
because	-	+	-	-	-	-	-	-	-	-
besides	-	-	-	-	-	-	-	-	-	+
but	-	-	-	-	-	+	-	-	-	+
depending on	-	-	-	+	-	-	-	-	-	-
despite	-	-	-	-	-	-	+	-	-	+
either	-	-	-	-	-	-	+	-	-	+
either or	-	-	-	-	-	-	+	-	-	+
else	-	-	-	+	-	-	+	-	-	+
even	-	-	-	-	+	-	-	-	-	+
even if	-	-	-	+	-	-	+	-	-	+
even though	-	-	-	-	-	-	+	-	-	+
except	-	-	-	-	-	+	-	-	-	-
far from	-	-	-	-	-	+	-	-	-	+
given	-	-	-	+	-	-	-	-	-	-
hence	-	+	+	-	-	-	-	-	-	-
how	+	-	-	-	-	-	-	-	+	-
however	-	-	-	-	-	-	+	-	-	-
if	-	-	-	+	-	-	-	-	-	-
in lieu of	-	-	-	-	-	+	-	-	-	+
in order that	-	-	-	-	-	-	-	-	-	+
in spite of	-	-	-	-	-	-	+	-	-	+
inasmuch as	+	-	-	-	-	-	-	-	-	-
instead	-	-	-	-	-	-	+	-	-	-
irrespective of	-	-	-	-	-	-	+	-	-	-
lest	-	+	-	-	-	-	+	-	-	-
moreover	-	-	-	-	+	-	-	-	-	-
neither	-	-	-	-	-	+	-	-	-	+
nevertheless	-	-	-	-	-	-	+	-	-	+
nonetheless	-	-	-	-	-	-	+	-	-	+

Conjunction	meaning									
	cy	cr	cm	cx	cq	cs	cz	cc	cn	ct
nor	-	-	-	-	-	+	+	-	-	-
notwithstanding that	-	-	-	-	-	-	+	-	-	+
on condition that	-	-	-	+	-	-	-	-	-	-
or	-	-	-	-	-	-	-	-	-	+
otherwise	-	-	-	+	-	-	+	-	-	+
rather than	-	-	-	-	-	-	-	-	-	+
regardless of	-	-	-	-	-	-	+	-	-	-
regarding	-	-	-	-	-	-	-	+	-	-
since	-	+	+	+	-	-	-	-	-	-
so	+	-	-	-	-	-	-	+	-	-
somehow	+	-	-	-	-	-	-	-	-	-
than	-	-	-	-	-	-	-	-	-	+
that	-	-	-	+	-	-	-	+	-	-
then	-	-	+	-	-	-	-	-	-	+
thereby	-	-	-	-	-	-	-	+	-	-
therefore	-	+	-	-	-	-	+	-	-	+
though	-	-	-	+	-	-	+	-	-	+
thus	+	-	-	-	-	-	-	-	-	-
unless	-	-	-	+	-	+	-	-	-	+
what	-	-	-	-	-	-	-	+	-	-
whatever	-	-	-	-	-	-	-	+	-	-
when	-	-	+	-	-	-	-	+	-	-
whenever	-	-	+	-	-	-	-	+	-	-
whereas	+	-	-	-	-	-	+	-	-	-
whether	-	-	-	-	-	-	-	-	-	+
why	-	+	-	-	-	-	-	-	-	-
yet	+	-	-	-	-	+	+	-	-	+

3 The sentence

In Part 2 we have operated with segments, indicating that a segment can be equal to a simple sentence or be part of it. The sentence, in our view, is any grammatically correct and meaningful word, or word sequence, that stretches from full stop to full stop, or from full stop to a Question or Exclamation Mark.

3.1 Simple sentence

The simple sentence, like the segment, is composed of several elements:

1. The Subject (Sj) is the performer of the action.
2. The Predicate or Verb, always expressed as a Verbal Tense (v), is the action (*arrive*, *sit*) or state (*is, was*, etc.).

3. The Object Direct (Od) is an object towards which the action is aimed directly.
4. The Object Indirect (Oi) is an object towards which the action is aimed indirectly.

The simple sentence can consist of a Subject only, a Verb only, a Subject and Verb only, a Subject, Verb and Object Direct only, or a Subject, Verb, Object Indirect and Object Direct only. It cannot consist of Subject, Verb and Object Indirect only, Object only, or Verb and Object only (except in Imperative sentences).

Other, less important elements of the sentence are:

5. The Complement (Subject, Object), which modifies the Subject or the Object.
6. The Infinitive, otherwise called The Infinitival Complement.
7. The Adverbs and the adverbial phrases, as modifiers of the Verb.
8. The Article, the Pronoun, the Numeral and the Adjective as modifiers of the Noun.

The difference between a segment and a Simple Sentence (in the traditional sense) is that the segment does not contain a Prepositional Adverbial Clause, though it contains Adverbs and Adverbial Phrases – their position in the segment is marked as **b**, **up**, **also**. For example, the Simple Sentence

(i)	*The book is*	*always*	*on the table.*
	A n are	up	on A n
	Sj v	b	bl
	Sj v		Cs

is composed of two segments. The Prepositional Adverbial Clause (bl) acts as a Complement Subject. In another example, the Prepositional Adverbial Clause (PAC) acts as Object (ii),

(ii)	*We arrived*	*at the station.*
	d v	at A n
	Sj v	bl
	Sj v	Od

because the Prepositional Adverbial Clause is the Object of the action.

The role of the Prepositional segments must be established algorithmically, by analysing the context in which they appear.

NB In length, the segment is equal to or shorter than a Simple Sentence or a Clause.

3.2 *Clause*

The Clause can be of two types.

On the one hand, it can be equal to a Simple Sentence, or joined to another such Simple Sentence to form a Complex or Compound Sentence by means of a Conjunction. For example:

    (iii)   *We waited, but she did   not   arrive.*
             d   v   but d shall also v
             Sj v   but Sj v

On the other hand, the Clause can be equal to a Simple Sentence, having appositional role (used as a Complement in the same way as a single word would be used as a Complement in the Simple Sentence), for example: *which was built*; *who came to visit us*, etc. Compare the sentences:

    (iv)   *Our baker, a man who benefits mankind,*
             O   n   d   who v   n
             Sj   Sj   Sj v   Od
             Sj   Cs
             built himself a new house in the neighbourhood.
             v   X   A G   n   in A n
             v   Oi   Od   bl
    (v)   *We met a woman, a friend of ours.*
             d   v A n   A n   of Os
             Sj v Od   Co

The examples above illustrate the difference between a segment and a Clause.

3.3 Complex Sentence

The Complex (or Compound) Sentence consists of Clauses. There are two main types of Clauses.

3.3.1   The Principal (or Main) Clause

This is the Independent Clause. All other Clauses in the Complex (or Compound) Sentence are dependent on it and modify it in one way or another. The Complex Sentence can have more than one Main Clause. For example (the segments are separated by /):

    (vi)   *I bought a sweet melon | on Friday | and*
             d v   A G   n   on FB   and
             | we ate it today, | though | it had to stay a
              d v R up   though it had to v
             few more days to ripen well.
             up   to v   up

The Main Clauses are underlined. The Main Clause is recognized algorithmically (Algorithm No 20). Example (vi) illustrates the positioning of the segments in a Complex Sentence.

NB On a purely grammatical basis, the main clause is the one that has a Subject, Verb and Object. However, on a purely semantic basis, it could be said that the sentence above has only one main clause: *I bought a sweet melon.* The other two main clauses provide more detailed information about the melon, therefore they are subordinate.

3.3.2   *The Subordinate or so-called Dependent Clause*

The Subordinate Clause is linked to the Main Clause or to another Subordinate Clause by means of a Conjunction. The choice of a given Conjunction depends on the meaning we want to express with the entire Complex (or Compound) Sentence. The Dependent Clauses, depending on whether they complement (refer to) the Subject, the Predicate (the Verb) or the Object of the Main Clause, are respectively called Subject Clause (vii), Predicate Clause (viii) and Object Clause (ix).

(vii)   *He agreed though   he objected at first.*
d   v   though d v   bm
Sj v

(vii a) *She is   what she must be.*
d   am what d shall be
Sj v   Cs

(viii)   *Your mother meant what   she said.*
O   n   v   what d v
Sj   v   Sj v

(viii a) *She knew what to say.*
d   v   what to v
Sj   v

(ix)   *I regard him as a very clever man.*
d v   R   as A b   G   n
Sj v   Od   Co

Some of these are Prepositional Clauses, because they start with a Preposition (iv above), others begin straight away with a Conjunction (iii above), still others start with both a Preposition and a Determiner (x), or a Conjunction and a Preposition (xi):

(x)   *You should write to all except   to him.*
d   shall v   to M except to R

(xi)   *We eat meat every day, except on Sunday.*
d   v n   each n   except on n

Those referring to the Predicate are called Prepositional Adverbial Clauses (*to him, to all* in (x)).

The reader can find more about the Sentence and the Clauses in the respective literature.

The above succinct description was meant only as a reminder of what the sentence really is and how it should be compared to the segment. In the light of this description, it can be seen that the segment can be equated only with the Simple Sentence (without the Prepositional Adverbial Clause) or with the Clause (without the Conjunctions).

For more information about what type of segments can follow after a particular Conjunction, the reader should refer to the Dictionary of Segments.

Since the segment is deprived of lexical meaning, we cannot provide rules on how to use the segments to generate Complex (or Compound) Sentences. We can, however, provide rules on how to make a Simple Sentence interrogative.

4 Creation of Interrogative Sentences

In English, the Interrogative Pronouns and the Auxiliary Verbs are used to create Interrogative Sentences. Algorithm No 22 describes how to do that, how to turn a segment into an Interrogative segment.

When we match a portion of text with a segment, we must have a list of all Interrogative segments as well. This list is very long, therefore we thought that it would be better to devise a simple algorithmic procedure to turn the segments into the Interrogative, instead of listing them.

4.1 Procedure to create Interrogative segments. Algorithm No 22

1. Is this **there**?
2. Yes. Is it followed by **are**, **is**, **were**?
2a. Yes. Record: are (is, were) + there + the rest of the segment. Read next segment. Go to 1. (For brevity we will use Go to 1).
2b. No. Go to 1.
3. No. Is this it?
4. Yes. Is it followed by: **was**, **is**?
4a. Yes. Record: **was (is)** + **it** + the rest of the segment. Go to 1.
4b. No. Is it followed by a **v** (Verb) ?
4c. Yes. Record: **did** (**do**, **does**) + **it** + **v** + ... (the rest of the segment). Go to 1.
4d. No. Go to 1.
5. No. Is this I?
6. Yes. Is I followed by: **are** (**is**, **were**, **was**)?
6a. Yes. Record: **are** (**is**, **was**, **were**) + **I** + ... (the rest of the segment). Go to 1.
6b. No. Is I followed by a v (Verb) ?
6c. Yes. Record: **did** (**do**, **does**) + **I** + **v** + ... (the rest of the segment). Go to 1.
6d. No. Go to 1.
7. No. Is this: Sj am Cs?
8. Yes. Record: am + Sj + Cs. Go to 1.

9. No. Is this: Sj + v + Oi + Od, or Sj + v + O, or Sj + v + Od + Co?

10. Yes. Record: **did** (**do**, **does**) + Sj + v + ...(the rest of the segment). Go to 1.

11. No. Is this: Sj am P2 ... (the rest of the segment)?

12. Yes. Record: am + Sj + P2 + ... (the rest of the segment). Go to 1.

13. No. Is this: Sj + Pi + ... (the rest of the segment)?

14. Yes. Record: **am** (**is**, **are**, **was**, **were**) + Sj + Pi + ... (the rest of the segment). Go to 1.

15. No. Stop. End of operation.

We can also use the modal Verbs and the **have** paradigm to create Interrogative segments in the same way as described in Algorithm No 22.

11 Further applications

The ultimate goal of Computational Linguistics is to teach the computer to understand Natural Language.

A computer's understanding of the meaning of a portion of text, in effect, amounts to identifying the meaning of that portion with a fixed meaning in its memory. If the computational linguists can supply the portions of meaning and establish the procedures to show how a portion of text can be matched with that fixed portion of meaning in a computer's memory, then Computational Linguistics will take a step further towards understanding the meaning of the entire sentence.

By definition, the text is any length of sentences connected by meaning. The text also contains pragmatic and novel information – something which cannot readily be seen in the sentence.

Can we imbue the segments with meaning and use them for identification of the meaning of the sentence?

Let us suppose for a moment that we have filled in the segments with actual words from the language, using the grammatical rules for concord and agreement, but ignoring the lexical meaning. Then we'll have a great, but nevertheless finite, number of grammatically correct statements, most of which will be utterly meaningless. The next thing we can do is to cross out from the list all meaningless statements, leaving only the meaningful ones. What we will have now is a finite number of meaningful statements composed of natural language words, for instance:

(i)   *People eat food.*

However, the number of these natural language statements will be beyond compute and at this stage we would not know how similar or distant in meaning these statements are when compared to one another. For example if we say:

(ii)   *Stanley wants a pet.* and
(iii)   *Stanley intends to buy a collie.*

the computer would not know, yet, that this amounts to the same thing – Stanley's desire to have a dog.

Let us now suppose, for a moment, that instead of natural language words, we use abbreviations for a particular type of meaning, like the abbreviations we have used in Part 2 of this book to mark words with identical meaning, and that we have an abbreviation for every conceivable lexical meaning. We expect that in any natural language there would be just over two thousand different lexical meanings, excluding the meanings of the subgroups of a group (see Georgiev, 1994–2001). Then, let us substitute the Parts of Speech in a segment with the respective meanings (abbreviated). As a result, we will have a great, but nevertheless finite, number of segments, filled in with the abbreviations of the semantic groups, which we will call *thought patterns*. The estimated number of thought patterns is over one million.

While the segments, as sequences of Parts of Speech, provide the syntactical frame of expression, the thought patterns presumably are the rails on which our thoughts run. They are the scope, the limits, of our understanding of the external reality, piece by piece, segmented, for better consumption. The thought patterns, in our view, will be the smallest descriptions of the external reality, also the smallest logical units, the smallest inferences made in our judgement of the outer world. The smallest because our aim will be to describe the text with them, to describe the external reality using pre-recorded statements and sentences, in the same way as the morphemes of the words or the words of the sentence form strings to express certain meaning. Being the smallest, they cannot be cut further like we cut the word into morphemes, or the sentence into words. They can be only joined together in sequences to form larger units.

Let us take as an example the word *head*. As a Noun (Georgiev, 1994–2001), it is met in the word-group RI-A (as part of the body) and also in the word-group HR (*chief, leader*); as a Verb, it is met in the group BFC (*guide, direct, lead, conduct, exercise guidance, head*). Let us then take as an example the following sentences:

(iv)　　*The head of the Russian delegation arrived in Geneva.*
　　　　A　　d　　of A　G　　　n　　　　v　　　in n

If we substitute the Parts of Speech with semantic groups (AF-EB for *Russia* and related words – state, located both in Europe and Asia, etc.; GZ-A for *delegation* and related words – *deputation*, etc.; CLA for *arrived* and related words – *come, get to, reach*, etc.; CU-T for *Geneva* and related words – city, used as headquarters of UN, located in Switzerland, etc.) we can present the above sentence in the following way:

(iv a)　A HR of A AF-EB GZ-A CLA in CU-T

This is a much closer approximation to the meaning of that sentence than that provided by the Parts of Speech.

Let us now consider the next example, where the word *head* will be used again, but with a different meaning.

(v)　　*John hit his head.*
　　　　d　　v　O　n

If we use OO to denote *hit* and the words related to it (*beat, pound, buffet, smite, knock,* etc.), then we can substitute (v) with semantic groups:

(v a)   l OO O RI-A

where **l** is a subgroup of **d** (denotes male) and RI-A is *head*, representing a subgroup of *body*.

In other words, this is an abridged presentation of *a male hit his head*. If we want to be less specific, we can replace **l** with **d** (to include male and female, singular and plural). If we want to be more specific, then we can replace **l** with *John*.

In another example, *head* will be coded differently:

(vi)   *He was asked to head the delegation.*
        d   am P2   to v   A n

and this sentence can be substituted with the thought pattern

(vi a)   l am DG to BFC A GZ-A

(DG represents all synonyms of *ask(ed)*, BFC substitutes all synonyms of *lead* and GZ-A marks the word *delegation* as a member of a class denoting a *group of people*, temporally assembled to represent a larger group of people.)

As we have seen, the word *head*, in all examples, figures only with one meaning – the meaning required in that particular context. This is one of the possible ways to disambiguate the lexical meaning of the word.

The thought patterns will be fixed in the computer's memory as constant concepts. Being constituents of the Sentence and not of the text as a whole, the thought patterns will allow for more detailed and precise description of reality, piece by piece, than the *scenes* described by Schank and Fano (1992: 175–88). Note that the scenes and the scripts in Schank's theory describe a whole text (situations in a story) and then are programmed to make logical inferences on individual sentences or other related texts, while the thought patterns will describe the meaning of individual sentences only, and can make logical inferences using the semantic paradigm(s). Compare for example:

CLA in CU-T
arrived in Geneva
came to Switzerland

Now we shall turn our attention briefly to a more specific problem related to the idea of thought patterns: what makes us understand those foreigners who speak the language brokenly? First, when they choose a word from a set of words sharing the same meaning, they often tend to choose the wrong word. For example, they might say

(vii)   *the leader of the Russian delegation*

instead of the more commonly used word *head*:

(viii)   *the head of the Russian delegation*

and still they will be understood correctly.

This is an example of what is well known in the literature as *norm of usage*. The norm of usage is the established preference of use of a certain word out of a set of words sharing the same meaning.

The use of thought patterns will have an immense advantage in human–computer communication, because they can accept both the established usage, the norm, and those usages which are less established or may even seem erroneous. For example:

(ix)   *the chief of the Russian deputation*

Secondly, a foreigner may wrongly arrange the semantic groups when forming a thought pattern. For example:

(x)   *People food eat.*
       d   n   v
       d   LQ IF

instead of

(x a)   *People eat food.*
         d   v   n
         d   IF LQ

where LQ is an abbreviation marking the class of words denoting *food* and IF marks all synonyms of *eat*. This arrangement (x) is common to some languages such as Turkish or German, where the Verb often ends the sentence. In this case, we will need a more sophisticated algorithm to understand and correct a sentence like (x).

And finally, a foreign speaker may arrange the segments of a sentence in a manner not quite permissible in English. For example:

(xi)   *Lily went to school by car.*
        d   v   to n   by n
        Sj   v   bdl   bi

may have the following arrangement of its three segments:

(xi a)   *Lily went to school by car.*
(xi b)   *By car Lily went to school.*
(xi c)   *To school Lily went by car.*
(xi d)   *By car to school Lily went.*
(xi e)   *To school by car Lily went.*
(xi f)   *Lily to school by car went.*
(xi g)   *Lily by car to school went.*
(xi h)   *Lily by car went to school.*
etc.

Example (xi f) is characteristic of Turkish, an agglutinative language, in which the Prepositional Adverbial Clauses, expressed as single words, are allowed to intervene between the Subject and the Verb. Naturally, not all these sequences of segments are permitted in English. In some languages some of the sequences are acceptable, in others they are not.

Since there are no rules to govern the arrangement of segments within the sentence – this is a task for text synthesis, not for text analysis – the computer software program developed on this basis will not be able to say which one of the above sentences is correct. The user will be alerted where the sentence is absolutely correct (xi a), because it is ambiguous, and his attention will also be drawn where it is needed most (xi f):

(xi a)   *Lily went to school by car.*
(xi aa) d   v   to n   by n
         Sj   v   bdl   bi
(xi ab) d   v   to v   by n
         Sj   v   Ic   bi

If the longer segment (xi ab) has precedence over the shorter one (xi aa), the sentence will be parsed incorrectly (to v = Ic). If the computer program is made so that it regards the Prepositions (in this case the Particle *to*) used after a Verb as ambiguous, the above sentence will have two parsings (xi aa, xi ab) and the user will be asked to intervene. In example (xi f) the user will be asked for help because *to school* has two different interpretations.

(xi f)   *Lily | to school | by car | went.*
(xi fa) d   to v   by n   v
(xi fb)   to n

The method described in this book is universal – it can be applied successfully to any other Natural Language. The author of this book has already applied it to the French language (Georgiev, 1997–2001b) and to the German language (Georgiev, 1996–2001b) to produce parsing software programs. The publication of the written results, in a similar form, is pending.

The segments as described in Part 2 can be used as a basis for construction of a spell-checking software program based on syntax, provided that additional grammatical rules are introduced to govern the concord in number and gender between its constituent words. Such a spell-checking program for the English language is already available on the software market under the name SYNTCHECK (Georgiev, 1993b). SYNTCHECK uses additional algorithms (which are not included in this book) – describing the agreement in number and gender between different word pairs within the sentence – and is able to spot those words that are spelt correctly from the orthographical point of view, but incorrectly from the grammatical point of view. Using the same method, the same author has developed versions for the German (Georgiev, 1996–2001a), French (Georgiev, 1997–2001a) and Italian (Georgiev, 2000–2001) languages.

On the other hand, the thought patterns, as outlined in this section, can be used to design a spell-check program based on meaning. The semantic groups of words will substitute the Parts of Speech in the segments to create thought patterns. The sequence of semantic groups in a thought pattern will represent the combinatorics of meaning permitted in the language (but not, yet, the norm of usage). Then if someone, instead of (x a), uses the expression (xii)

> (xii)   *Houses eat food.* (expression in Natural language)
>   n   v   n   (segment)
>   AB-D IF LQ   (thought pattern)

(where AB marks the meaning of the class of words denoting *building, construction, erection*, and AB-D is a subclass denoting *living quarters*), the computer will reject it as meaningless, because this thought pattern will not be registered in its memory and therefore it will not be regarded as truthful. However, the computer can acknowledge this particular thought pattern, and register it in its memory only on the condition that it is accepted as allegorical.

Appendix 1: List of Prepositions and Conjunctions and their most characteristic meanings

(* marks the presence of a particular meaning, the dash (-) marks its absence)

Preposition/ Conjunction List No 1	Meaning												
	bs 1	br 2	bc 3	bl 4	bm 5	bn 6	bz 7	bx 8	bq 9	by 10	bp 11	bu 12	bv 13
aboard	-	-	-	*	-	-	-	-	-	-	-	-	-
about	-	*	*	*	*	-	-	-	*	*	*	*	-
above	-	-	*	*	-	-	-	-	*	*	-	-	-
according	-	-	-	-	-	-	-	-	-	*	-	-	-
across	-	-	-	*	-	-	-	-	-	-	-	-	-
after	-	-	-	*	*	-	-	-	-	-	-	-	-
against	-	-	-	*	-	-	*	-	-	-	*	-	-
ahead of	-	-	-	*	*	-	-	-	-	-	-	-	-
albeit	-	-	-	-	-	-	-	*	-	-	-	-	-
along	-	-	-	*	-	-	-	-	-	-	-	-	-
also	-	-	-	-	-	-	-	-	-	-	-	-	-
although	-	-	-	-	-	-	*	-	-	-	-	-	-
altogether	-	-	-	-	-	-	-	-	-	*	-	-	-
among	-	-	-	*	-	-	-	-	-	-	-	-	-
and	-	-	-	-	-	-	-	-	-	-	-	-	-
anyway	-	-	-	-	-	-	*	-	-	-	-	-	-
apart from	*	-	-	-	-	-	*	-	-	-	-	-	-
around	-	-	-	*	*	-	-	-	-	-	-	-	-
as	-	*	*	-	*	*	*	*	-	*	-	-	-
as as	-	-	-	-	-	-	-	-	-	*	-	-	-
as yet	-	-	-	-	*	-	*	-	-	-	-	-	-
at	-	*	*	*	*	*	-	*	*	*	*	-	*
because	-	*	-	-	-	-	-	-	-	-	-	-	-
before	-	-	-	*	*	-	-	-	-	-	-	-	-
behind	-	-	-	*	*	-	-	-	-	-	-	-	-
beside	-	-	-	*	-	-	-	-	-	-	-	-	-
besides	*	-	-	-	-	-	*	*	-	*	-	-	-

Preposition/ Conjunction List No 1	bs 1	br 2	bc 3	bl 4	bm 5	bn 6	bz 7	bx 8	bq 9	by 10	bp 11	bu 12	bv 13
between	-	-	-	*	*	-	-	-	-	-	-	-	-
beyond	-	-	-	*	-	-	-	-	-	-	-	-	-
both	-	-	-	-	-	-	-	-	*	-	-	-	-
but	*	-	-	-	-	-	*	-	-	-	-	-	-
by	-	*	-	*	*	*	*	-	*	*	*	-	-
concerning	-	-	-	-	-	-	-	-	-	-	-	*	-
depending on	-	-	-	-	-	-	-	*	-	-	-	-	-
despite	*	-	-	-	-	-	*	-	-	*	-	-	-
down	-	-	-	*	-	-	-	-	-	-	-	-	-
during	-	-	-	-	*	-	-	-	-	-	-	-	-
either or	-	-	-	-	-	-	-	*	-	-	-	-	-
else	-	-	-	-	-	-	*	*	-	-	-	-	-
even	-	-	-	-	-	-	*	-	-	*	-	-	-
even if	-	-	-	-	-	-	*	*	-	-	-	-	-
even though	-	-	-	-	-	-	*	-	-	-	-	-	-
except	*	-	-	-	-	-	-	-	-	-	-	-	-
far from	*	-	-	*	-	-	*	-	-	-	-	-	-
for	-	*	-	-	*	-	-	-	*	-	*	*	-
from	*	*	*	*	*	-	-	-	-	-	*	-	-
given	-	-	-	-	-	-	-	*	-	-	-	-	-
hence	-	*	-	-	*	-	-	-	-	-	-	-	-
how	-	-	-	-	-	*	-	-	-	*	-	-	-
however	-	-	-	-	-	-	*	-	-	-	-	-	-
if	-	-	-	-	-	-	-	*	-	-	-	-	-
in	-	*	*	*	*	*	*	*	*	*	*	*	*
inasmuch as	-	-	-	-	-	-	-	-	-	*	-	-	-
in lieu of	*	-	-	-	-	-	-	-	-	-	-	-	-
in order that	*	-	-	-	-	-	*	-	-	-	-	-	-
inside	-	-	-	*	*	-	-	-	-	-	-	-	-
in spite of	-	-	-	-	-	-	*	-	-	-	-	-	-
instead	*	-	-	-	-	-	-	-	-	-	-	-	-
into	*	-	*	*	-	*	-	-	-	-	-	-	-
in view of	-	*	*	-	-	-	-	*	-	-	-	-	-
irrespective (of)	-	-	-	-	-	*	-	-	-	-	-	-	-
lest	*	-	-	-	-	-	-	-	-	-	-	-	-
like	-	-	-	-	-	*	-	-	-	*	-	-	-
moreover	-	-	-	-	-	-	*	-	-	-	-	-	-
near	-	-	-	*	-	-	-	-	-	-	-	-	-
needless	*	-	-	-	-	-	*	-	-	-	-	-	-
neither nor	*	-	-	-	-	-	*	-	-	-	-	-	-
nevertheless	-	-	-	-	-	*	-	-	-	-	-	-	-
next	-	-	-	*	*	-	-	-	-	-	-	-	*

Preposition/ Conjunction List No 1	Meaning												
	bs 1	br 2	bc 3	bl 4	bm 5	bn 6	bz 7	bx 8	bq 9	by 10	bp 11	bu 12	bv 13
nonetheless	-	-	-	-	-	-	*	-	-	-	-	-	-
nor	*	-	-	-	-	-	*	-	-	*	-	-	-
notwithstanding	-	*	-	-	-	-	*	-	-	-	-	-	-
of	*	*	*	-	-	-	-	-	-	-	-	*	-
on	-	*	*	*	*	*	-	-	*	*	*	*	*
once	-	-	-	-	*	-	-	-	-	-	-	-	*
on condition	-	-	-	-	-	-	-	*	-	-	-	-	-
onto	-	-	-	*	-	-	-	-	-	-	-	-	-
or	-	-	-	-	-	-	*	*	-	-	-	-	-
otherwise	*	-	-	-	-	-	*	*	-	-	-	-	-
over	-	-	*	*	*	-	-	-	*	-	-	*	*
past	-	-	-	*	*	-	-	-	-	-	-	-	-
per	-	-	-	-	-	-	-	-	*	-	-	-	-
perhaps	-	-	-	-	-	-	-	*	-	-	-	-	-
prior (to)	-	-	-	-	*	-	-	-	-	-	-	-	-
provided (that)	-	-	-	-	-	-	-	*	-	-	-	-	-
rather than	*	-	-	-	-	-	*	-	-	*	-	-	-
regarding	-	-	*	-	-	-	-	-	-	-	-	-	-
round	-	-	-	*	*	-	-	-	-	-	-	-	-
since	-	*	-	-	*	-	*	*	-	-	-	-	-
so	-	-	*	-	-	-	-	*	-	*	-	-	-
somehow	-	-	*	-	-	*	-	-	-	*	-	-	-
somewhat	-	-	-	-	-	-	-	-	-	*	-	-	-
somewhere	-	-	-	*	-	-	-	-	-	-	-	-	-
than	*	-	-	-	-	-	*	-	-	-	-	-	-
that	-	-	*	-	-	-	-	-	-	-	-	-	-
then	-	-	-	-	*	-	-	-	-	-	-	-	-
thereby	-	-	*	-	-	-	-	-	-	-	-	-	-
therefore	-	-	-	-	-	-	*	*	-	*	-	-	-
though	-	-	-	-	-	-	*	*	-	-	-	-	-
through	-	-	-	*	*	-	-	-	-	-	-	-	-
throughout	-	-	-	*	*	-	-	-	-	-	-	-	-
thus	-	-	-	-	-	-	-	-	-	*	-	-	-
to	-	*	-	*	*	-	-	-	*	-	*	-	-
towards	-	-	-	*	*	-	-	-	-	-	*	-	-
under	-	-	*	*	-	-	-	*	*	-	-	-	-
unless	*	-	-	-	-	-	*	*	-	-	-	-	-
until/till	-	-	-	-	*	-	-	-	-	-	-	-	-
upon	-	*	-	*	-	-	-	-	-	-	-	-	-
via	-	-	-	*	*	-	-	-	-	-	-	-	*
what	-	-	*	-	-	-	-	-	-	-	-	-	-
whatever	-	-	*	-	-	-	*	-	-	-	-	-	-

Preposition/ Conjunction List No 1	bs 1	br 2	bc 3	bl 4	bm 5	bn 6	bz 7	bx 8	bq 9	by 10	bp 11	bu 12	bv 13
when	-	-	*	-	*	-	-	-	-	-	-	-	-
whenever	-	-	*	-	*	-	-	-	-	-	-	-	-
where	-	-	*	*	-	-	-	-	-	*	-	-	-
whereas	-	-	-	-	-	-	*	-	-	-	-	-	-
whether	-	*	-	-	-	-	-	*	-	-	-	-	-
which	-	-	*	-	-	-	-	-	-	-	-	-	-
while	-	-	-	-	*	-	-	-	-	-	-	-	-
who	-	-	-	-	-	-	-	-	-	-	-	-	-
whom	-	-	-	-	-	-	-	-	-	-	-	-	-
whose	-	-	-	-	-	-	-	-	-	-	-	-	-
why	-	*	-	-	-	-	-	-	-	-	-	-	-
with	-	*	*	-	-	*	-	-	*	-	*	*	-
within	-	-	-	*	*	-	-	-	*	-	-	-	-
without	*	-	-	-	-	-	-	-	-	-	-	-	-
yet	*	-	-	-	-	-	*	-	-	-	-	-	-

Appendix 2: Internet downloads

Instructions on how to download and use the additional files. The Dictionary of Segments, the full text of the algorithms (flow charts) and a commercial copy of the software program SYNTPARSE can be downloaded at http://www.langsoft.ch/eag/eag_app.htm.

SYNTPARSE needs a password to install on Windows. This password is: sparse2. Please type in the password when prompted to do so. Note that the password is case sensitive. SYNTPARSE does not need a password to run on LINUX and UNIX Operating Systems (DOS mode only).

One of the text files contains all algorithms (No 1–No 22). The other text file contains the Dictionary of Segments. Both files are compressed for different Operating Systems. For Windows they are in zip format. For LINUX and UNIX they are in tar.gz format. The text file called Segments contains approximately 27,000 syntactically correct sequences of Parts of Speech allowed by English grammar and usage (in certain positions the Parts of Speech are substituted by words or by abbreviations for semantic groups). The segments are arranged alphabetically and presented in the order used by the computer program for identification of a portion of text with a segment: first come the Nominal Segments, followed by the Verbal Segments and finally come the segments that start with an Auxiliary word (mainly Conjunction or Preposition). The reader can find detailed information on how to interpret and use the segments in Part 2 of this book. Apart from its usefulness for the algorithms, the Dictionary of Segments can be used for reference by anyone who writes in English and wishes to check if the syntactical expression of his (her) sentence is in accordance with that allowed by English syntax. Then the user must perform the operations of identification of a portion of text with a segment from the Dictionary of Segments, as described in Algorithm No 7: if a segment (or segments) is found to match the sentence, then that sentence can be considered to be syntactically correct (but not, yet, semantically).

Since the parsing of the segments (and hence that of sentences) is pre-recorded, the Dictionary of Segments can be used for reference by anyone who teaches or studies English Syntax and Parsing.

The text information is provided as ASCII files, to ensure maximum compatibility for a wide range of PCs, including later Macs.

The access to the files (Algorithms or Segments) is the same as that to any other text file: the user must have a Word Processor on the hard disk, or if not a Word Processor must be installed and opened. The usual commands, common to all Word Processors, are 'open' or 'open, file name' if the user has already loaded the file on the hard disk. When the file *Segments* is opened, the user should use the commands 'search' ('find', 'locate', etc., available on the menu, usually under 'edit') and enter the search pattern (the segment or the initial part of the segment), or 'go to' (page number), or use the keys 'Page Up' or 'Page Down' in order to find the desired segment. Those readers who do not have a PC at their disposal ought to find a way to obtain a print-out of the Dictionary of Segments.

General index of abbreviations

NB Some of the abbreviations such as d', n', l, k are used only in the Dictionary of Wordforms (DW).

1 Alphabetical list of one-letter abbreviations

=	equal to
+	plus
"	the second word marked with " refers to the previous one marked with the same sign (except in Genitive of the Noun, as in N"'s)
'	the second word marked with ' refers to the previous one marked '
*	the segment is grammatically incorrect or incomplete
A	Article (definite and indefinite)
a(n)	**Indefinite Article**
b	Adverb, less, just, only, still
C	Preposition including all Prepositions having adverbial nature such as inside, over, above, outside, near, etc.
d	EBB, Personal Pronoun Nominal Case, Noun denoting a person, one, others, abbreviation, some, G + d + name, d + name's + G + n, d + name's + n, d + of + A + n, name, d + name, G + d, whoever, d + of + name + of + name, A G d of A G G n, some, G + G + G + d, d + of + n + name, d + of + G + n, name + of + A + G + G + n, A + d + of + A + G + n, A + d + of + n, G + N"'s + G + d, A + S + d, A + S + d + of + A + G + n, name + of + name, M + d, A + N"'s + G + G + d, A + G + n denoting a group of people, G + n denoting a group, A + d, A + G + d + of + n, A + d + of + A + G + N"'s + G + G + n, A + G + G + n denoting a group of people, A + d + of + I + G + n, A + d + of + N"'s + G + n, another + d, etc.
	(NB **G** are optional; **N"'s = G**!) Note that here **d** stands for both masculine and feminine gender; **d** is a subclass of the Noun and marks the semantic group 'a human being'; **d** has its own subclasses.
d'	**d** plural (used only in DW)
F	Abbreviation
G	Adjective (incl. -er,- est) as an Attribute or Predicative, more
h	A Noun used in singular only (used only in DW)

I	Indicative Pronoun, last, next
i	Indicative Pronoun, such, Article
j	An Adjective, Numeral Ordinal, Adverb and Participle 1st that can be used with **be** and its paradigm as a Predicative or Complement, e.g. ready, sure, busy, more, steady, sunny, etc.
k	**d** female (used only in DW)
k'	**k** plural (used only in DW)
l	**d** male (used only in DW)
l'	**l** plural (used only in DW)
M	Numeral Cardinal, UK, figure (number), EBL
m	Numeral Cardinal, figure (number)
N	Noun
n	Noun (singular or plural)
n'	Noun plural (used only in DW)
"n"	Noun used as a quotation and put in Inverted Commas
O	Possessive Pronoun (nominative)
P	Gerund
p	Preposition (used only in DW)
q	A Noun used in the plural only (used only in DW)
R	Personal Pronoun Objective Case, EBB, other, another, one, name, others, both, Noun
r	Geographical name
S	Numeral Ordinal, last, previous, former (S = G; S = n)
T	Numeral denoting a repetition: once, twice, etc., many times, half, M times, score of times, half the time
V	Verb
v	Main Verb (including have and do, excluding the Auxiliary Verbs)
v'	3rd person singular of the Present Tense
W	Mathematical sign
X	Reflexive Pronoun
Z	Reciprocal Pronoun

2 Abbreviations of two or more letters

AA	Adverb or Adjective
Abbr.	Abbreviation
Adj	Adjective
Adv	Adverb
Aj	Adjective
almost	almost, nearly
along	along, alongside
also	not, also, Adverb, even, only, still, too
am	am, are, was, were, is
among	among, amid, amongst
ANV	Adjective or Noun or Verb
are	are, is, was, were
AV	Adjective or Verb
b change	Adverbial clause for change
b means	Adverbial clause for means

b opposition	Adverbial clause for opposition
ba	Adverbial clause for activity
bb	Adverbial clause for togetherness and joint action
bc	Adverbial clause for circumstances
bdl	Adverbial clause for direction and location
be	Adverbial clause for togetherness
bf	Adverbial clause for result
bg	Adverbial clause for 'stoppage'
bh	Adverbial clause denoting starting point
bi	Adverbial clause for instrument, means
bj	Adverbial clause for appearance
bk	Adverbial clause for source
bl	Adverbial clause for location
bm	Adverbial clause for time
bn	Adverbial clause for manner
bo	Adverbial clause for purpose
bp	Adverbial clause for purpose
bq	Adverbial clause for quantity
br	Adverbial clause for reason
bs	Adverbial clause for separation
bt	Adverbial clause for 'clothes'
bu	Adverbial clause for concern
bv	Adverbial clause for sequence
bw	Adverbial clause for persuasion
bx	Adverbial clause for condition
by	Adverbial clause for comparison
bz	Adverbial clause for opposition
called	called, named, denominated, entitled, termed
can	can, should, will, would, would better, ought to, must, have to
cc	Conjunction for circumstances
cm	Conjunction for time
cn	Conjunction for manner
Co	Complement Object
cq	Conjunction for addition
cr	Conjunction for reason
Cs	Complement Subject
cs	Conjunction for exclusion
ct	Conjunction for alternative (option)
cx	Conjunction for condition
cy	Conjunction for comparison
cz	Conjunction for opposition
Dem. Pr	Demonstrative Pronoun
despite	despite, notwithstanding
did	did, do, does
DS	Dictionary of Segments
DW	Dictionary of Wordforms
each	each, every
EAH	seam, strip, band, ribbon
EAI	come back, return, go back
EAJ	endorse, sign, approbate, approve, give one's consent, etc.

EAL	except, with the exception (of), with the exclusion of, without, etc.
EAM	give rise to, sprout, give birth to, etc.
EAN	at the back of one's mind, subconsciously
EAO	forward, ahead
EAP	somewhere else, not here, elsewhere
EAQ	already, at times, sometimes, now and then, often, occasionally, periodically, intermittently, once, never, some day, always, no longer, one day, no more, never more, never again, ever (EAQ is a subgroup of HA)
EAR	next, afterwards, after that, hereafter
EAS	indeed, of course, yes, no doubt
EAT	confide in, trust
EAU	all, everything
EAV	too, as well, also
EAW	reportedly, perhaps, possibly, probably, presumably, may be, undoubtedly, no doubt, indeed, certainly, etc.
EAY	going on, continuing, in progress
EAZ	in public, in the open, outdoors, outside
EBA	notwithstanding, nevertheless, after all
EBB	anyone, someone, somebody, anybody, any person, everyone, everybody, no one, no body, whomever, nobody, one, each one of R, others, other people
EBC	whatever, anything, everything, something, nothing, the thing, the things
EBD	for now, for the time being, at present, currently, presently
EBF	good night, goodbye, hello, farewell
EBI	taking into consideration, taking into account, given, considering, having in mind
EBK	nearly, almost, approximately
EBL	half, 1/3, 1/4, etc.
EBM	goodbye, farewell, goodnight, good afternoon
EBN	day, morning, dusk, sunrise, sunset, evening, lunch, lunch time, afternoon, night
EBO	tens, dozens, hundreds, thousands, millions, score, none
EBP	20s, 30s, 40s, 50s, 60s, 70s, 80s, 90s, ...
EBQ	breakfast, lunch, supper, dinner, sunrise, sunset, dawn
EBR	a hundred, a thousand, a million, a dozen, etc.
EBS	Christmas, Easter, New Year, Holy Week, etc.
EBT	now, yesterday, tomorrow
EBU	better, best, worst, worse, well
EBW	uncommunicative, taciturn, speechless, reticent, spellbound
end	end, start, close, closure, middle, beginning
except	except, save, apart from, with the exception of, excluding
FB	words denoting time (period of time)
FB-BD	1950, 1960, 1970, 1980, 1990, etc.
FB-BE(A–L)	Months
FB-BH(A–H)	Days of the week
FB-BL	50s, 60s, 70s, 80s, 90s, etc.
FB-BM	seasons
future	future, present, past

goodnight	goodnight, goodbye, farewell
greeting	goodbye, good afternoon, good morning, etc.
HA	endlessly, permanently, perpetually, eternally, ceaselessly, non-stop, unendingly, continuously, unceasingly, constantly, uninterruptedly, incessantly, everyday, indefinitely, daily, steadily, endemically, cronically, persistently, continually, invariably, gradually, by degrees, bit by bit, step by step, by and by, little by little, in stages, progressively, successively, for days on end, for months on end, every day, intermittently, for years on end, unabatedly, for ever, for ever and ever, all the time, always, day and night, ever, evermore, all the way through, day by day, day after day, daily
had	have, had
has	has, have, had
have	have
heading(s)	heading, title (usually in italics)
hence	hence, therefore, that's why
high	high, low
Ic	Infinitival Complement
Indef. Pr	Indefinite Pronoun
Indic. Pr	Indicative Pronoun
inside	inside, outside
Inter. Pr	Interrogative Pronoun
JD	Winds (North, South, East, West)
JE	words denoting measure
JE(A-D)	words denoting measure (subgroup)
JE-D	words denoting distance
JE-Dn	words denoting distance
just	just, Adverb, do, does, did, also, even
last	past, recent, last, next, early, late, coming, only, former, previous, later, latter
late	late, early
less	many, less, few, the greater part, best, worse, little, most, much, more, Adverb, very, even, further, not much, a little, a lot
LQ	look and its synonyms
more	more, less, Adjective
morning	morning, evening, afternoon
much	much, more, little
NA	Noun or Adjective
name	name (proper)
near	near, close, far, far away
nearly	nearly, approximately, almost
neither	neither, either, nor
NG	Nominal Word Group
no	no
not	not
NP	Noun Phrase
N"s	Noun expressing possessiveness: -'s, -s' (Genitive of the Noun)
NV	Noun or Verb
Od	Object Direct
other	other, another

off	Prepositions and other words used with the Prepositional and Phrasal or idiomatic Verbs: apart, by, upon, over, forth, up, down, away, out, in, into, at, with, along, together, through, across, round, around, aside, adrift, about, home, aback, ahead, for, clear, plain, part, back, alone, charge, right, loose, fast, secret, astray, place, behind, abroad, open, busy, alongside, high, aloud, from, past
Oi	Object Indirect
one	one, ones
ones	one, ones
Os	Possessive Pronoun (dative)
outset	outset, beginning
PA	Participle (-ed) or Adjective
PAC	Prepositional Adverbial Clause
PANV	Participle (-ing) or Adjective or Noun or Verb
PAV	Participle (-ing) or Adjective or Verb
PC	Personal computer
P1	Participle 1st
P2	Participle 2nd
Pi	Participle '-ing'
Poss. Pr	Possessive Pronoun
PPNC	Personal Pronoun Nominal Case
PPOC	Personal Pronoun Objective Case
Pr	Predicative
PS	Part of Speech
PU	monetary unit (pound, dollar, etc.)
PV	Participle (-ed) or Verb
Pv	Participle '-ing' (equivalent to 'to + v')
QJ	words denoting colour
Rec. Pr	Reciprocal Pronoun
Refl. Pr	Reflexive Pronoun
Rel. Pr	Relative Pronoun
RM	record to memory
round	round, around
shall	do, does, did, shall, should, can, could, dare, may, might, will, would, have to, ought to, must, have to
should	should, will, would, may, might, shall, must
Sj	Subject
some	some, certain, most
still	still, yet
TCi	Participle '-ing' of TCv (communication)
TCn	Nouns from the group TCn (communication)
TCv	Verb, from the semantic group 'speech and communication'
TE	words denoting group(s) of people
that	that (does not refer to previous Noun)
that'	that (refers to previous Noun)
title	Sir, Von, Dr, Mr, Miss, etc.
today	today, yesterday, tomorrow
too	Adverb, too, as well, also
towards	towards, toward
UF	something, nothing, everything, all, anything

UG	marriage, wedding, death, birth
UG'	within, inside, outside, abroad, beyond
UI	UG, UL, anywhere, everywhere, nowhere, somewhere, down, up, afar, overseas, over here, over there, throughout, elsewhere, around, EAZ, worldwide, out there
UJ	beside, near, next, alongside, against, opposite
UK	all, a few, several, some, many, any, lots of, a lot, a number, a couple (of), less, much, more, most, far more, none, every, few, so little, all the, almost all the, a great deal, a great many, a good deal, all of R, so many, large number(s) (of), certain, much more, each, each one (of), tens of thousands, EBO of, other, another, a few more, quite a lot (of), any other, far too much, half the, half a(n), the whole lot, very few, very many and other words and phrases denoting number or quantity
UL	outside, inside, downstairs, upstairs, here, there
under	under, beneath, below
until	until, till
up	The same list as for 'off' plus **b** (all Adverbs) – only in the segment or at the end of the segment (not at the start of a segment!)
up	up, off, out, down, over, in (only when at the beginning of a segment)
VAP	Verb or Adjective or Participle (-ed)
VG	Verbal group
VNP	Verb or Noun or Participle (-ed)
VP	Verbal phrase
was	was, is
West	West, South, East, North
yes	yes, no
Z's	Reciprocal Pronoun

References

Brill, E. and Mooney, R. J. (1997), 'An overview of empirical natural language processing', in *AI Magazine*, 18 (4): 13–24.

Chomsky, N. (1957), *Syntactic Structures*. The Hague: Mouton.

Curme, G. O. (1955), *English Grammar*. New York: Barnes and Noble.

Dowty, D. R., Karttunen, L. and Zwicky, A. M. (eds) (1985), *Natural Language Parsing*. Cambridge: Cambridge University Press.

Garside, R. (1986), 'The CLAWS word-tagging system', in R. Garside, G. Leech and G. Sampson (eds) *The Computational Analysis of English*. Harlow: Longman.

Gazdar, G. and Mellish, C. (1989), *Natural Language Processing in POP-11*. Reading, UK: Addison-Wesley.

Georgiev, H. (1976), 'Automatic recognition of verbal and nominal word groups in Bulgarian texts', in *t.a. information, Revue International du traitement automatique du langage*, 2, 17–24.

Georgiev, H. (1991), 'English Algorithmic Grammar', in *Applied Computer Translation*, Vol. 1, No. 3, 29–48.

Georgiev, H. (1993a), 'Syntparse, software program for parsing of English texts', demonstration at the Joint Inter-Agency Meeting on Computer-assisted Terminology and Translation, The United Nations, Geneva.

Georgiev, H. (1993b), 'Syntcheck, a computer software program for orthographical and grammatical spell-checking of English texts', demonstration at the Joint Inter-Agency Meeting on Computer-assisted Terminology and Translation, The United Nations, Geneva.

Georgiev, H. (1994–2001), *Softhesaurus, English Electronic Lexicon*, produced and marketed by LANGSOFT, Sprachlernmittel, Switzerland; platform: DOS/Windows.

Georgiev, H. (1996–2001a), *Syntcheck, a computer software program for orthographical and grammatical spell-checking of German texts*, produced and marketed by LANGSOFT, Sprachlernmittel, Switzerland; platform: DOS/Windows.

Georgiev, H. (1996–2001b), *Syntparse, software program for parsing of German texts*, produced and marketed by LANGSOFT, Sprachlernmittel, Switzerland; platform: DOS/Windows.

Georgiev, H. (1997–2001a), *Syntcheck, a computer software program for orthographical and grammatical spell-checking of French texts*, produced and marketed by LANGSOFT, Sprachlernmittel, Switzerland; platform: DOS/Windows.

Georgiev, H. (1997–2001b), *Syntparse, software program for parsing of French texts*, produced and marketed by LANGSOFT, Sprachlernmittel, Switzerland; platform: DOS/Windows.

Georgiev, H. (2000–2001), *Syntcheck, a computer software program for orthographical and grammatical spell-checking of Italian texts*, produced and marketed by LANGSOFT, Sprachlernmittel, Switzerland; platform: DOS/Windows.

Giorgi, A. and Longobardi, G. (1991), *The Syntax of Noun Phrases: Configuration, Parameters and Empty Categories*. Cambridge: Cambridge University Press.

Graver, B. D. (1971), *Advanced English Practice*. Oxford: Oxford University Press.

Grisham, R. (1986), *Computational Linguistics*. Cambridge: Cambridge University Press.

Harris, Z. S. (1982), *A Grammar of English on Mathematical Principles*. New York: Wiley.

Hausser, R. (1989), *Computation of Language*. Berlin: Springer.

Hornby, A. S. (1958), *A Guide to Patterns and Usage in English*. London: Oxford University Press.

Kavi, M. and Nirenburg, S. (1997), 'Knowledge-based systems for natural language', in A. B. Tucker (ed.) *The Computer Science and Engineering Handbook*. Boca Raton, FL: CRC Press, Inc., 637–53.

Koverin, A. A. (1972), 'Grammatical analysis, on a computer, of French scientific and technical texts' (in Russian), PhD thesis, Leningrad University, Russia.

Leech, S. and Svartvik, J. (1975), *A Communicative Grammar of English*. London: Longman.

Manning, C. and Schütze, H. (1999), *Foundations of Statistical Natural Language Processing*. Cambridge, MA: MIT Press.

Marcus, M. P. (1980), *A Theory of Syntactic Recognition for Natural Language*. Cambridge, MA: MIT Press.

McEnery, T. (1992), *Computational Linguistics*. Wilmslow, UK: Sigma Press.

Mihailova, I. V. (1973), 'Automatic recognition of the nominal group in Spanish texts' (in Russian), in R. G. Piotrovskij (ed.) *Injenernaja Linguistika*. St Petersburg: Politechnical Institute, 148–75.

Primov, U. V. and Sorokina, V. A. (1970), 'Algorithm for automatic recognition of the nominal group in English technical texts' (in Russian), in R. G. Piotrovskij (ed.) *Statistika Teksta, II*. Minsk: Politechnical Institute.

Pullum, G. K. (1984), 'On two recent attempts to show that English is not a CFL', *Computational Linguistics*, 10 (3–4), 182–6.

Quirk, R. and Greenbaum, S. (1983), *A University Grammar of English*. London: Longman.

Quirk, R., Greenbaum, S., Leech, G. and Svartvic, J. (1972), *Grammar of Contemporary English*. London: Longman.

Reichman, R. (1985), *Getting Computers to Talk like You and Me*. Cambridge, MA: MIT Press.

Sestier, A. and Dupuis, L. (1962), 'La place de la syntaxe dans la traduction automatique des langues. Esquisse d'un nouveau système de description grammaticale et de son utilisation pour la reconstruction des structures grammaticales', *Ingénieurs et Techniciens*, No. 1555, 43–50.

Schank, R. and Fano, A. (1992) 'Knowledge, memory, learning and teaching. A survey of our research', in *t.a.l., Traitement Automatique des Langues*, Vol. 33, No. 1–2.

Shanks, D. (1993), 'Breaking Chomsky's rules', *New Scientist*, February, 26–30.

Shieber, S. M. (1985), 'Evidence against the non-context-freeness of natural language', in *Linguistics and Philosophy*, 8, 333–43.

Stannard, A. (1974), *Living English Structure*. London: Longman.

Urdang, L. (ed.) (1968), *The Random House Dictionary of the English Language* (College Edition). New York: Random House.

Venev, Y. (1990), *Elsevier's Dictionary of Mathematical and Computational Linguistics*. Amsterdam: Elsevier.

Index of terms